MPEG-V

MPEG-V

BRIDGING THE VIRTUAL AND REAL WORLD

KYOUNGRO YOON

SANG-KYUN KIM

JAE JOON HAN

SEUNGJU HAN

MARIUS PREDA

ELSEVIER

AMSTERDAM • BOSTON • HEIDELBERG • LONDON
NEW YORK • OXFORD • PARIS • SAN DIEGO
SAN FRANCISCO • SINGAPORE • SYDNEY • TOKYO
Academic Press is an imprint of Elsevier

Academic Press is an imprint of Elsevier
125 London Wall, London EC2Y 5AS, UK
525 B Street, Suite 1800, San Diego, CA 92101-4495, USA
225 Wyman Street, Waltham, MA 02451, USA
The Boulevard, Langford Lane, Kidlington, Oxford OX5 1GB, UK

Notices

Knowledge and best practice in this field are constantly changing. As new research and experience broaden our understanding, changes in research methods, professional practices, or medical treatment may become necessary.

Practitioners and researchers must always rely on their own experience and knowledge in evaluating and using any information, methods, compounds, or experiments described herein. In using such information or methods they should be mindful of their own safety and the safety of others, including parties for whom they have a professional responsibility.

To the fullest extent of the law, neither the Publisher nor the authors, contributors, or editors, assume any liability for any injury and/or damage to persons or property as a matter of products liability, negligence or otherwise, or from any use or operation of any methods, products, instructions, or ideas contained in the material herein.

ISBN: 978-0-12-420140-8

British Library Cataloguing-in-Publication Data
A catalogue record for this book is available from the British Library.

Library of Congress Cataloging-in-Publication Data
A catalog record for this book is available from the Library of Congress.

For Information on all Academic Press publications
visit our website at http://store.elsevier.com/

Typeset by MPS Limited, Chennai, India
www.adi-mps.com

Publisher: Todd Green
Acquisition Editor: Tim Pitts
Editorial Project Manager: Charlie Kent
Production Project Manager: Jason Mitchell
Designer: Matthew Limbert

CONTENTS

ACKNOWLEDGMENT

This book would not be possible without the hard work of all the MPEG-V contributors that, meeting after meeting, during 3 years, built a consistent architecture supporting multi-sensorial user experiences, bringing innovative ideas and giving them a shape in terms of standard specifications. We would like to express our honor and satisfaction for working in such a challenging environment. Naming all the MPEG-V contributors would require a few pages and, probably, would not be complete, however, we would like to express special thanks to Jean Gelissen from Philipps and Sanghyun Joo from ETRI, the original initiators of the project and to Leonardo Chiariglione from Cedeo for the significant help in positioning MPEG-V in the MPEG eco-system.

AUTHOR BIOGRAPHIES

Kyoungro Yoon is a professor in School of Computer Science and Engineering at Konkuk University, Seoul, Korea. He received the BS degree in electronic and computer engineering from Yonsei University, Korea, in 1987, the MSE degree in electrical and computer engineering from University of Michigan, Ann Arbor, in 1989, and the PhD degree in computer and information science in 1999 from Syracuse University, USA. From 1999 to 2003, he was a Chief Research Engineer and Group Leader in charge of development of various product-related technologies and standards in the field of image and audio processing at the LG Electronics Institute of Technology. Since 2003, he joined Konkuk University as an assistant professor and has been a professor since 2012. He actively participated in the development of standards such as MPEG-7, MPEG-21, MPEG-V, JPSearch, and TV-Anytime and served as a co-chair for Ad Hoc Groups on User Preferences, chair for Ad Hoc Group on MPEG Query Format. He is currently serving as the chair for Ad Hoc Group on MPEG-V, the chair for Ad Hoc Group on JPSearch, and the chair for the Metadata Subgroup of ISO/IEC JTC1 SC29 WG1 (a.k.a. JPEG). He also served as an editor of various international standards such as ISO/IEC 15938-12, ISO/IEC 23005-2/5/6, and ISO/IEC 24800-2/5. He has co-authored over 40 conference and journal publications in the field of multimedia information systems. He is also an inventor/co-inventor of more than 30 US patents and 70 Korean patents.

Sang-Kyun Kim received the BS, MS, and PhD degrees in computer science from University of Iowa in 1991, 1994, and 1997, respectively. In 1997, he joined the Samsung Advanced Institute of Technology as a researcher. He was a senior researcher as well as a project leader on the Image and Video Content Search Team of the Computing Technology Lab until 2007. Since 2007, he joined Myongji University as an assistant Professor and has been an associate Professor in the Department of Computer Engineering since 2011. His research interests include digital content (image, video, and music) analysis and management, image search and indexing, color adaptation, mulsemedia adaptation, sensors and actuators, VR, and media-centric-IoT. He actively participated in the multimedia standardization activities such as MPEG-7, MPEG-21, MPEG-A,

MPEG-V, as a co-chair and a project editor. He serves currently as a project editor of MPEG-V International Standards, i.e. ISO/IEC 23005-2/3/4/5, and 23005-7. He has co-authored over 40 conference and journal publications in the field of digital content management and mulsemedia simulation and adaptation. He is also an inventor/co-inventor of more than 25 US patents and 90 Korean patents.

Jae Joon Han has been a principal researcher at Samsung Advanced Institute of Technology (SAIT) in Samsung Electronics, Korea since 2007. He received the BS degree in electronic engineering from Yonsei University, Korea, in 1997, the MS degree in electrical and computer engineering from the University of Southern California, Los Angeles, in 2001, and the PhD degree in electrical and computer engineering from Purdue University, West Lafayette, IN, in August 2006. Since receiving the PhD degree, he was at Purdue as a Postdoctoral Fellow in 2007. His research interests include statistical machine learning and data mining, computer vision, and real-time recognition technologies. He participated in the development of standards such as ISO/IEC 23005 (MPEG-V) and ISO/IEC 23007 (MPEG-U), and served as the editor of ISO/IEC 23005-1/4/6. He has co-authored over 20 conference and journal publications. He is also an inventor/co-inventor of three US patents and 70 filed international patent applications.

Seungju Han is currently a senior researcher at Samsung Advanced Institute of Technology (SAIT) in Samsung Electronics, Korea. He received the PhD degree in electrical and computer engineering in 2007, from the University of Florida, USA. Since 2007, he has joined Samsung Advanced Institute of Technology as a research engineer. He participated in the development of standards such as ISO/IEC 23005 (MPEG-V) and ISO/IEC 23007 (MPEG-U), and served as the editor of ISO/IEC 23005-2/5. He has authored and co-authored over 25 research papers in the field of pattern recognition and human–computer interaction. He is also an inventor/co-inventor of four US patents and 70 filed international patent applications.

Marius Preda is an associate professor at Institut MINES-Telecom and Chairman of the 3D Graphics group of ISO's MPEG (Moving Picture Expert Group). He contributes to various ISO standards with technologies in the fields of 3D graphics, virtual worlds, and augmented reality and has received several ISO Certifications of Appreciation. He leads a research team with a focus on Augmented Reality, Cloud Computing, Games and Interactive Media and regularly presents results in journals and at speaking engagements worldwide. He serves on the program committee international conferences and reviews top-level research journals.

After being part of various research groups and networks, in 2010 he founded a research team within Institut MINES-Telecom, called GRIN – GRaphics and INteractive media. The team is conducting research at the international level cooperating with academic partners worldwide and industrial ICT leaders. Selected results are showcased on www.MyMultimediaWorld.com.

Academically, Marius received a degree in Engineering from Politehnica Bucharest, a PhD in Mathematics and Informatics from University Paris V and an eMBA from Telecom Business School, Paris.

PREFACE

Traditional multimedia content is typically consumed via audio-visual (AV) devices like displays and speakers. Recent advances in 3D video and spatial audio allow for a deeper user immersion into the digital AV content, and thus a richer user experience. The norm, however, is that just two of our five senses – sight and hearing – are exercised, while the other three (touch, smell, and taste) are neglected.

The recent multitude of new sensors map the data they capture onto our five senses and enable us to better perceive the environment both locally and remotely. In the literature, the former is referred to as "Augmented Reality", and the latter as "Immersive Experience". In parallel, new types of actuators produce different kinds of multi-sensory effect. In early periods such effects were mostly used in dedicated installations in attraction parks equipped with motion chairs, lighting sources, liquid sprays, etc., but it is more and more to see multi-sensory effects produced in more familiar environments such as at home.

Recognizing the need to represent, compress, and transmit this kind of contextual data captured by sensors, and of synthesizing effects that stimulate all human senses in a holistic fashion, the Moving Picture Experts Group (MPEG, formally ISO/IEC JTC 1/SC 29/WG 11) ratified in 2011 the first version of the MPEG-V standard (officially known as "ISO/IEC 23005 – Media context and control"). MPEG-V provides the architecture and specifies the associated information representations that enable interoperable multimedia and multimodal communication within Virtual Worlds (VWs) but also with the real world, paving the way to a "Metaverse", i.e. an online shared space created by the convergence of virtually enhanced reality and physically persistent virtual space that include the sum of all Virtual Worlds and Augmented Realities. For example, MPEG-V may be used to provide multi-sensorial content associated to traditional AV data enriching multimedia presentations with sensory effects created by lights, winds, sprays, tactile sensations, scents, etc.; or it may be used to interact with a multimedia scene by using more advanced interaction paradigms such as hand/body gestures; or to access different VWs with an avatar with a similar appearance in all of them.

In the MPEG-V vision, a piece of digital content is not limited to an AV asset, but may be a collection of multimedia and multimodal objects forming a scene, having their own behaviour, capturing their context, producing effects in the real world, interacting with one or several users, etc. In other words, a digital item can be as complex as an entire VW. Since a standardizing VW representation is technically possible but not aligned with industry interests, MPEG-V offers interoperability between VWs (and between any of them and the real world) by describing virtual objects, and specifically avatars, so that they can "move" from one VW to another.

This book on MPEG-V draws a global picture of the features made possible by the MPEG-V standard, and is divided into seven chapters, covering all aspects from the global architecture, to technical details of key components – sensors, actuators, multi-sensorial effects – and to application examples.

At the time this text was written (November 2014), three editions of MPEG-V have been published and the technical community developing the standard is still very active. As the main MPEG-V philosophy is not expected to change in future editions, this book is a good starting point to understand the principles that were at the basis of the standard. Readers interested in the latest technical details can see the MPEG-V Web-site (http://wg11.sc29.org/mpeg-v/).

Marius Preda
Leonardo Chiariglione

CHAPTER 1

Introduction to MPEG-V Standards

Contents

1.1 INTRODUCTION TO VIRTUAL WORLDS

The concept of a virtual world has become a part of our everyday lives so recently that we have not even noticed the change. There have been various attempts at defining a virtual world, each with its own point of view. The worlds that we are currently experiencing, from the viewpoint of information technology, can be divided into three types: the real world, virtual worlds, and mixed worlds. Conventionally, a virtual world, also referred to frequently as virtual reality (VR), is a computer-generated environment, giving the participants the impression that the participants are present within that environment [1]. According to Milgram and Kishino [1], real objects are those having actual existence that can be observed directly or can be sampled and resynthesized for viewing, whereas virtual objects are those that exist in essence or effect, but not formally or actually, and must be simulated.

Recently, Gelissen and Sivan [2] redefined a virtual world as an integration of 3D, Community, Creation, and Commerce (3D3C). Here, 3D indicates a 3D visualization and navigation for the representation of a virtual world, and 3C represents the three key factors that make a virtual

MPEG-V.
DOI: http://dx.doi.org/10.1016/B978-0-12-420140-8.00001-9

Figure 1.1 A virtual gaming world (from *World of Warcraft*).

world closer to the real world, which can be characterized by daily interactions for either economic (creation and commerce) or noneconomic/cultural (community) purposes.

Virtual worlds can also be divided into gaming and nongaming worlds. A virtual gaming world is a virtual world in which the behavior of the avatar (user) is goal-driven. The goal of a particular game is given within its design. *Lineage* [3] and *World of Warcraft* [4] are examples of virtual gaming worlds. Figure 1.1 shows a screen capture from *World of Warcraft*. In contrast, a nongaming virtual world is a virtual world in which the behavior of the avatar (user) is not goal-driven. In a nongaming virtual world, there is no goal provided by the designer, and the behavior of the avatar depends on the user's own intention. An example of a nongaming virtual world is *Second Life* by Linden Lab, a captured image of which is shown in Figure 1.2 [5].

A virtual world can provide an environment for both collaboration and entertainment [6]. Collaboration can mainly be enabled by the features of the virtual world, such as the 3D virtual environments in which the presence, realism, and interactivity can be supported at a higher degree than in conventional collaboration technology, and avatar-based interactions through which the social presence of the participants and the self-presentation can be provided at a higher degree than in any other existing environment.

Figure 1.2 A nongaming virtual world (from *Second Life*).

1.2 ADVANCES IN MULTIPLE SENSORIAL MEDIA

1.2.1 Basic Studies on Multiple Sensorial Media

Along with the sensations associated with 3D films and UHD display panels, the development of Multiple Sensorial Media (MulSeMedia), or 4D media, has received significant attention from the public. 4D content generally adds sensorial effects to 3D, UHD, and/or IMAX content, allowing audiences to immerse themselves more deeply into the content-viewing experience. Along with the two human senses of sight and hearing, sensorial effects such as wind, vibration, and scent can stimulate other senses, such as the tactile and olfaction senses. MulSeMedia content indicates audiovisual content annotated with sensory effect metadata [7].

The attempts to stimulate other senses while playing multimedia content have a long history. Sensorama [8,9] which was an immersive VR motorbike simulator, was a pioneer in MulSeMedia history. As a type of futuristic cinema, Sensorama rendered sensorial effects with nine different fans, a vibrating seat, and aromas to simulate a blowing wind, driving over gravel, and the scent of a flower garden or pizzeria. Although Sensorama was not successful in its day, its technology soon became a pioneer of current 4D theaters and the gaming industry.

The significance of olfactory or tactile cues has been reported in many previous studies [10–14]. Dinh et al. [10] reported that the addition of tactile, olfactory, and auditory cues into a VR environment increases the

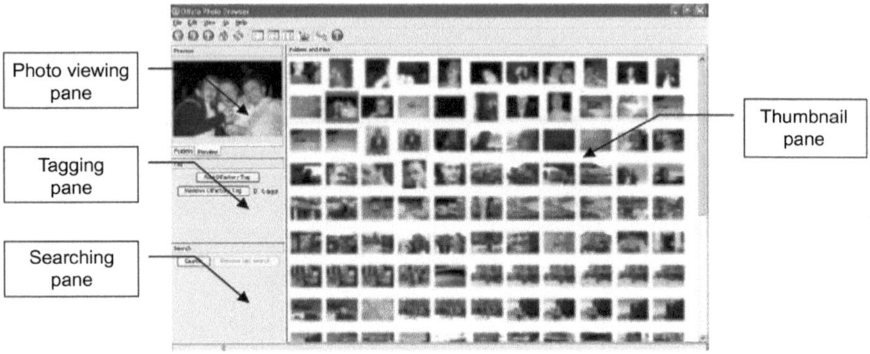

Figure 1.3 Search and retrieve based on odor [13].

user's sense of presence and memory of the environment. Bodnar et al. [11] reported that the olfactory modality is less effective in alarming users than the other modalities such as vibration and sound, but can have a less disruptive effect on continuing the primary task of the users. Ryu and Kim [12] studied the effectiveness of vibro-tactile effects on the whole body to simulate collisions between users and their virtual environment.

Olfactory cues can be used to evoke human memories. Brewster et al. [13] presented a study on the use of smell for searching through digital photo collections, and compared text- and odor-based tagging (Figure 1.3). For the first stage, sets of odors and tag names from the user descriptions of different photos were generated. The participants then used these to tag their photos, returning two weeks later to answer questions regarding these images. The results showed that the performance when using odors was lower than that from simple text searching but that some of the participants had their memories of their photos evoked through the use of smell.

Ghinea and Ademoye [14] presented a few design guidelines for the integration of olfaction (with six odor categories) in multimedia applications. Finally, Kannan et al. [15] encompassed the significance of other senses incorporated in the creation of digital content for the packaging industry, healthcare systems, and educational learning models.

1.2.2 Authoring of MulSeMedia

The difficulties in producing MulSeMedia content mainly lie in the time and effort incurred by authoring the sensory effects. For the successful industrial deployment of MulSeMedia services, the provisioning of an easy and efficient means of producing MulSeMedia content plays a critical role. Figure 1.4 shows examples of the authoring tools used to create digital content with sensorial effects.

(A)
(B)
(C)
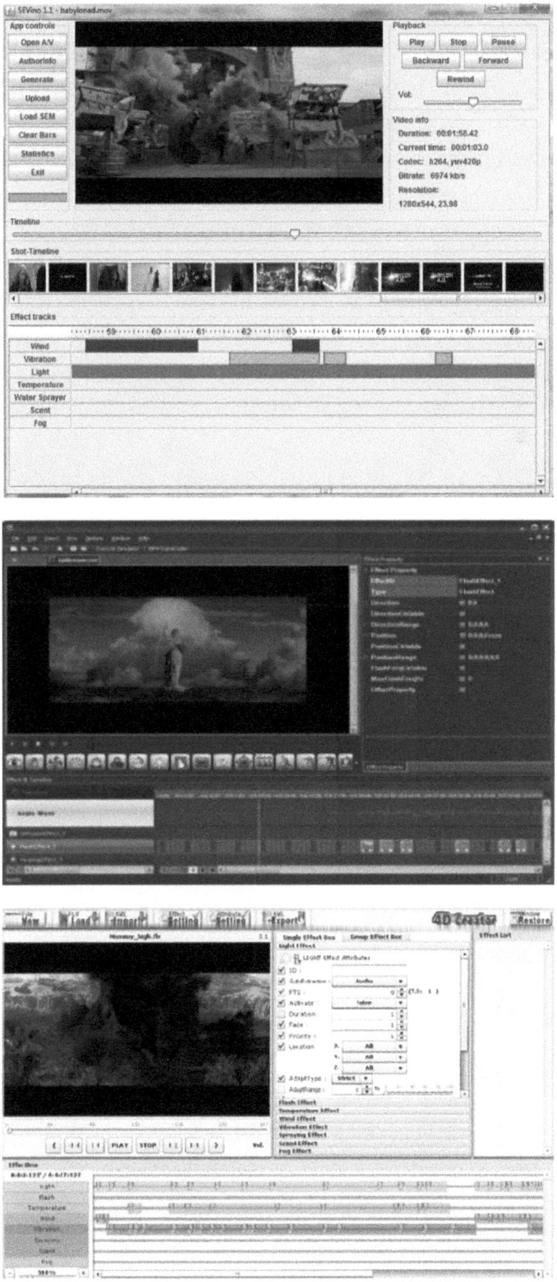

Figure 1.4 Authoring tools for sensorial effects: (A) SEVino by Waltl et al. [18,19], (B) RoSEStudio by Choi et al. [16], and (C) SMURF by Kim [17].

Waltl et al. [18,19] presented a sensory effect authoring tool called SEVino (Figure 1.4A), which can verify XML instances from the Java Architecture for XML Binding (JAXB) complying with the XML schema specified in MPEG-V, Part 3 (which is described in Chapter 2). Choi et al. [16] presented an authoring tool known as RoSEStudio (Figure 1.4B) with a framework for streaming services with sensorial effects to bring about an at-home 4D entertainment system based on the MPEG-V standard. Kim [17] presented an authoring tool known as SMURF (Figure 1.4C), which not only can create *GroupOfEffects* but also supports the *Declaration* and *ReferenceEffect* for ordinary users to easily create their own desired sensorial effect metadata. Figure 1.5 shows 20 icons indicating sensorial effects such as wind, temperature, scent, fog, light, vibration, motion, and tactile sensations.

The authoring of MulSeMedia content can be boosted by extracting sensorial information automatically from the content itself. In other words, sensory effects can be generated automatically by extracting sensorial (physical and emotional) properties from the content and by mapping the major attributes of the extracted properties to the sensory effects [7]. This can speed up the authoring process significantly.

Extracting physical properties such as the color characteristics from the content was achieved by Waltl et al. [19] and Timmerer et al. [20]. In their

Figure 1.5 Sensorial effect menu icons [16].

works, ambient light devices were controlled using automatic color calculations (e.g., averaging the RGB or dominant colors in the RGB, HSV, and HMMD spaces) to enable an immediate reaction to color changes within the content. Kim et al. [7] extracted the color temperature from the content to convert them into four categories of emotional properties (i.e., hot, warm, moderate, and cool). The extracted emotional properties are in turn mapped to temperature effects to author the MulSeMedia content automatically.

The sensory effects created by different authoring tools can be visualized through sensory effect simulators. Kim et al. [21] presented a sensible media simulator (Figure 1.6) for a 4D simulation in an automobile environment and the implementation of sensorial actuators. Waltl et al. [19] briefly described a simulator (SESim) to evaluate the quality of the multimedia experience presented to the users.

1.2.3 Quality of Experience of MulSeMedia

It is important to know how digital content enriched with additional sensorial effects actually affects the level of satisfaction. Therefore, the quality

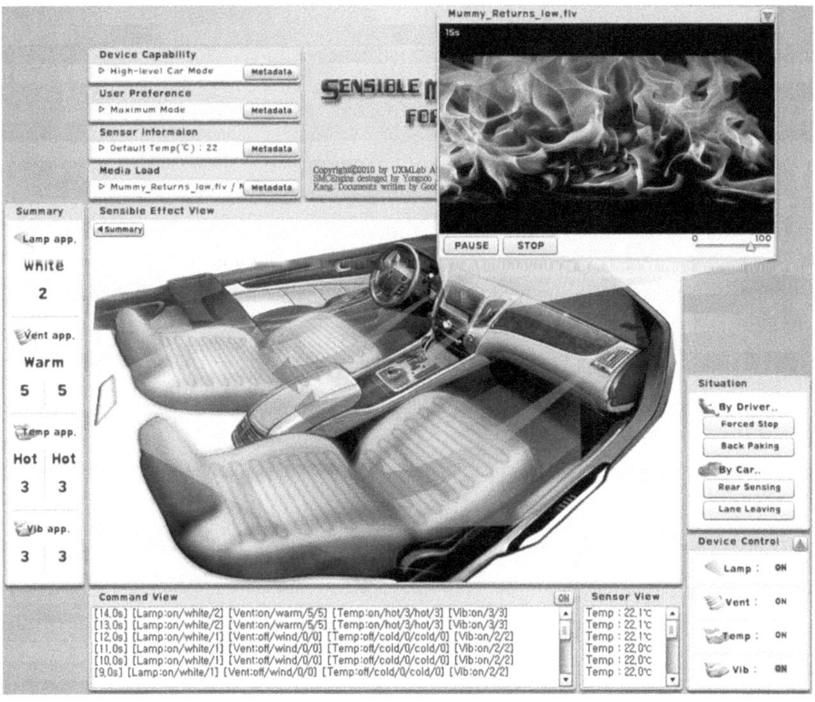

Figure 1.6 Sensorial effect simulation [21].

of experience regarding sensorial effects is measured through a careful experimental design. In this section, publicly known test setups along with regulated test procedures are described as well as a few experimental results of the quality of experience (QoE) of MulSeMedia.

1.2.3.1 Test Setups

Waltl et al. [18] collected a total of 76 video sequences from different genres, i.e., action, documentaries, sports, news, and commercial sequences, and described them based on their sensorial effects (i.e., wind, vibration, and light). They opened a dataset comprising a number of video sequences from different genres as a means to inspire similar researches. Furthermore, they described possible test setups using off-the-shelf hardware for conducting subjective quality assessments. The setup for one amBX system consists of two fans, two light-speakers, a wall washer, a Wrist Rumbler, and a subwoofer (left-most side of Figure 1.7A). The middle of Figure 1.7A shows the test setup using two amBX systems. The third test setup (right-most side of Figure 1.7A) consists of two amBX systems and two sets of Cyborg Gaming Lights.

Figure 1.7B shows the actual test setup depicted on the right-most side of Figure 1.7A.

Waltl et al. [22] presented a demonstration setup that uses stereoscopic 3D and sensory devices, i.e., fans, vibration panels, and lights (Figure 1.7C). This chapter reported that the combination of 3D content with sensorial effects allows further improvement in the viewing experience for users.

1.2.3.2 Test Procedures

Rainer et al. [23] presented recommendations for the test setups and methods used in the MulSeMedia experience. Figure 1.8 shows the experimental procedures for a MulSeMedia viewing experience. In the first stage, the test participants have to read the introduction, which explains the purpose of the actual experiment. In the second stage, some demographic and educational information of the participants is acquired using a pre-questionnaire. The training phase is provided to eliminate the surprise effect and help the participants become familiar with the stimulus presentation. The main evaluation adheres to the recommendations of ITU P.910 and P.911 [24,25] regarding the test methods and design. Two of the main evaluation methods used, i.e., DCR and DSCQS, are presented in Figure 1.9. Finally, a post-questionnaire was provided to ask the participants whether they had already participated in a similar experiment and to provide them a chance to give their feedback.

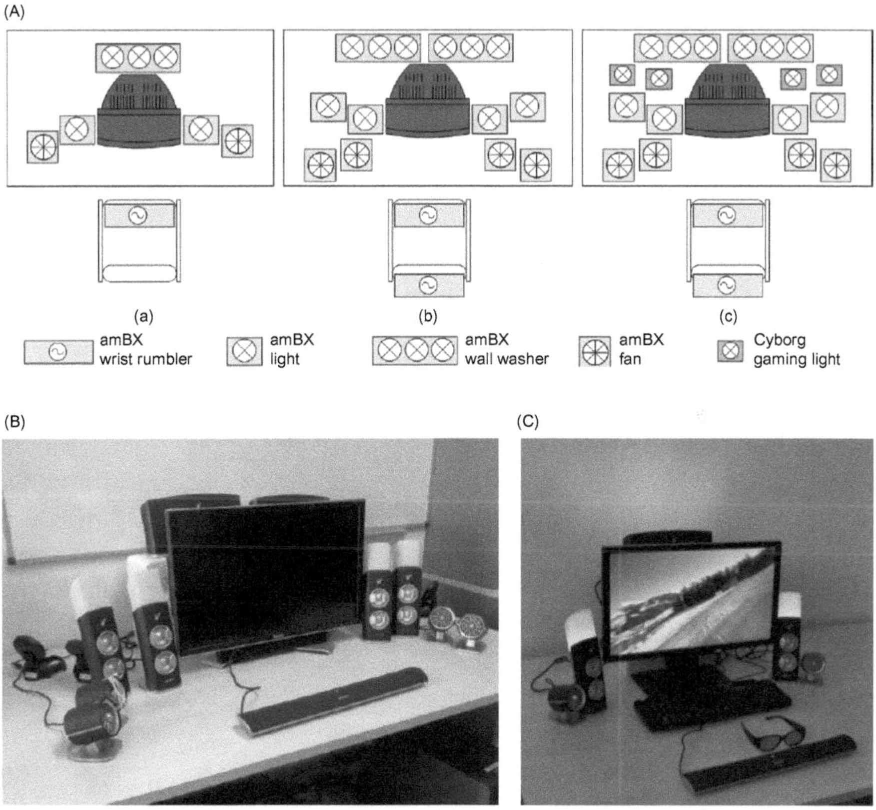

Figure 1.7 Sensorial effect test setups [18,22].

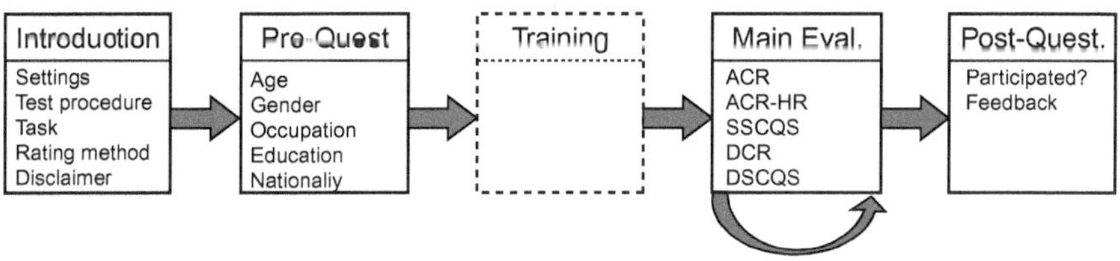

Figure 1.8 Test procedure for the sensorial effects [23].

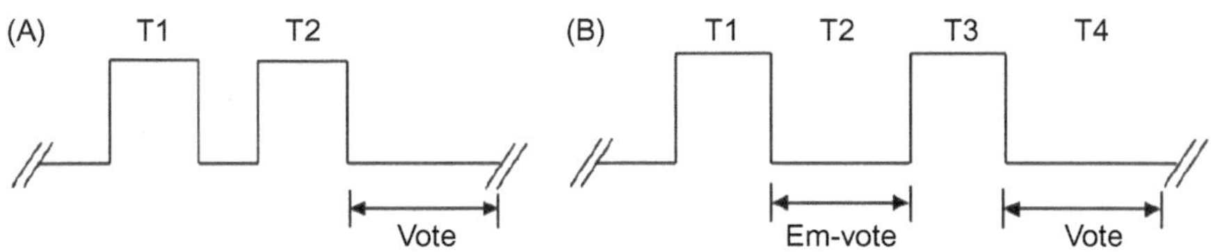

Figure 1.9 (A) DSR and (B) DSCQS [23].

Figure 1.9A shows the Degradation Category Rating (DCR) method. In T1, the reference content is presented, and in T2, the content with sensorial effects is shown. Between T1 and T2, a gray screen is presented to the participants. Figure 1.9B shows the Double Stimulus Continuous Quality Scale (DSCQS) method. T1 shows the presentation of a video sequence without sensorial effects. T2 illustrates the rating of emotions and their intensity. T3 shows a presentation of the same video sequence with sensorial effects, and finally, T4 provides the rating of the emotions and their intensity for the video sequence with sensorial effects.

1.2.3.3 Experimental QoE Results for Sensorial Effects

Waltl et al. [26] investigated the QoE based on various video bit-rates of multimedia contents annotated with sensorial effects (e.g., wind, vibration, and light). The results show that the level of satisfaction of a video sequence with sensorial effects is higher than that of a video without sensorial effects. Timmerer et al. [20] presented the QoE test results for wind, vibration, and lighting effects for the action, sports, documentary, news, and commercial genres, which indicate that the action, sports, and documentary genres benefit more from sensorial effects than the news and commercial genres.

Rainer et al. [27] presented the emotional response of users and an enhancement of the QoE of Web video sequences. In particular, the authors' QoE experiments were conducted in Austria and Australia to investigate whether geographical and cultural differences affect elicited emotional responses of the users.

Timmerer et al. [28] derived a utility model for sensory experiences using their previous QoE experimental results. The aim of this utility model was to estimate the QoE of multimedia content with sensorial effects as compared with the QoE of multimedia content without sensorial effects. The proposed utility model shows that a linear relationship exists between the QoE without sensorial effects and the QoE with sensorial effects.

Kim et al. [21] presented the relationship between the QoE with sensorial effects and the learning types of the participants. The experimental results showed that stimulations from the vibration effects generated greater satisfaction in people with a high tactile perception capability at a statistically significant level. Stimulations through vibration effects generated more satisfaction in people with a low visual perception level as well. This indicates that vibration effects can be assumed to be a high priority for people with a high tactile perception capability and/or a low visual perception capability. Kim et al. [7] also showed that the sequences with temperature effects automatically generated through a color temperature estimation clearly enhanced the level of satisfaction.

Yazdani et al. [29] analyzed the electroencephalogram (EEG) of five participants during their perception of both unpleasant and pleasant odorous stimuli. They identified the regions of the brain cortex that are active during the discrimination of unpleasant and pleasant odor stimuli.

1.3 HISTORY OF MPEG-V

MPEG-V shares a similar view of virtual and real worlds, except that its definition of a real world is tighter, and that of a virtual world has been extended as compared to their conventional definitions. In MPEG-V, the sampled and resynthesized environments of the real world are no longer considered real worlds and are viewed as virtual worlds. Therefore, movies or video sequences depicting the real world are also considered another representation of a virtual world. Such a change in the definitions of real and virtual worlds has made it possible to develop the concepts of virtual-to-real and real-to-virtual adaptations.

Creating and enjoying films in 3D have become popular, a breaking point being the 3D movie, *Avatar*, which had unprecedented success owing to its 3D effects. One reason for this success is the ability to immerge the user into the story through the creation of a full audiovisual environment. Additionally, by providing more effects on top of the audiovisual effects, it is possible to obtain more immersion in terms of user experience. One possibility is to add special effects provided by (sensorial) actuators, so-called 4D effects, which affect senses other than seeing and hearing. Other modalities, such as olfaction, mechanoreception, equilibrioception, or thermoception may be stimulated, giving the feeling of being part of the media content, and resulting in a meaningful and consistent user experience. In particular, 4D movies that include sensorial effects such as wind, vibration, lighting, and scent can stimulate the human sensory system using actuators such as fans, motion chairs, lighting devices, and scent generators. Such rendering of sensorial effects in the real world is an example of a virtual-to-real adaptation.

It is also well known that user interaction is a powerful means to improve the user experience. Interacting with digital content, thereby changing it from a linear content, as in the case of traditional movies, allows users to be not only spectators but also actors. The success of complex video games that create an entire universe is an indicator of the role such an interaction can play. More generally, virtual worlds are typical applications using 3D technologies, allowing the user to interact and change both the storyline and the environment. A notable example is *Second Life*, which allows users to project themselves into virtual characters (called avatars). Through their avatar, the user can live a virtual life; communicate with others, perform daily activities, and own virtual assets such as houses and other types of property. In massive multiplayer online role-playing games (MMORPG) such as *World of Warcraft* or *Lineage*, users can operate their characters in a virtual world and cooperate with others to fulfill missions. Such 3D games immerse users in a virtual world by providing a fictional environment that can otherwise only be experienced in their imagination.

Moreover, controlling virtual worlds with sensors provides an even more immersive media experience. The effective control of objects in such virtual worlds has been developed in many ways: the motions of users captured from a set of sensors are used to control game characters. The recently developed "Kinect" sensor can capture the full-body skeleton of each user and use captured data to manipulate objects in a virtual world. In addition, some pioneering technologies are used to capture brain waves to recognize the user's intention and/or internal state. These activities for controlling the avatars or objects of a virtual world by sensing the real environment and real objects can be viewed as an example of a real-to-virtual adaptation.

Because each of these technologies related to immersive multisensorial experiences is based on proprietary products, there is no standard way for representing the data from sensors and actuators in the real world, and no common way to interface with a virtual world. As a result, each proprietary virtual world has also been isolated from other virtual worlds. This hinders users when migrating from one virtual world to another, and therefore, when a virtual world loses its interest, all assets produced and the entire community itself are lost. To increase the usability of each virtual world and their interoperability, and improve the controls and increase the quality of the user experience, the MPEG community has developed the MPEG-V standard (ISO/IEC 23005) with the intention of offering a common information representation format. The standardization work in MPEG-V was initiated in 2008, and the second version of the standard was published in 2013 [30–36].

MPEG-V was initiated in 2008 based on two separate projects with different objectives. One is the Metaverse EU project whose objective is to provide a framework for interoperability between heterogeneous virtual worlds [2,37]. The other is the Single Media Multiple Devices (SMMD) project of ETRI, Korea, whose objective is to develop technology providing new media services with sensory effects using multiple devices [38].

Metaverse project-related proposals were first submitted at the 81st MPEG meeting in Lausanne, Switzerland, in July 2007, and SMMD project-related proposals were first submitted at the 82nd MPEG meeting in Shenzhen in October 2007. The Metaverse project was renamed MPEG-V, and is focused on the exchange of information between virtual worlds. The SMMD project was renamed Representation of Sensory Effects (RoSE), and is focused on the representation of sensory effects for new types of media services.

At the 87th meeting in Lausanne, Switzerland, in February 2009, the two on-going projects of MPEG-V and RoSE were merged into the MPEG-V standard, which deals with both virtual and real worlds. The architecture and introduction of the standard was given in Part 1 of MPEG-V. The control information was provided in Part 2. Representations of the sensory effects and sensory effect metadata were given in Part 3, and the representation of avatars was provided in Part 4. Committee drafts of the first edition were released at the 89th meeting in London in July 2009. At the 90th meeting in Xian, China, in October 2009, discussions were held on the subdivision of the control information of Part 2, which was finally divided into two separate parts at an Ad Hoc meeting in Paris in December 2009, i.e., the control information in Part 2, and the data formats for interaction devices in Part 5. At the 91st Kyoto meeting, the common tools and types from each part of the standard were extracted and became the newly added Part 6. Finally, the reference software is provided in Part 7.

The first edition of the complete set of MPEG-V specifications was published in early 2011. At the 91st Kyoto meeting in January 2010, the need for binary representations of the MPEG-V tools for a greater transfer efficiency was raised, and work on the second edition of the standard was started. After creating a binary representation of all existing tools in the first edition, as well as new sensory effects and other additional tools, the second edition was finally published in 2013.

Currently, the third edition of the standard is progressing with the addition of more effects, devices, and sensors.

1.4 ORGANIZATIONS OF MPEG-V

MPEG-V (Media context and control), published in ISO/IEC 23005, provides an architecture and specifies the associated information representations to enable bridges between the real world and digital content, and to increase the interoperability between virtual worlds. MPEG-V is applicable in various business models/domains for which audiovisual contents can be associated with sensorial effects that need to be rendered on appropriate actuators and/or benefit from well-defined interactions with an associated virtual world.

A well-defined connection between the real and virtual worlds is needed to reach simultaneous reactions in both worlds. This is done in MPEG-V by defining an architecture that provides interoperability at various levels. Efficient, effective, intuitive, and entertaining interfaces between users and virtual worlds are of crucial importance for their wide acceptance and use of such technologies. To improve the process of creating virtual worlds, a better design methodology and better tools are indispensable.

The MPEG-V standard consists of the following parts: Part 1: Architecture [30]; Part 2: Control Information [31]; Part 3: Sensory Information [32]; Part 4: Virtual World Object Characteristics [33]; Part 5: Formats for Interaction Devices [34]; Part 6: Common Types and Tools [35]; and Part 7: Conformance and Reference Software [36].

Part 1 provides an overview of MPEG-V along with the architecture and various use cases or applications of the MPEG-V standard.

Part 2 provides the tools for a description of the capabilities of the actuators and sensors, the user's preferences regarding the sensory effects, and their preferences in terms of the sensor adaptations. Altogether, these tools are called the control information, and are used for the detailed and personalized control of the actuators and sensors. The control information is provided using the Control Information Description Language (CIDL) with the Device Capability Description Vocabulary (DCDV), Sensor Capability Description Vocabulary (SCDV), User's Sensory Preference Vocabulary (USPV), and Sensor Adaptation Preference Vocabulary (SAPV), whose syntaxes are defined using the XML schema.

Part 3 provides the tools for a description of the sensorial effect in synchronization with the media content. The descriptions of the sensorial effect or sensory effect metadata (SEM) are defined using the Sensory Effect Description Language (SEDL) with the Sensory Effect Vocabulary (SEV) based on the XML schema.

Part 4 defines the characteristics of a virtual-world object to provide tools enabling the interoperability between virtual worlds. It also provides tools for the description or metadata of avatars and virtual objects. The metadata describe the characteristics of the avatars and virtual objects in terms of their nature, character, and appearance, to name a few, but do not provide the actual shape, texture, or rendering information.

Part 5 specifies the interfaces or data formats for an interoperable exchange of information to/from the sensors and actuators. These interfaces are defined by the Interaction Information Description Language (IIDL) with the Device Command Vocabulary (DCV) and Sensed Information Vocabulary (SIV) based on the XML schema. The DCV defines the data formats used as commands to the actuators. The SIV defines the data formats used for transferring sensed information from a sensor to the adaptation engine or to the information destination.

Part 6 specifies the syntax and semantics of the data types and tools that are common to more than one part of the MPEG-V standard. In the appendix of this part of the standard, the classification schemes for various sets of terms, such as the unit and scent types, are also defined.

Part 7 provides the reference software and specifies the conformance using a Schematron.

Figure 1.10 shows a diagram of the MPEG-V system architecture and its data transition scenarios. The MPEG-V specifications are used for three different types of media exchanges between real and virtual worlds. The first media exchange is the information adaptation from a virtual world into the real world (Figure 1.10A). It accepts sensorial effect data (specified in MPEG-V, Part 3) and/or Virtual World Object Characteristics (MPEG-V, Part 2) as contextual inputs; accepts Actuator Capability and/or Actuation Preferences (MPEG-V, Part 2) and/or Sensed Information (MPEG-V, Part 5) as control parameters; and generates Actuator Commands (MPEG-V, Part 5) to the real-world actuators. The VR adaptation engine converts (or adapts) either the Virtual World Object Characteristics or the sensorial effect data from a virtual world into the Actuator Commands in the real world in accordance with the input control parameters. The manner in which the adaptation engine is implemented is not within the scope of the MPEG-V standardization. The second media exchange is the information adaptation from the real world into a virtual world. The real-to-virtual adaptation engine accepts Sensed Information (MPEG-V, Part 5) from sensors as the real-world context; accepts Sensor Capability and/or Sensor Adaptation

(A)

(B)

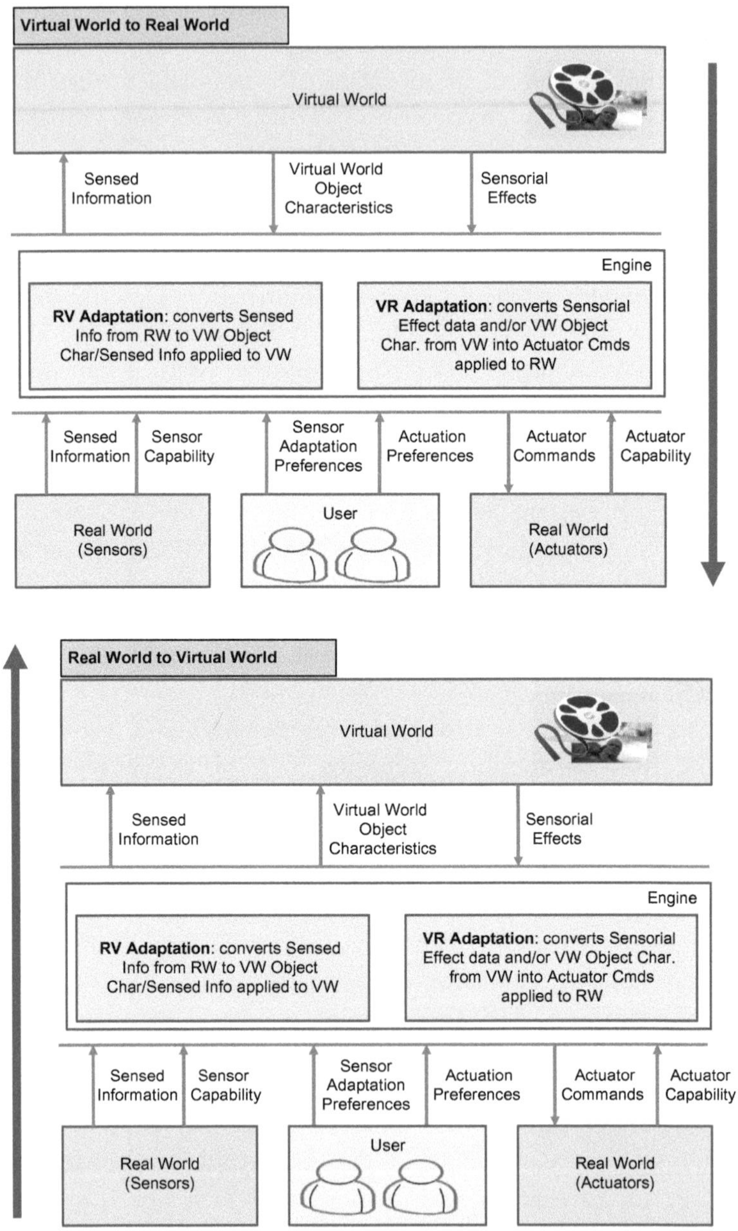

Figure 1.10 MPEG-V architectures and data transition scenarios: (A) a virtual- into real-world scenario, (B) a real- into virtual-world scenario, and (C) a virtual- into virtual-world scenario.

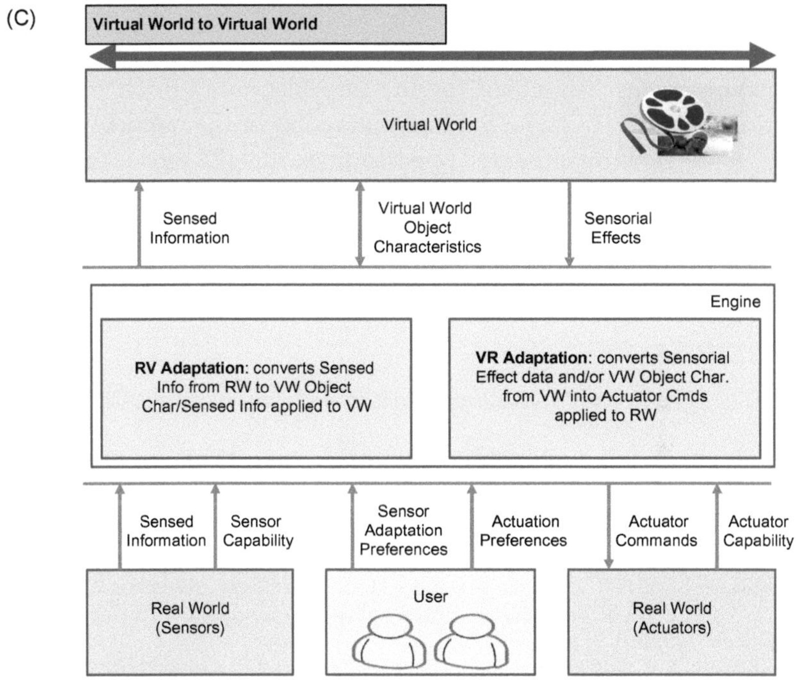

Figure 1.10 (Continued).

Preferences (MPEG-V, Part 2) as control parameters; and generates Virtual World Object Characteristics (MPEG-V, Part 4) and/or adapted Sensed Information (MPEG-V, Part 5) to the associated virtual-world objects (Figure 1.10B). The RV adaptation engine converts (or adapts) the sensed information from the real-world sensors into the Virtual World Object Characteristics and/or the adapted sensed information of a virtual world in accordance with the input control parameters. Finally, information exchange between virtual worlds is conducted by adapting proprietary Virtual World Object Characteristics into the normatively specified Virtual World Object Characteristics (MPEG-V, Part 4) (Figure 1.10C).

1.5 CONCLUSION

MPEG-V (ISO/IEC 23005) provides the architecture and necessary associated information representation supporting the information exchanges between the real and virtual worlds, and the information exchange between virtual worlds. To support the information exchanges, the information between the two worlds should be adapted by considering the capabilities of each world and the user preferences regarding the information. Each component for the information adaption is addressed in sections of ISO/IEC 23005. Finally, adoption of the standardized information representation provides opportunities for 4D broadcasting, natural interaction with intelligent sensors within any virtual world, seamless interaction between real and virtual worlds, and the importing of virtual characters and objects between virtual worlds.

REFERENCES

[1] P. Milgram, F. Kishino, A taxonomy of mixed reality visual displays, IEICE Trans. Inf. Syst. E77-D (12) (1994).
[2] J.H.A. Gelissen, Y.Y. Sivan, The Metaverse1 case: historical review of making one virtual worlds standard (MPEG-V), J. Virtual Worlds Res. 4 (3) (2011).
[3] Lineage. <http://lineage.plaync.com>, (last accessed on 20.09.14).
[4] World of WarCraft. <http://www.battle.net/wow/>, (last accessed on 20.09.14).
[5] Second Life. <http://secondlife.com>, (last accessed on 20.09.14).
[6] S. van der Land, A.P. Schouten, B. van der Hooff, F. Feldberg, Modelling the Metaverse: a theoretical model of effective team collaboration in 3D virtual environments, J. Virtual Worlds Res. 4 (3) (2011).
[7] S.-K. Kim, S.-J. Yang, C. Ahn, Y. Joo, Sensorial information extraction and mapping to generate temperature sensory effects, ETRI J. 36 (2) (2014) 232–241.
[8] H. Rheingold, Virtual Reality, Summit Books, New York, NY, 1991 (Chapter 2).
[9] J.J. Kaye, Making scents: aromatic output for HCI, Interactions 11 (1) (2004) 48–61.
[10] H.Q. Dinh, N. Walker, L.F. Hodges, C. Song, A. Kobayashi, Evaluating the importance of multisensory input on memory and the sense of presence in virtual environments, in: Proceedings—Virtual Reality Annual International Symposium, 1999, pp. 222–228.
[11] A. Bodnar, R. Corbett, D. Nekrasovski, AROMA: ambient awareness through olfaction in a messaging application: Does olfactory notification make "scents?" in: Sixth International Conference on Multimodal Interfaces, 2004, pp. 183.
[12] J. Ryu, G.J. Kim, Using a vibro-tactile display for enhanced collision perception and presence, in: VRST '04: Proceedings of the ACM Symposium on Virtual Reality Software and Technology, ACM, New York, NY, 2004, pp. 89–96.
[13] S.A. Brewster, D.K. McGookin, C.A. Miller, Olfoto: designing a smell-based interaction, in: CHI 2006: Conference on Human Factors in Computing Systems, 2006, p. 653.
[14] G. Ghinea, O.A. Ademoye, Olfaction-enhanced multimedia: perspectives and challenges, Multimed. Tools Appl. (2010) 1–26.
[15] R. Kannan, S.R. Balasundaram, F. Andres, The role of mulsemedia in digital content ecosystem design, in: Proceedings of the International Conference on Management of Emergent Digital EcoSystems, 2010, pp. 264–266.
[16] B. Choi, E.-S. Lee, K. Yoon, Streaming media with sensory effect, in: Proceedings of the International Conference on Information Science and Application, Jeju Island, Republic of Korea, April 26–29, 2011, pp. 1–6.
[17] S.-K. Kim, Authoring multisensorial content, Signal Process. Image Commun. 28 (2) (2013) 162–167.
[18] M. Waltl, C. Timmerer, B. Rainer, H. Hellwagner, Sensory effect dataset and test setups, in: IEEE Proceedings of the Fourth International Workshop Quality Multimedia Experience, 2012, pp. 115–120.

[19] M. Waltl, C. Timmerer, H. Hellwagner, A test-bed for quality of multimedia experience evaluation of sensory effects, in: Proceedings of the International Workshop Quality Multimedia Experience, San Diego, CA, July 29–31, 2009, pp. 145–150.
[20] C. Timmerer, M. Waltl, B. Rainer, H. Hellwagner, Assessing the quality of sensory experience for multimedia presentations, Signal Process. Image Commun. 27 (8) (2012) 909–916.
[21] S.-K. Kim, Y.-S. Joo, Y. Lee, Sensible media simulation in an automobile application and human responses to sensory effects, ETRI J. 35 (6) (2013) 1001–1010.
[22] M. Waltl, B. Rainer, S. Lederer, et al., A 4D multimedia player enabling sensory experience, in: IEEE Proceedings of the Fifth International Workshop Quality Multimedia Experience, 2013, pp. 126–127.
[23] Rainer, B., Timmerer, C., Waltl, M., Recommendations for the subjective evaluation of sensory experience, in: Fourth International Workshop on Perceptual Quality of Systems, 2013.
[24] ITU-T Rec. P.910, Subjective Video Quality Assessment Methods for Multimedia Applications, April 2008.
[25] ITU-T Rec. P.911, Subjective Audiovisual Quality Assessment Methods for Multimedia Applications, December 2008.
[26] M. Waltl, C. Timmerer, H. Hellwagner, Improving the quality of multimedia experience through sensory effects, in: IEEE Proceedings of the Second International Workshop Quality Multimedia Experience, 2010, pp. 124–129.
[27] B. Rainer, M. Waltl, E. Cheng et al., Investigating the impact of sensory effects on the quality of experience and emotional response in web videos, in: IEEE Proceedings of the Fourth International Workshop Quality Multimedia Experience, 2012, pp. 115–120.
[28] C. Timmerer, B. Rainer, M. Waltl, A utility model for sensory experience, in: IEEE Proceedings of the Fifth International Workshop Quality Multimedia Experience, 2013, pp. 224–229.
[29] A. Yazdani, E. Kroupi, J. Vesni, T. Ebrahimi, Electroencephalogram alterations during perception of pleasant and unpleasant odors, in: IEEE Proceedings of the Fourth International Workshop Quality Multimedia Experience, Yarra Valley, Australia, 2012, pp. 272–277.
[30] ISO/IEC 23005-1: 2014 Information technology—Media context and control—Part 1: Architecture, January 2014.
[31] ISO/IEC 23005-2:2013 Information technology—Media context and control—Part 2: Control information, November 2013.
[32] ISO/IEC 23005-3:2013 Information technology—Media context and control—Part 3: Sensory information, November 2013.
[33] ISO/IEC 23005-4:2013 Information technology—Media context and control—Part 4: Virtual world object characteristics, November 2013.
[34] ISO/IEC 23005-5: 2013 Information technology—Media context and control—Part 5: Data formats for interaction devices, November 2013.
[35] ISO/IEC 23005-6: 2013 Information technology—Media context and control—Part 6: Common types and tools, November 2013.
[36] ISO/IEC 23005-7: 2014 Information technology—Media context and control—Part 7: Conformance and reference software, January 2014.
[37] Metaverse, <http://www.metaverse1.org>, (last accessed on 20.09.14).
[38] B.S. Choi, S.H. Joo, H.Y. Lee, Sensory effect metadata for SMMD media service, in: Proceedings of the Fourth International Conference on Internet and Web Applications and Services, Venice/Mestre, Italy, May 2009.

CHAPTER 2

Adding Sensorial Effects to Media Content

Contents

2.1 INTRODUCTION

MPEG-V, Part 3: Sensory information (ISO/IEC 23005-3), specifies the Sensory Effect Description Language (SEDL) [1] as an XML schema-based language that enables one to describe sensorial effects (SEs) such as light, wind, fog, and vibration that trigger human senses. The actual SEs are not part of the SEDL but are defined within the Sensory Effect Vocabulary (SEV) for extensibility and flexibility, allowing each application domain to define its own SEs. A description conforming to SEDL is referred to as Sensory Effect Metadata (SEM) and may be associated with any type of multimedia content (e.g., movies, music, Web sites, games). The SEM is used to steer actuators such as fans, vibration chairs, and lamps using an appropriate mediation device to increase the user experience. That is, in addition to the audiovisual (AV) content of a movie, e.g., the user will also perceive other effects such as those described above, giving the user the sensation of being part of the particular media content, which

MPEG-V.
DOI: http://dx.doi.org/10.1016/B978-0-12-420140-8.00002-0

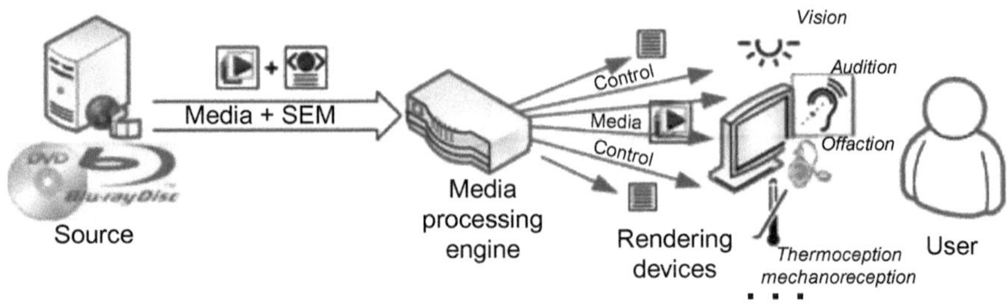

Figure 2.1 Concept of MPEG-V SEDL [1].

will result in a worthwhile, informative user experience. The concept of receiving SEs in addition to AV content is depicted in Figure 2.1.

The media and corresponding SEM may be obtained from a Digital Versatile Disc (DVD), Blu-ray Disc (BD), or any type of online service (i.e., download/play or streaming). The media processing engine, which is also referred to as the adaptation engine, acts as the mediation device and is responsible for playing the actual media content resource and accompanied SEs in a synchronized way based on the user's setup in terms of both the media content and rendering of the SE. Therefore, the media processing engine may adapt both the media resource and the SEM according to the capabilities of the various rendering devices.

The SEV defines a clear set of actual SEs to be used with the SEDL in an extensible and flexible way. That is, it can be easily extended with new effects or through a derivation of existing effects thanks to the extensibility feature of the XML schema. Furthermore, the effects are defined based on the authors' (i.e., creators of the SEM) intention independent from the end user's device setting, as shown in Figure 2.2.

The sensory effect metadata elements or data types are mapped to commands that control the actuators based on their capabilities. This mapping is usually provided by the Virtual-to-Real adaptation engine and was deliberately not defined in this standard, i.e., it is left open for industry competitors. It is important to note that there is not necessarily a one-to-one mapping between elements or data types of the SE data and ACs. For example, the effect of hot/cold wind may be rendered on a single device with two capabilities, i.e., a heater or air conditioner, and a fan or ventilator.

As shown in Figure 2.3, the SEs can be adjusted into adapted SEs (i.e., defined in MPEG-V, Part 5, as device commands) in accordance with the capabilities of the actuators (ACs, defined in MPEG-V, Part 2) and actuation preferences (APs, defined in MPEG-V, Part 2, as user sensory preferences).

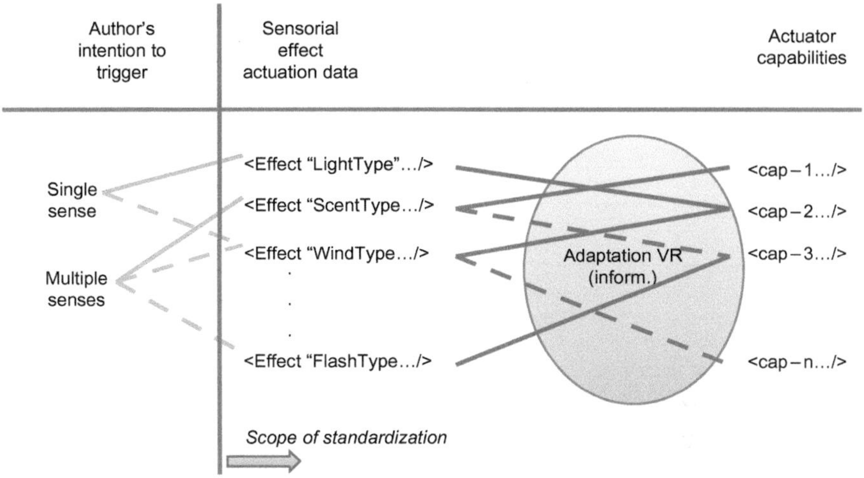

Figure 2.2 Mapping of author's intentions to SE data and actuator capabilities (ACs) [2].

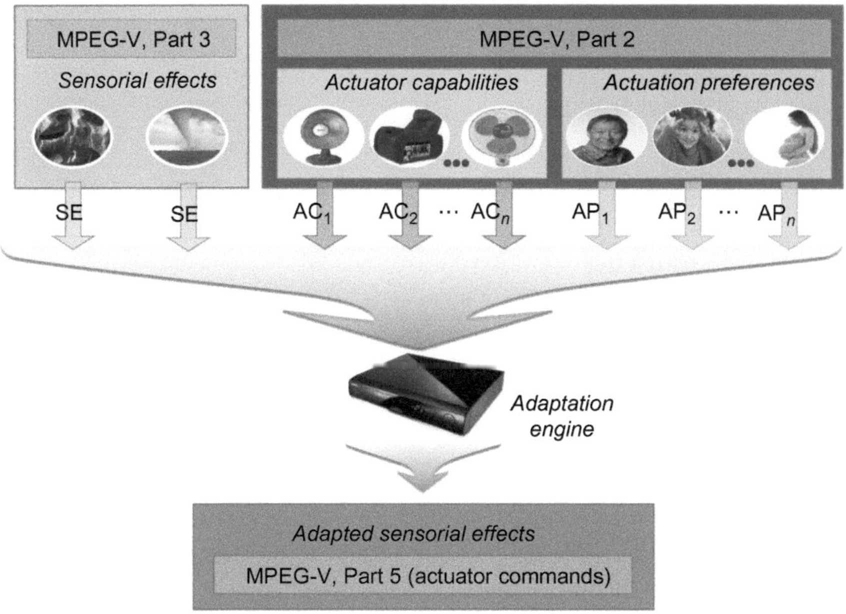

Figure 2.3 The adapted SEs (actuator commands defined in MPEG-V, Part 5) generated by combining SEs with ACs and user's APs.

Figure 2.4 shows an example of combining SEs (SEs in MPEG-V, Part 3) with sensed information (SI in MPEG-V, Part 5) to generate adapted actuator commands (ACmd in MPEG-V, Part 5). For example, the SE corresponding to the scene might be cooling the temperature to

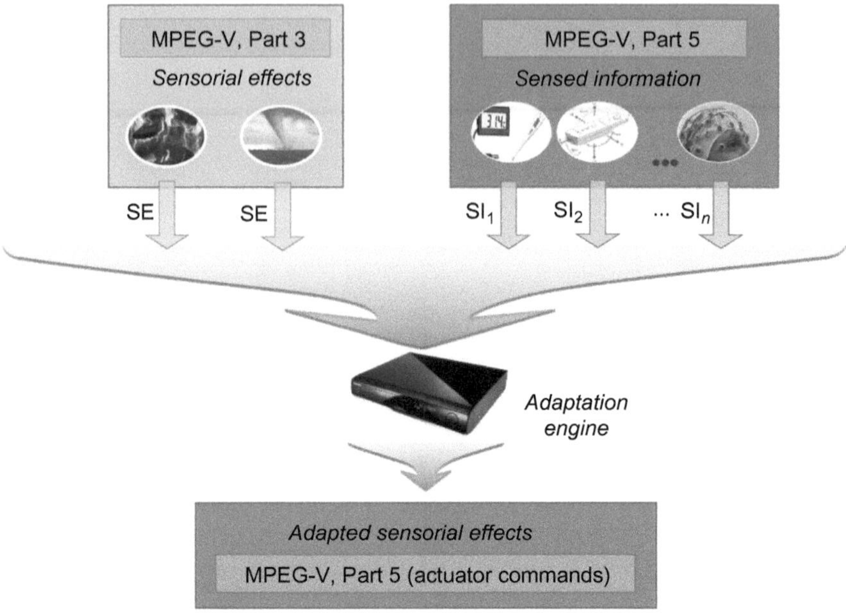

Figure 2.4 The adapted SEs (actuator commands defined in MPEG-V, Part 5) generated by combining SEs with SI.

5°C and adding a wind effect with 100% intensity. Assume instead that the current room temperature is 12°C. It would be unwise to deploy the cooling and wind effect as described in the SE data because the current temperature inside the room is already low, and users may feel uncomfortable with the generated SEs. Therefore, a sensor measures the room temperature and the adaptation engine generates the adapted SEs (i.e., ACmds), which are a reduced wind effect (20% intensity) and a heating effect (20°C), for instance.

This chapter is organized as follows. Section 2.2 describes the details of the SEDL. Section 2.3 presents the SEV, which specifies the data formats used for creating SEs. Section 2.4 presents XML instances using SEDL and SEV. Finally, Section 2.5 concludes the chapter.

2.2 SENSORY EFFECT DESCRIPTION LANGUAGE

2.2.1 SEDL Structure

The SEDL is a language providing basic building blocks to instantiate sensory effect metadata defined by the MPEG-V standard based on XML that can be authored by content providers.

2.2.2 Base Data Types and Elements of SEDL

There are two base types in the SEDL. The first base type is `SEMBaseAttributes`, which includes six base attributes and one base attribute Group. The schema definition of `SEMBaseAttributes` is shown in Table 2.1. The `activate` attribute describes whether the SE shall be activated.

The `duration` attribute describes the duration of any SE rendering. The `fade` attribute describes the fade time within which the defined `intensity` is reached. The `alt` attribute describes an alternative effect identified by the uniform resource identifier (URI). For example, an alternative effect is chosen because the original intended effect cannot be rendered owing to a lack of devices supporting this effect. The `priority` attribute describes the priority for effects with respect to other effects in the same group of effects sharing the same point in time when they should become available for consumption. A value of 1 indicates the highest priority, and larger values indicate lower priorities. The `location` attribute describes the location from where the effect is expected to be received from the user's perspective according to the *X*, *Y*, and *Z* axes, as depicted in Figure 2.5. A classification scheme that may be used for this purpose is `LocationCS`, as defined in Annex A of ISO/IEC 23005-6. For example, `urn:mpeg:mpeg-v:01-SI-LocationCS-NS:left:*:midway` defines the location as follows: left on the *X*-axis, any location on the *Y*-axis, and midway on the *Z*-axis. That is, it describes all effects on the left-midway side of the user. The `SEMAdaptabilityAttributes` contains two attributes related to the adaptability of the SEs. The `adaptType` attribute describes the preferred

Table 2.1 Schema definition of `SEMBaseAttributes`

```
<attributeGroup name="SEMBaseAttributes">
  <attribute name="activate" type="boolean" use="optional"/>
  <attribute name="duration" type="positiveInteger" use="optional"/>
  <attribute name="fade" type="positiveInteger" use="optional"/>
  <attribute name="alt" type="anyURI" use="optional"/>
  <attribute name="priority" type="positiveInteger" use="optional"/>
  <attribute name="location" type="mpeg7:termReferenceType"
   use="optional"/>
  <attributeGroup ref="sedl:SEMAdaptabilityAttributes"/>
</attributeGroup>

<attributeGroup name="SEMAdaptabilityAttributes">
  <attribute name="adaptType" type="sedl:adaptTypeType" use="optional"/>
  <attribute name="adaptRange" type="sedl:adaptRangeType" default="10"
   use="optional"/>
</attributeGroup>
```

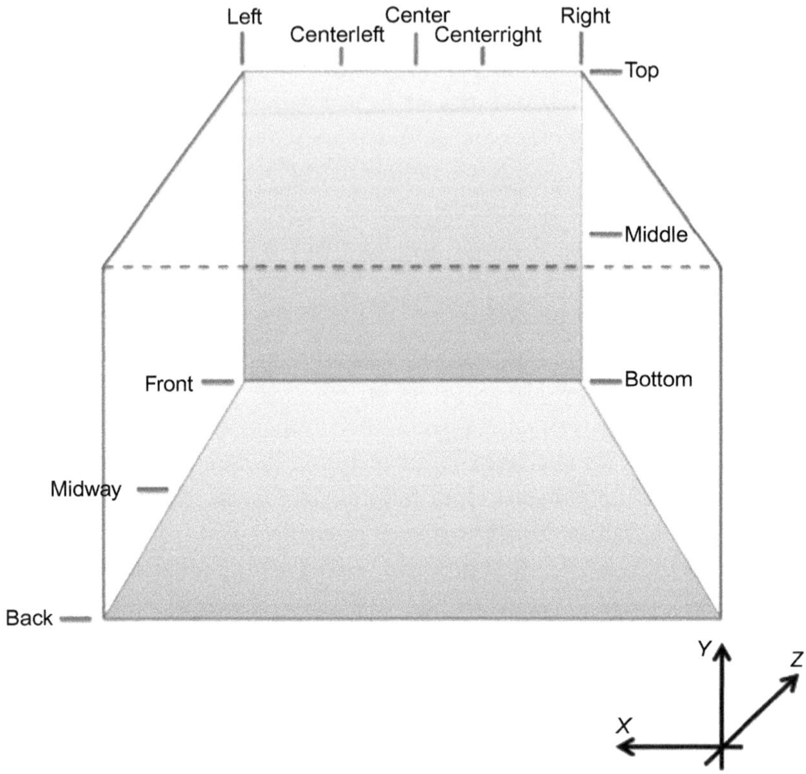

Figure 2.5 Location model for SEs and reference coordinate system.

type of adaptation using the following possible instantiations: `strict`, i.e., an adaptation by approximation may not be performed, i.e., an adaptation by approximation may be performed with a smaller effect value than the specified effect value, i.e., an adaptation by approximation may be performed with a greater effect value than the specified effect value, and i.e., an adaptation by approximation may be performed between the upper and lower bounds specified by `adaptRange`. The `adaptRange` attribute describes the upper and lower bounds in terms of percentage for `adaptType`.

There are five base elements (Table 2.2), i.e., `Declaration`, `GroupOfEffects`, `Effect`, `ReferenceEffect`, and `Parameter`, which are explained in detail in the following sections, extended from the abstract `SEMBaseType` type (the top-most base type in SEDL). This structure of having an abstract type is a way of providing extensibility in the standard that allows any elements having the extended type of `SEMBaseType` to be used when each element is instantiated. `SEMBaseType` has an `id` attribute that identifies the `id` of `SEMBaseType` (Table 2.3 and Figure 2.6).

Table 2.2 Schema definition of base elements in SEDL

```
<element name="Declarations" type="sedl:DeclarationsType"/>
<element name="GroupOfEffects" type="sedl:GroupOfEffectsType"/>
<element name="Effect" type="sedl:EffectBaseType"/>
<element name="ReferenceEffect" type="sedl:ReferenceEffectType"/>
<element name="Parameter" type="sedl:ParameterBaseType"/>
```

Table 2.3 Schema definition of SEMBaseType

```
<complexType name="SEMBaseType" abstract="true ">
  <complexContent>
    <restriction base="anyType">
      <attribute name="id" type="ID" use="optional"/>
    </restriction>
  </complexContent>
</complexType>
```

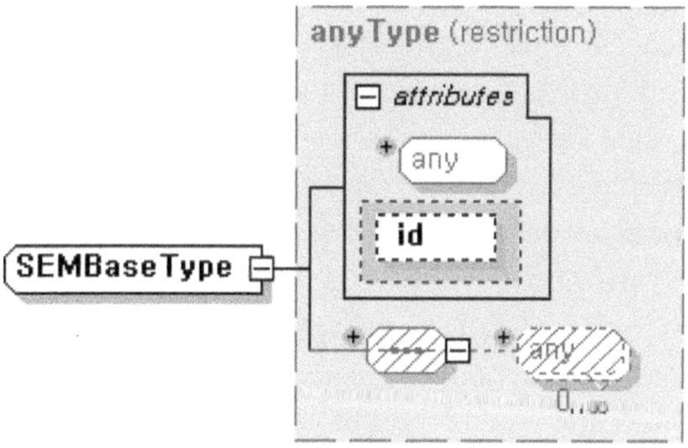

Figure 2.6 Definition of the SEMBaseType type.

2.2.3 Root Element of SEDL

Table 2.4 shows the schema definition of the SEM root element of SEDL along with the structure diagram shown in Figure 2.7. The SEM root element can contain the DescriptionMetadata element; unlimited repetitions of the Declarations element, GroupOfEffects element, Effect element, and ReferenceEffect element; and anyAttribute, which can identify the process units and associating time information. The DescriptionMetadata element, Declarations element, GroupOfEffects element, Effect element, and ReferenceEffect element types are explained in the following sections in detail.

Table 2.4 Schema definition of `SEM` root element

```
<element name="SEM">
  <complexType>
    <sequence>
      <element name="DescriptionMetadata"
       type="sedl:DescriptionMetadataType" minOccurs="0" maxOccurs="1"/>
      <choice maxOccurs="unbounded">
        <element ref="sedl:Declarations"/>
        <element ref="sedl:GroupOfEffects"/>
        <element ref="sedl:Effect"/>
        <element ref="sedl:ReferenceEffect"/>
      </choice>
    </sequence>
    <anyAttribute namespace="##other" processContents="lax "/>
  </complexType>
</element>
```

The `anyAttribute` contains `siAttributeList`, which holds properties related to the process unit fragmentation, i.e., `anchorElement`, `puMode`, and `encodesAsRAP`, and properties related to the time information, i.e., `timescale`, `ptsDelta`, `absTimeScheme`, `absTime`, and `pts`. There is a rule that the `SEM` element must have a `timescale` attribute. `siAttributeList` is the XML streaming instruction defined in ISO/IEC 21000-7 (MPEG-21). The XML streaming instructions allow first identifying the process units in an XML document, and second, assigning time information to these units. These instructions are particularly required when an entire XML document is fragmented into small pieces of (e.g., well formed) XML documents for effective streaming or storing purposes. The `GroupOfEffects` element, `Effect` element, and `ReferenceEffect` element can again contain `siAttributeList` to describe the properties related to the fragmentation and time information.

Table 2.5 shows an instance of the `SEM` root element including several attributes used to identify the namespaces, as well as an example of the `siAttributeList` attribute. The puMode and timescale in the SEM root element are inherited to the child anchor elements. The `puMode` "ancestorDescendants" indicates that each process unit contains the anchor element, its ancestor, and descendent element. The `timescale` specifies the timescale, i.e., the number of ticks per second.

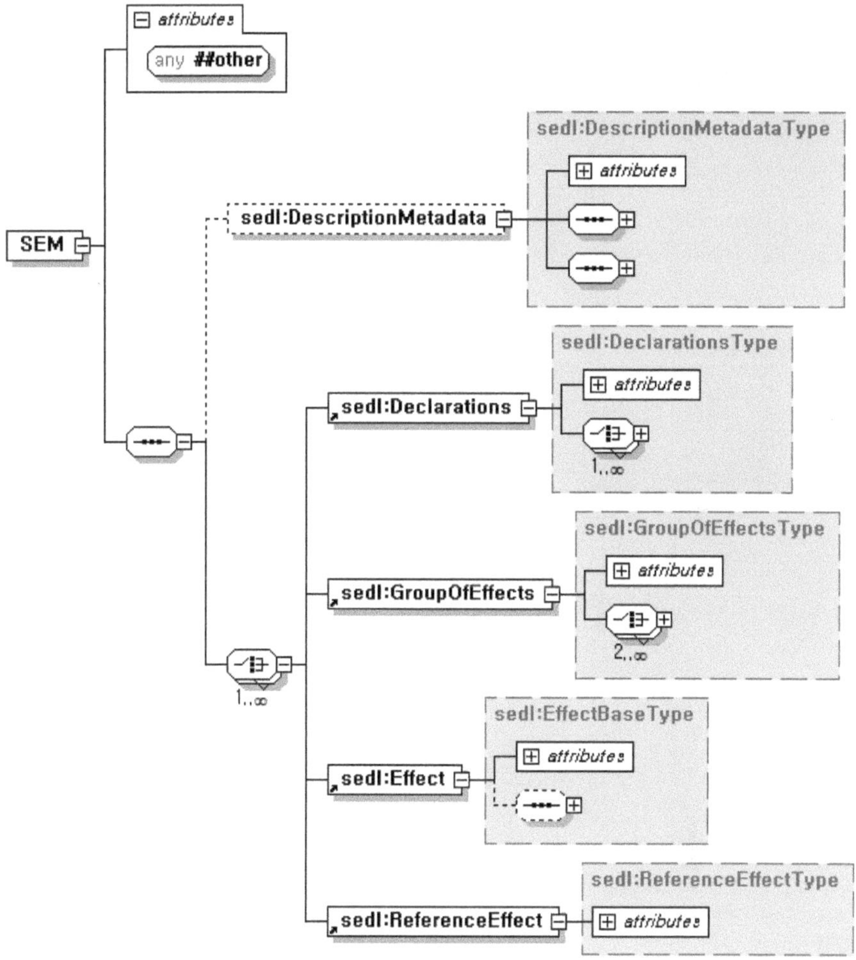

Figure 2.7 Structure diagram of the SEM root element.

Table 2.5 Example instance of SEM root element

```
<?xml version="1.0"?>
<SEM
xmlns:xsi="http://www.w3.org/2001/XMLSchema-instance"
xmlns="urn:mpeg:mpeg-v:2010:01-SEDL-NS"
xmlns:sev="urn:mpeg:mpeg-v:2010:01-SEV-NS"
xmlns:mpeg7="urn:mpeg:mpeg7:schema:2004"
xmlns:si="urn:mpeg:mpeg21:2003:01-DIA-XSI-NS"
xsi:schemaLocation="urn:mpeg:mpeg-v:2010:01-SEV-NS MPEG-V-SEV.xsd"
si:puMode="ancestorsDescendants" si:timeScale="1000">

...
</SEM>
```

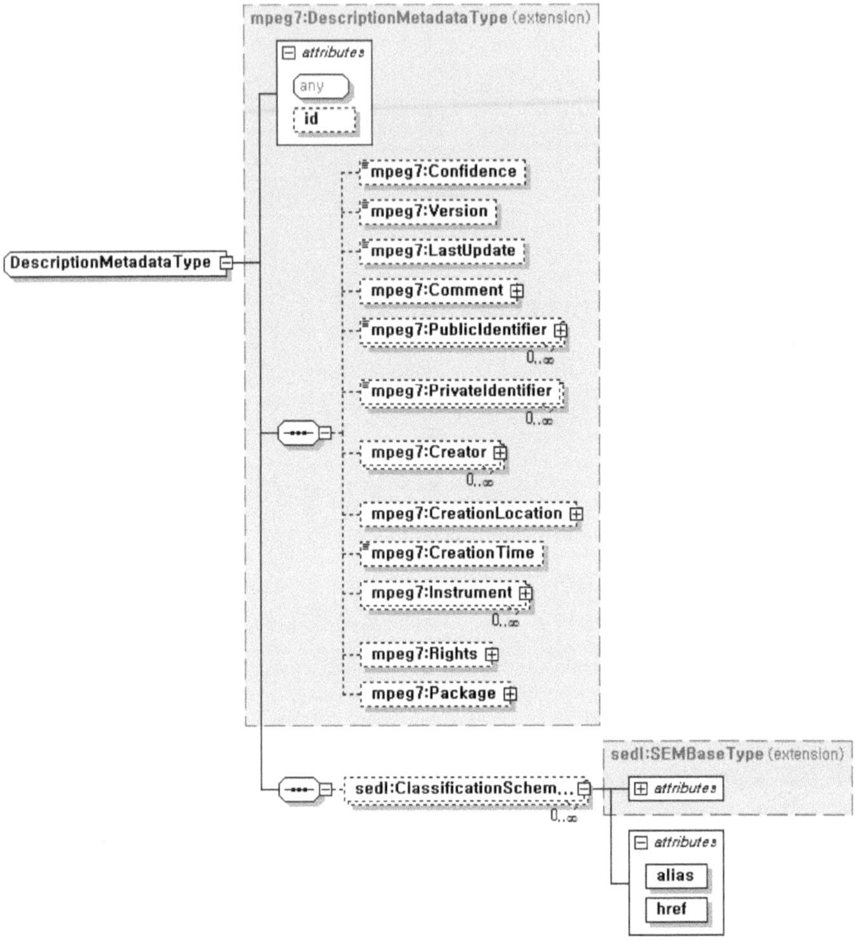

Figure 2.8 Structure diagram of `DescriptionMetadataType`.

2.2.4 Description Metadata

The `DescriptionMetadata` element describes general information about the SE metadata, such as the creation information or classification scheme alias. As shown in Table 2.4, the `DescriptionMetadata` element extends `DescriptionMetadataType`, which again extends the `MPEG7:DescriptionMetadataType`. As shown in Figure 2.8, `MPEG7:DescriptionMetadataType` describes the general information such as the creators, version, creation time, and proper information. `DescriptionMetadataType` also contains the `ClassificationSchemeAlias` element, which describes an `alias` for

Table 2.6 Example instance of the `DescriptionMetadata` element and its usage in a light effect

```
<sedl:DescriptionMetadata>
 <sedl:ClassificationSchemeAlias href="urn:mpeg:mpeg-v:01-SI-ColorCS-NS"
alias="COLOR"/>
</sedl:DescriptionMetadata>
<sedl:Effect xsi:type="sev:LightType" intensity-value="50.0" intensity-
range="0.00001 32000.0" duration="28" color=":COLOR:amber" si:pts="0"/>
```

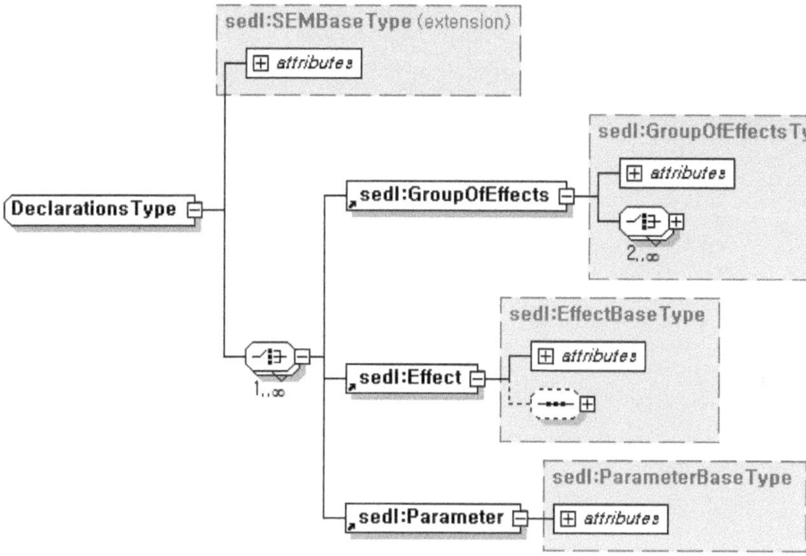

Figure 2.9 Structure diagram of `DeclarationsType`.

a classification scheme referenced by a URI. An example instance of the `ClassificationSchemeAlias` element of `DescriptionMetadataType` is shown in Table 2.6. In this instance, the URI of the classification scheme, `urn:mpeg:mpeg-v:01-SI-ColorCS-NS`, is replaced by the `alias` "COLOR" such that the light effect specifies its light `color` attribute as ":COLOR:amber" instead of using "urn:mpeg:mpeg-v:01-SI-ColorCS-NS:amber."

2.2.5 Declarations

The `Declarations` type, which extends the `SEMBaseType` type, describes a declaration of sensory effects, groups of sensory effects, or the parameters (Figure 2.9). In other words, an element defined by the `Declarations` type can contain an unbounded number of effects, groups of effects, or parameters that can be referenced later by the `ReferenceEffect` element.

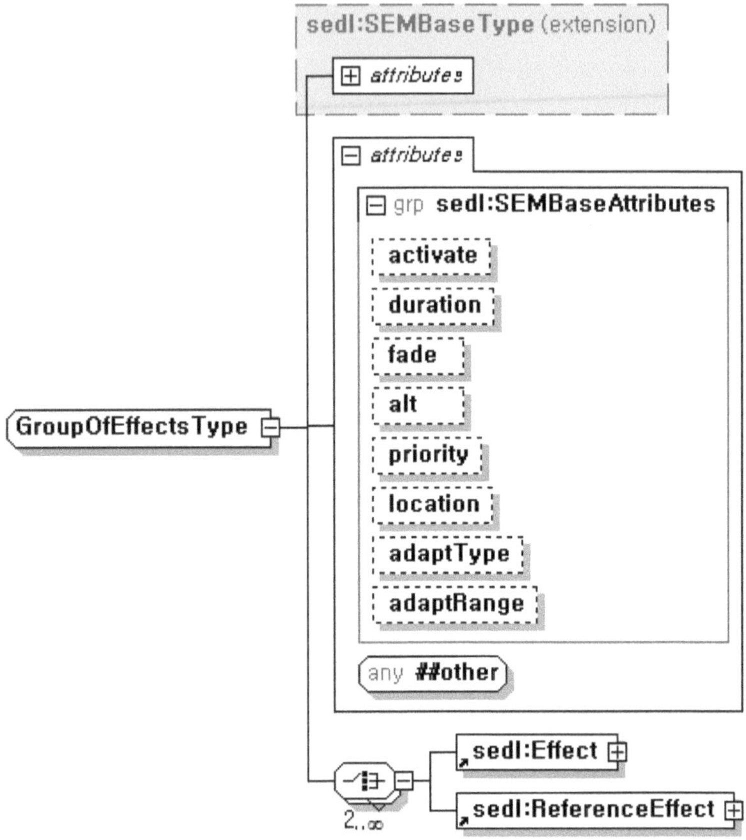

Figure 2.10 Structure diagram of `GroupOfEffectsType`.

For example, if a group of effect called "explosion," which is composed of light, scent, and vibration effects, is declared in the `Declarations` element, it can be reused several times during the last part of a movie sequence using `ReferenceEffect` elements.

2.2.6 Group of Effects

`GroupOfEffectsType`, which extends `SEMBaseType`, describes a group of two or more SEs (Figure 2.10). The SE elements in `GroupOfEffects` can be defined by either `EffectBaseType` or `ReferenceEffectType`. There are several rules applied for implementing `GroupOfEffects`. `GroupOfEffects` will have a timestamp (i.e., `pts`, `ptsDelta`, or `absTime`). Outside of the

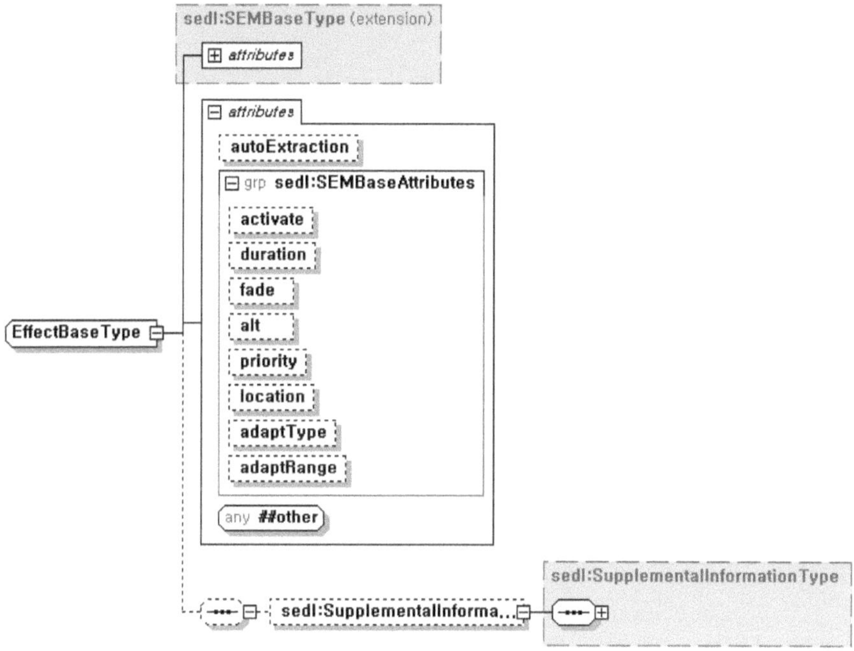

Figure 2.11 Structure diagram of `EffectBaseType`.

`Declarations`, `GroupOfEffects` shall not have both `pts` and `absTime` at the same time because if these two attributes contain different timestamps, the decoder cannot decide which one to follow for rendering the SEs. `GroupOfEffects` within `Declarations` will have only `ptsDelta` as a timestamp. This means that SEs in `GroupOfEffects` within the `Declarations` may have different starting times. The `GroupOfEffects` element can contain the `siAttributeList` to describe the properties related to the fragmentation and time information for effective XML streaming.

2.2.7 Effect

`EffectBaseType` extends `SEMBaseType` and provides a base abstract type for a subset of types defined as part of the sensory effect metadata types (Figure 2.11). `EffectBaseType` contains the `siAttributeList` in `anyAttribute` to describe the properties related to the fragmentation and time information for effective XML streaming. This type includes the `autoExtraction` attribute, which describes the automatic extraction of SEs

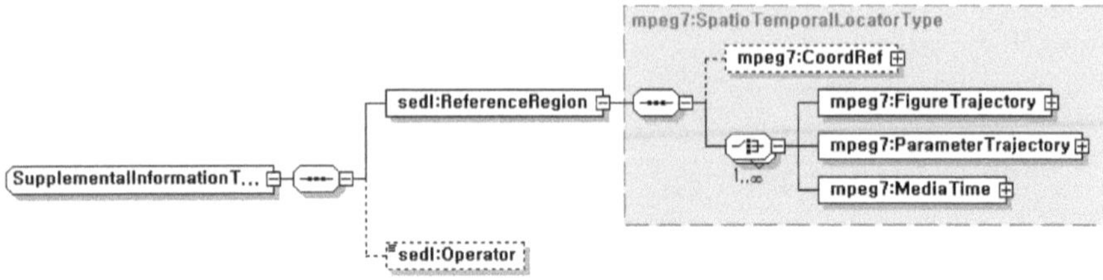

Figure 2.12 Structure diagram of `SupplementalInfomationType`.

and their major attributes such as the `intensity-value` from the media resource such as a video or audio sequence.

This type also includes the `SupplementalInformation` element with `SupplementalInformationType` (Figure 2.12) to describe the reference region (i.e., `ReferenceRegion` element) for an automatic extraction from a video sequence, and the `Operator` element, which describes how to extract SEs from the reference region of the video sequence. The `Operator` element can be specified as either `average` or `dominant`.

The following rules shall be referenced to generate the valid `Effect` metadata.

1. At the least, `activate`, `duration`, or `fade` shall be defined.
2. `Effect` outside of `GroupOfEffects` shall have a timestamp (i.e., `pts`, `ptsDelta`, or `absTime`).
3. `Effect` within `GroupOfEffects` shall have only `ptsDelta` for a timestamp.
4. `Effect` shall not have both `pts` and `absTime` at the same time.
5. `Effect` within `Declarations` shall have only `ptsDelta` for a timestamp.
6. If `duration` is defined, `activate` may not be defined.
7. If `fade` and `duration` are defined, `activate` may not be defined.
8. If `fade` is defined, the intensity is also defined.
9. If `fade` and `duration` are defined, `fade` must be less than or equal to `duration`.

2.2.8 Reference Effect

`ReferenceType` describes a reference to a SE, groups of SEs, or parameters (Figure 2.13). The `uri` attribute describes a reference to a SE, groups of SEs, or parameters by a URI. `ReferenceEffectType` contains `siAttributeList` in `anyAttribute` to describe the properties related to fragmentation and time information for effective XML streaming.

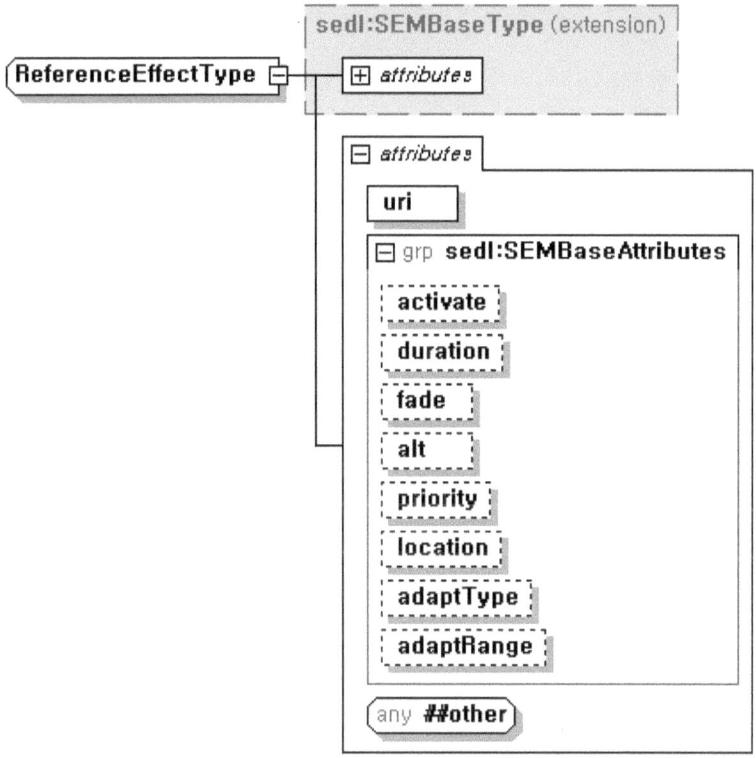

Figure 2.13 Structure diagram of `ReferenceEffectType`.

The following rules shall be referenced to generate valid `ReferenceEffect` metadata.

1. `ReferenceEffect` outside of `GroupOfEffects` shall have a timestamp (i.e., `pts`, `ptsDelta`, or `absTime`).
2. `ReferenceEffect` within `GroupOfEffects` shall have only `ptsDelta` for a timestamp.
3. `ReferenceEffect` shall not have both `pts` and `absTime` at the same time.
4. `ReferenceEffect` within `Declarations` shall have only `ptsDelta` for a timestamp.

2.2.9 Parameters

`ParameterBaseType` simply extends `SEMBaseType`, as shown in Figure 2.14. `ColorCorrectionParameterType` is the only type of parameter supporting the color correction effect. The parameters define the color characteristics of the content provider's display device along with the

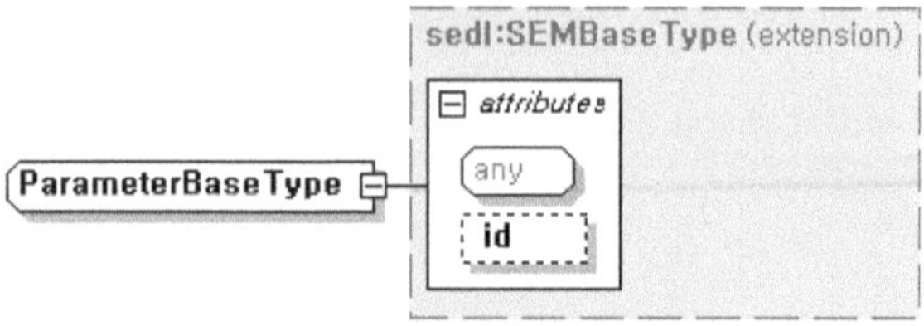

Figure 2.14 Structure diagram of ParameterBaseType.

lighting conditions surrounding the content provider. The parameters passing through this type enable reproducing the display colors of the consumer side, which are exactly the same as the colors created by the content provider. ColorCorrectionParameterType contains five elements: ToneReproductionCurves, ConversionLUT, ColorTemperature, InputDeviceColorGamut, and IlluminanceOfSurround. The ToneReproductionCurves element represents the characteristics (e.g., gamma curves for R, G, and B channels) of the provider's display device. The ConversionLUT element is a look-up table (matrix), which converts an image between an image color space (e.g., RGB) and a standard connection color space (e.g., CIE XYZ). The ColorTemperature element describes the white point setting (e.g., D65, D93) of the content provider's display device. The InputDeviceColorGamut element describes an input display device's color gamut, which is represented by the chromaticity values of the R, G, and B channels at the maximum Digital-to-Analog (DAC) values. The IlluminanceOfSurround element describes the illuminance level of the provider's viewing environment. The illuminance is represented in *lux*. Figure 2.15 shows the structure of ColorCorrectionParameterType.

2.3 SENSORY EFFECT VOCABULARY: DATA FORMATS FOR CREATING SEs

The SEDL provides a high-level structure, and as described in this chapter, only provides abstract elements through which the extended type of individual SEs can be instantiated. The data format for creating the metadata of each individual SE is defined as a sensory effect vocabulary in this standard. Table 2.7 shows the list of SEs defined in ISO/IEC 23005-3:2013. There are 15 SEs currently defined, and all of them are defined as extensions of EffectBaseType with the exception of FlashType and PassiveKinestheticMotionType. FlashType is defined as an extension of

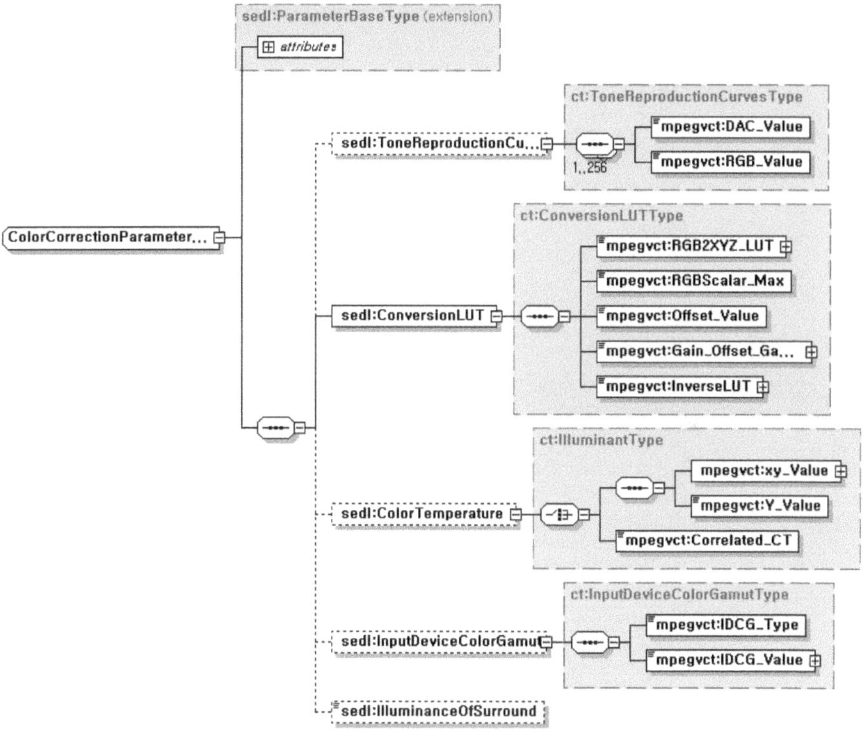

Figure 2.15 Structure diagram of `ColorCorrectionParameterType`.

Table 2.7 Sensory effect vocabulary defined in ISO/IEC 23005-3:2013

Type name	Base type
`LightType`	`EffectBaseType`
`FlashType`	`LightType`
`TemperatureType`	`EffectBaseType`
`WindType`	`EffectBaseType`
`VibrationType`	`EffectBaseType`
`SprayingType`	`EffectBaseType`
`ScentType`	`EffectBaseType`
`FogType`	`EffectBaseType`
`ColorCorrectionType`	`EffectBaseType`
`RigidBodyMotionType`	`EffectBaseType`
`PassiveKinestheticMotionType`	`RigidBodyMotionType`
`PassiveKinestheticForceType`	`EffectBaseType`
`ActiveKinestheticType`	`EffectBaseType`
`TactileType`	`EffectBaseType`
`ParameterizedTactileType`	`EffectBaseType`

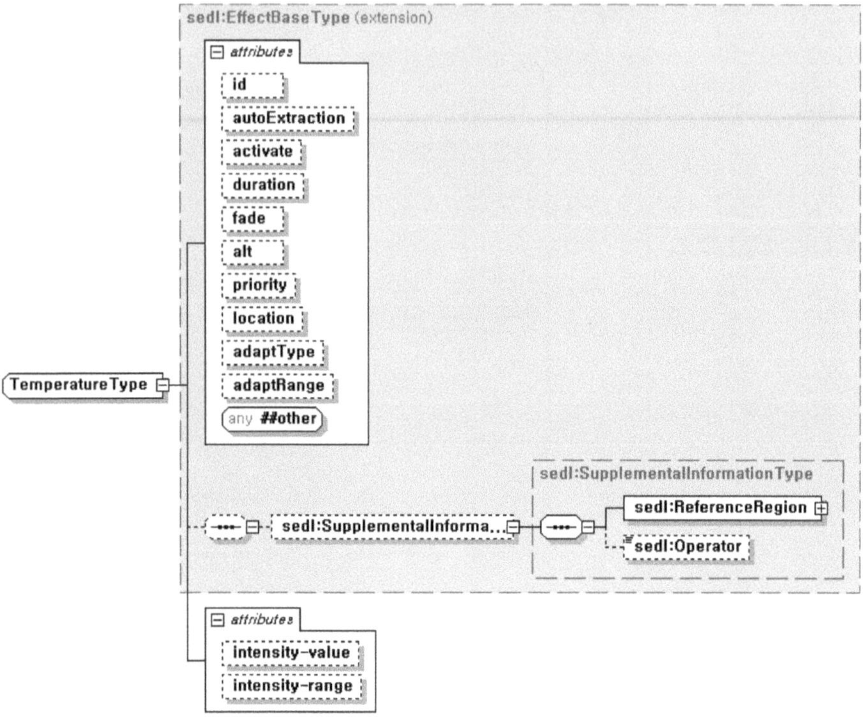

Figure 2.16 Structure diagram of `TemperatureType`.

`LightType` because a flash effect is a special variation of light and inherits all characteristics of the light effect. `PassiveKinestheticMotionType` is defined as an extension of `RigidBodyMotionType` because the passive kinesthetic motion effect is again a special variation of a rigid body motion, and inherits all characteristics of the rigid body motion effect.

Among these 15 SE types, `TemperatureType`, `WindType`, `VibrationType`, and `FogType` have only the `intensity-value` and `intensity-range` attributes and the elements and attributes inherited from `EffectBaseType`. As represented by the name of each type, the SEs related to temperature, wind, vibration, and fog can be described using these four types. Figure 2.16 shows the structure of `TemperatureType` as a representative of these four types, whose structures, with the exception of the semantics, are identical. The `intensity-value` attribute of the SEs expresses the absolute intensity in units defined in the semantics with respect to the `intensity-range` that the specific SE can produce. The default units of `TemperatureType`, `WindType`, `VibrationType`, and `FogType` are Celsius, Beaufort, Hertz (Hz), and ml/h, respectively.

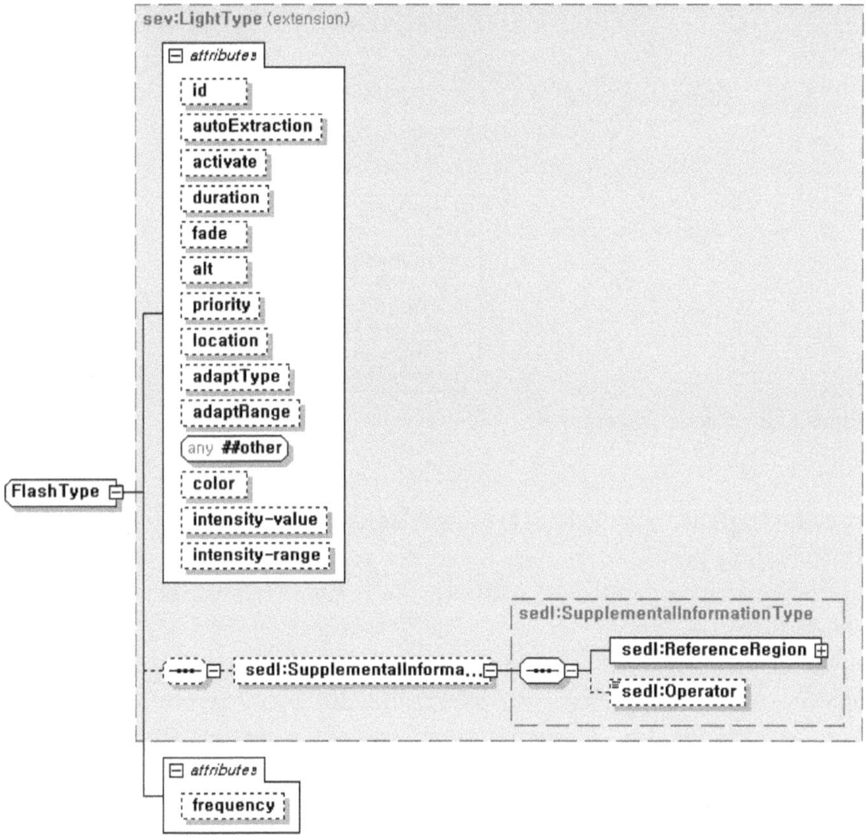

Figure 2.17 Structure diagram of `FlashType`.

The `LightType` can describe any light effects, including colored light effects. This type has another attribute, i.e., `colorType`, which is defined as a common type in ISO/IEC 23005-6:2013. The `color` attribute is either defined through `mpeg7:termReferenceType` or the RGB values. For an `mpeg7:termReferenceType` description, a classification scheme called "ColorCS" is defined in Annex A of ISO/IEC 23005-6:2013. For example, "urn:mpeg:mpeg-v:01-SI-ColorCS-NS:amber" indicates the color amber. On the other hand, the RGB value #FF0000 indicates an 8-bit representation of the color red. The `intensity-value` attribute of the `LightType` expresses the absolute intensity in terms of lux within the `intensity-range`.

The `FlashType` inherits all characteristics of `LightType`, and contains an additional attribute called `frequency`, which describes the number of flickers of light per second. Figure 2.17 shows the structure of `FlashType` type.

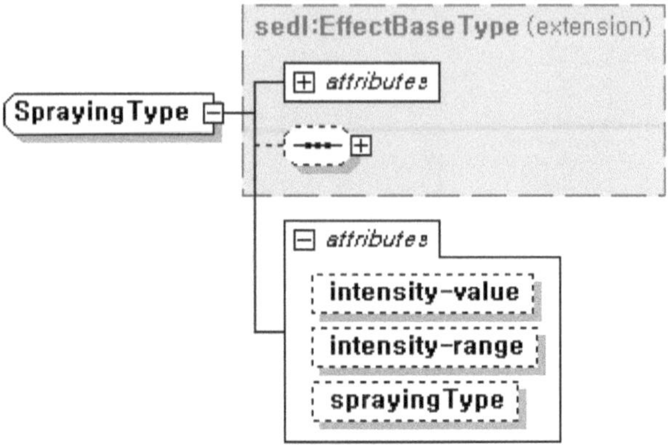

Figure 2.18 Structure diagram of `SprayingType`.

`SprayingType` and `ScentType` can describe any liquid type (possibly including powder type) spraying effects and scent, respectively. These two effects have another attribute, i.e., `mpeg7:termReferenceType`, in addition to the `intensity-value` and `intensity-range` attributes. The `sprayingType` attribute is used in `SprayingType` to identify the sprayed material based on the spraying effect, and the `scent` attribute is used in `ScentType` to identify a specific scent generated by the scent effect. In addition, `mpeg7:termReferenceType` provides a mechanism for referencing a specific term from a predefined classification scheme using a URI-type addressing mechanism. Figure 2.18 shows the structure of `SprayingType`. The attributes from `EffectBaseType` and the elements from `SupplementalInformationType` have been omitted from the figure for brevity.

`ColorCorrectionType` specifies a type of SE that can generate a color correction effect. The main purpose of a color correction effect is to reproduce the color of the visual content within images or video sequences based on the content provider's intention or the conditions of the display devices used on the consumer side. For example, broadcasters, digital content providers such as movie studios, advertisement companies, and Internet shopping providers are making considerable efforts in expressing the colors of their products or ads digitally as originally intended. In other words, the vivid colors that the content providers originally intended to show to consumers are effectively delivered by taking into account the display environment including the display device characteristics and ambient light. To maintain the color quality of the regions or

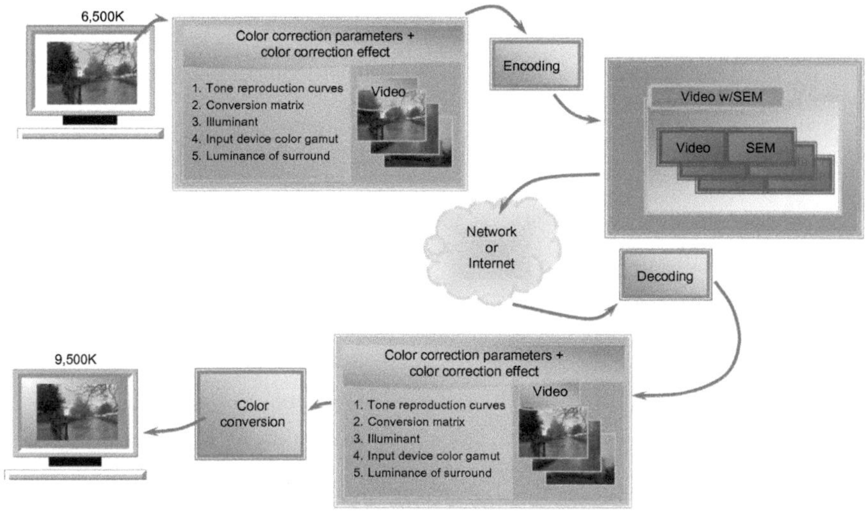

Figure 2.19 Example of the color reproduction process using `ColorCorrectionParameterType` with `ColorCorrectionType`.

objects within the images or video sequences, a consistent color reproduction process between the original visual content and the display device is required. Along with `ColorCorrectionParameterType` described in the previous section, `ColorCorrectionType` helps achieve this purpose. Figure 2.19 shows an example of the color reproduction process using color correction parameters and a color correction effect.

In addition to the elements and attributes inherited from `EffectBaseType`, `ColorCorrectionType` can optionally designate the regions (i.e., `SpatialTemporalLocator` or `SpatialTemporalMask`) within a video segment where the color correction effect is to be applied. If no regions are specified, the color correction effect is applied to the entire scene. The `intensity-value` attribute describes the intensity of the color correction effect in terms of "on" and "off" with respect to 1 (on) and 0 (off). The `intensity-range` describes the range of intensity values fixed as 0 (off) or 1 (on) by default. Figure 2.20 shows the structure of `ColorCorrectionType`.

`RigidBodyMotionType` can describe the movement of a rigid object such as a motion chair. `RigidBodyMotionType` is one of the most complex types of SE. In addition to the elements and attributes inherited from `EffectBaseType`, it includes the `MoveTowards`, `TrajectorySamples`, `Incline`, `Shake`, `Wave`, `Spin`, `Turn`, and `Collide` elements to specify the motion of a rigid object. `MoveTowards` covers the three-dimensional

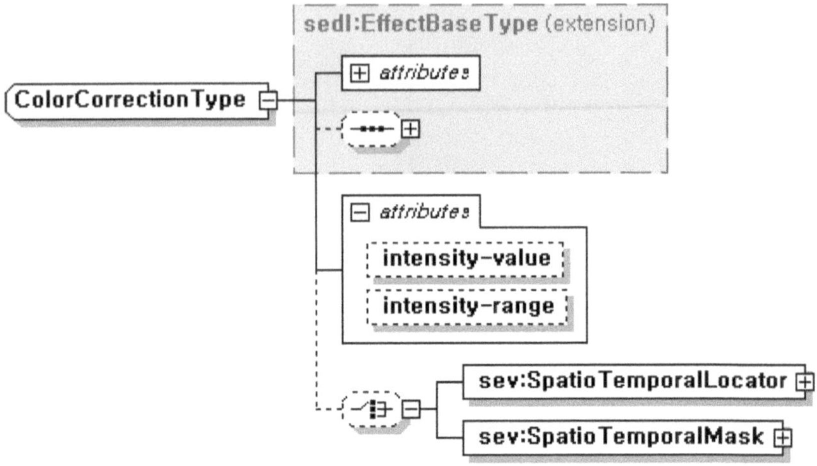

Figure 2.20 Structure diagram of `ColorCorrectionType`.

movements with six degrees of freedom (6 DoF), which means changing the location without a rotation; in addition, this element has six attributes to describe motion. The two attributes, `directionH` and `directionV`, provide the horizontal and vertical directions of the object to be moved with respect to its origin in terms of angle. Figure 2.21 shows the horizontal and vertical direction models for `directionH` and `directionV`, respectively.

The two attributes, `speed` and `acceleration`, provide the desired speed and acceleration of the object in cm/s and cm/s^2, respectively. The two attributes, `distance` and `distance-range`, describe the distance between the origin and destination in cm and in terms of its possible range, respectively.

The `TrajectorySamples` element describes a set of positions and orientation samples that the rigid object will follow. The trajectory samples are described through an $m \times 6$ matrix, where m denotes the number of trajectory samples, and the six columns contain the trajectory positions (Px, Py, Pz) and trajectory orientations (Ox, Oy, Oz) in order.

The `Incline` element describes pitching, yawing, and rolling motion of 6 DoF, which mean changing the rotation without changing the location of a rigid body object. The `InclineType` has 12 attributes, of which three attributes of `pitch`, `yaw`, and `roll` describe the rotating angle along the X, Y, and Z axes in counterclockwise angle, respectively, along with their feasible angle ranges defined in `pitch-range`, `yaw-range`, and `roll-range`. The three attributes, `pitchSpeed`, `yawSpeed`, and `rollSpeed`, describe the desired rotating speed of a rigid object along the X, Y, and Z axes, respectively,

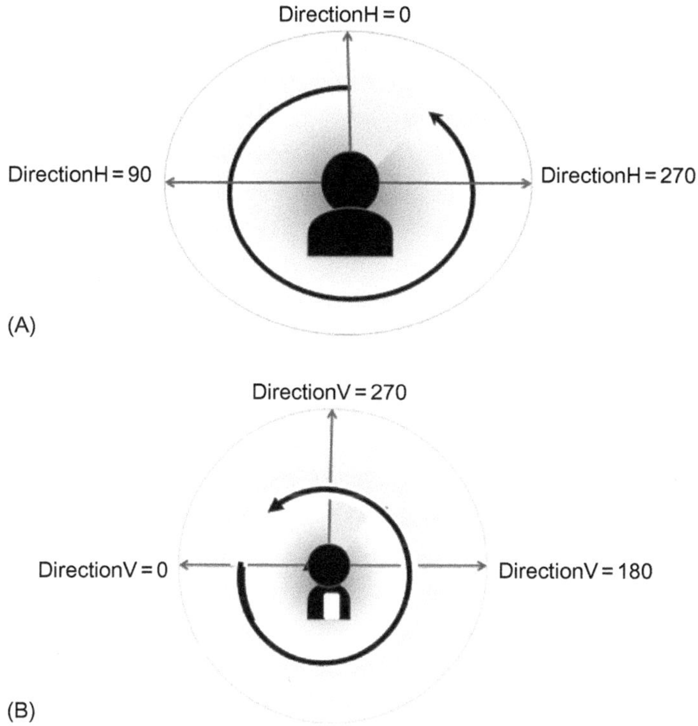

Figure 2.21 (A) Horizontal and (B) vertical direction models for a `MoveToward` pattern from left to right.

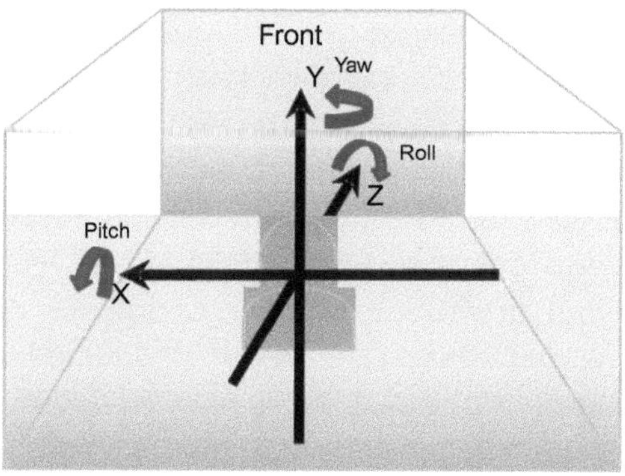

Figure 2.22 Reference coordinate system.

counterclockwise in degrees/s, and the last three attributes, `pitchAcceleration`, `yawAcceleration`, and `rollAcceleration`, describe the desired rotating acceleration of the device along the *X*, *Y*, and *Z* axes, respectively, counterclockwise in degrees/s^2.

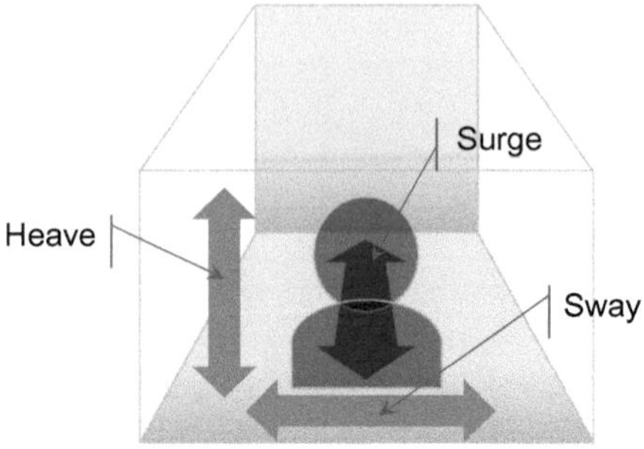

Figure 2.23 Direction model for shaking motion.

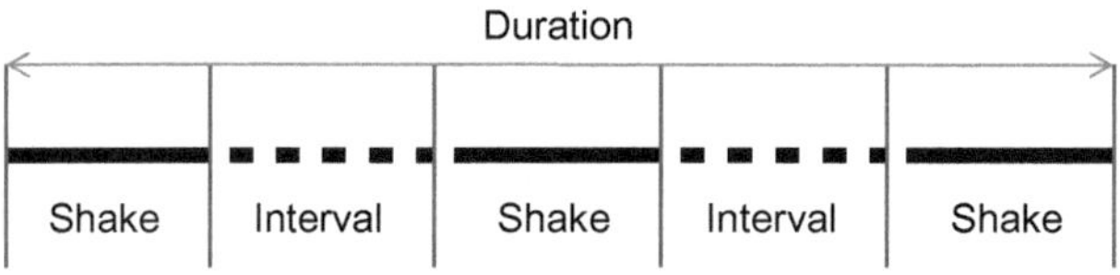

Figure 2.24 Example `interval` in the series of shaking motions.

The *X*, *Y*, and *Z* directions for any actuator defined in this section are commonly defined by adapting a right-hand coordinate system, as shown in Figure 2.22.

The *X*-axis is defined in the direction of the left-hand side of the user facing the screen. The *Y*-axis is defined in the reverse direction of gravity. The *Z*-axis is defined in the direction of the user's front facing the screen.

The `Shake` element describes continuously repeated movement from one side to the other. This element has five attributes, of which the `direction` attribute describes the direction of the shaking motion. An example of the `direction` attribute is shown in Figure 2.23. The `count` attribute describes the number of shaking motions during the given `duration` of time. The `distance` and `distance-range` attributes describe the distance between the two ends of the shaking motion in cm and its feasible distance range. The `interval` attribute describes a break in time between each shaking motion, as shown in Figure 2.24.

The `Wave` element describes a continuous up and down motion like tidal movements. This element has six attributes, of which the `direction` and `startDirection` attributes define the direction of wave motion (e.g., front to rear, left to right), and its initial starting up or down direction (Figure 2.25). The `distance` and `distance-range` attributes describe the distance of a wave

Figure 2.25 (A and B) Starting direction of a wave motion.

amplitude (between the top and bottom of the wave motion) in cm and its feasible distance range. The `interval` attribute describes a break in time between each shaking motion, as shown in Figure 2.24.

The `Spin` element describes continuous turning with respect to the centerpoint of the rigid object without changing its location. This element has three attributes, of which the `direction` attribute defines the direction of the spinning motion with respect to the three axes (e.g., pitch, yaw, and roll spinning). The `count` attribute describes the number of spins during the given `duration` of time. The `interval` attribute describes a break in time between each shaking motion, as shown in Figure 2.26.

The `Turn` element describes the motion of moving objects toward a certain direction left or right. This element has two attributes, of which the `direction` and `speed` attributes define the turning direction in terms of angle and its turning speed in degrees/s, respectively.

The `Collide` element describes the motion of a moving object colliding against something. This element has three attributes, of which the `directionH` and `directionV` attributes share the same semantics with those in `MoveTowards`, which provide the horizontal and vertical directions of the object to be moved with respect to the origin of the object in terms of angle and collision speed in degrees/s, respectively.

There also are five effect types defined to support haptic effects: passive kinesthetic motion, passive kinesthetic force, active kinesthetic, tactile, and parameterized tactile effects.

`PassiveKinestheticMotionType` (Figure 2.27) supports the trajectory motion guided by a kinesthetic device. A user grabs this kinesthetic device softly, and the device guides the user's hand according to the recorded motion trajectory (Figure 2.28). This type extends `RigidBodyMotionType`, which contains the `TrajectorySamples` element. The `updateRate` attribute describes the number of data updates per second.

The `PassiveKinestheticForceType` (Figure 2.29) supports a passive kinesthetic force/torque effect delivered by a kinesthetic device. A user grabs this kinesthetic device softly, and the device guides the user's hand

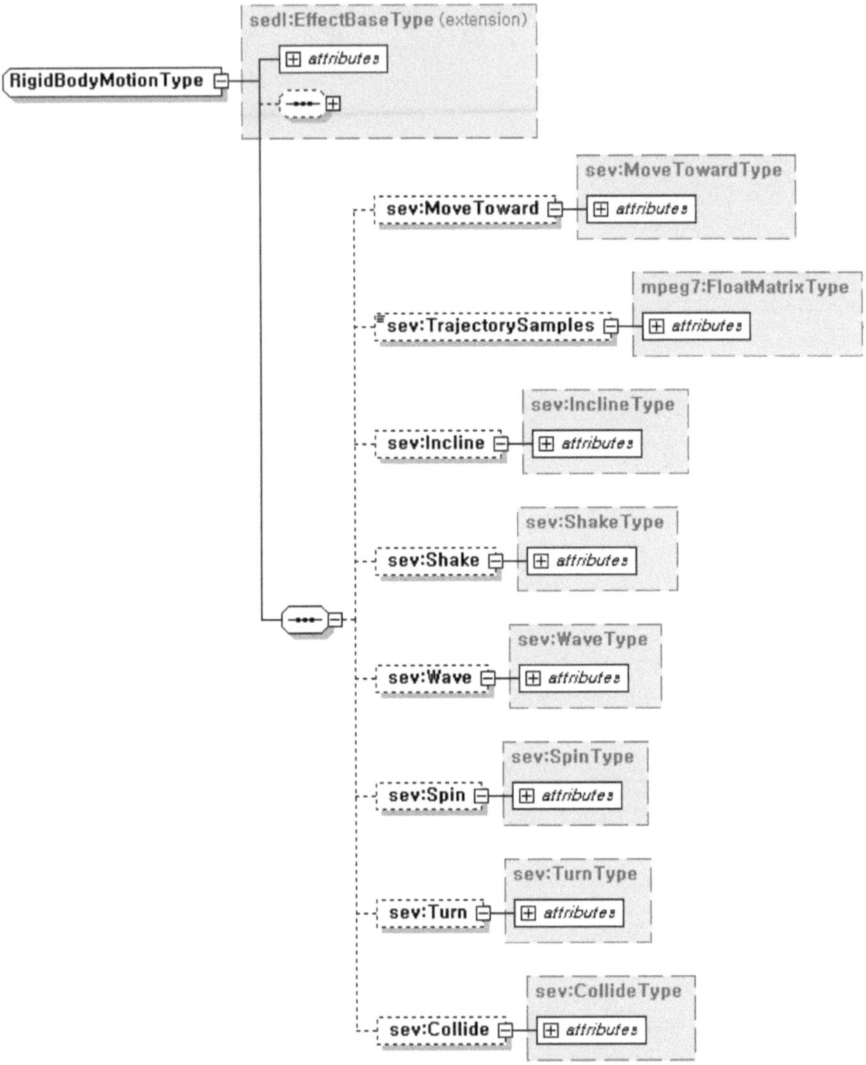

Figure 2.26 Structure diagram of `RigidBodyMotionType`.

according to the recorded histories of the force/torque. This type contains the `PassiveKinestheticForce` element, which is an $m \times 6$ matrix, where m rows denote the number of samples and the six columns contain three forces (Fx, Fy, and Fz in newton [N]) and three types of torques (Tx, Ty, and Tz in N-mm) in order. The `updateRate` attribute describes the number of data updates per second.

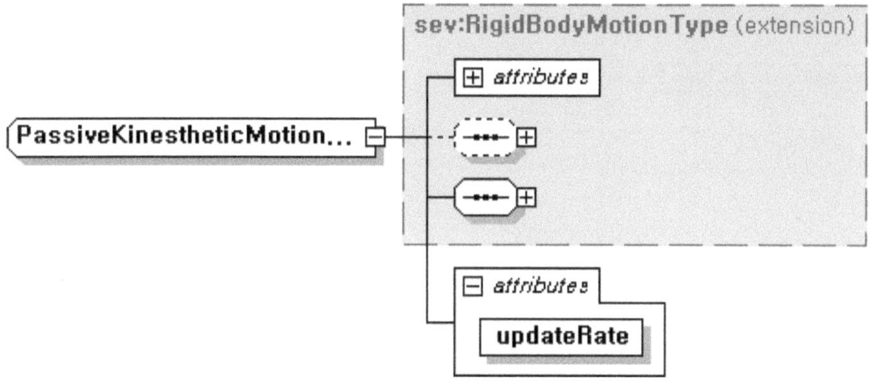

Figure 2.27 Structure diagram of `PassiveKinestheticMotionType`.

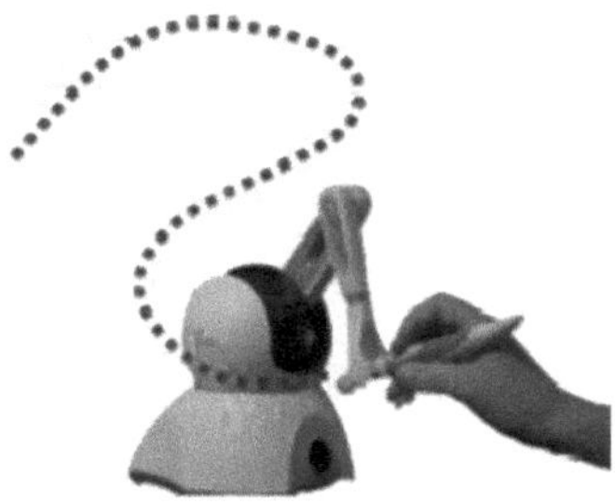

Figure 2.28 Example of `PassiveKinestheticMotion`.

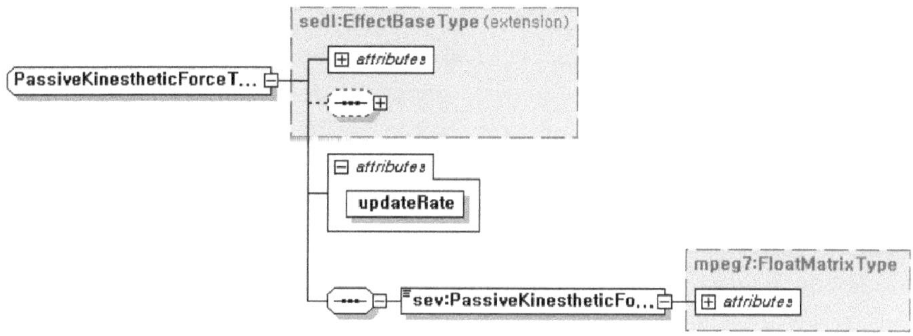

Figure 2.29 Structure diagram of `PassiveKinestheticForceType`.

`ActiveKinestheticType` (Figure 2.30) supports the active kinesthetic force/torque effect delivered by an object (or a virtual object) when a user touches it. This type contains the `ActiveKinesthetic` element, which describes three forces (`fx`, `fy`, and `fz` in newton) and three types of torques (`tx`, `ty`, and `tz` in N-mm).

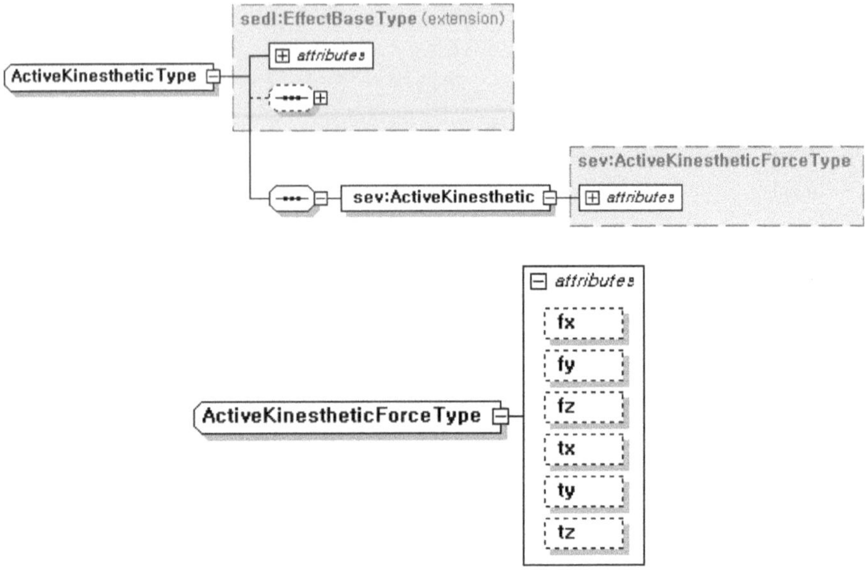

Figure 2.30 Structure diagram of `ActiveKinestheticType`.

`TactileType` was designed to support devices composed of an array of actuators, such as a tactile display, by touching the user to provide a feeling similar to actually touching the surface of a certain object. By extending `EffectBaseType`, `TactileType` has two additional attributes, `tactileEffect` and `updateRate`, and a choice between two elements, `ArrayIntensity` and `TactileRecource`. The `tactileEffect` attribute describes the type of tactile effect, e.g., vibrotactile, pressure-tactile, or thermal-tactile, as defined in Annex A.2.8 of MPEG-V, Part 6. The `updateRate` attribute describes the number of data updates per second. The `ArrayIntensity` element provides the intensity value of individual actuator of an array type of tactile device. For a thermal-tactile effect, the intensity is specified in degrees Celsius. For the vibrotactile effect, the intensity is specified in mm (amplitude). For the pressure-tactile effect, the intensity is specified in N-mm^2. The `TactileRecource` element points to either a tactile video or audio file. For example, a tactile video file describes the tactile intensities in terms of the video grayscale (0–255), whereas a tactile audio file describes the tactile intensities in the form of a waveform. Such grayscale (0–255) or waveform values can be converted into levels based on the number of levels that the tactile device can produce. Figure 2.31 shows the structure of `TactileType`. `ParameterizedTactileType` contains a base waveform that can

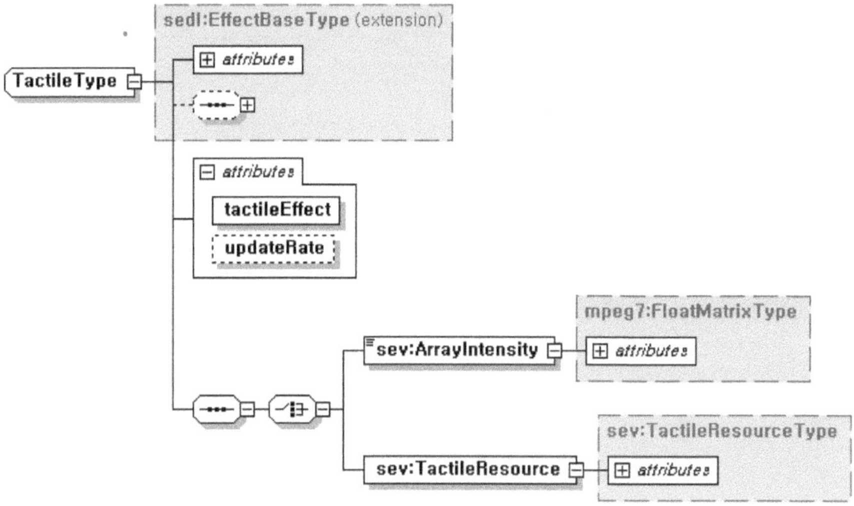

Figure 2.31 Structure diagram of `TactileType`.

be produced by combining several properties such as the amplitude, signal length, DC offset, and phase delay to create patterned tactile effects. Again, this base waveform can be used to create a block waveform comprising the periodical repetitions of the base tactile effect.

2.4 CREATING SEs

An effective and easy sensory effect authoring tool using the technologies described in this chapter is important for content providers when creating 4D content. Several authoring tools have been proposed to assign sensory effect metadata to AV content [3–5]. The sensory effect authoring tools support user-friendly graphic interfaces for easy SEM authoring, automatic XML instance validation functions, and convenient Web accessibility (Figure 2.32). The sensory effect metadata created by the content providers are carried by either DVDs or broadcasting networks and consumed by the Virtual-to-Real adaptation engine, which is embedded in consumer electronics to produce the final adapted ACmds. The sensory effect metadata can be attached to other multimedia content, such as games, simulations, and educational multimedia aid materials.

As previously described in this chapter, the `SEM` root element, `GroupOfEffects` element, `Effect` element, and `ReferenceEffect` element in ISO/IEC 23005-3 (MPEG-V, Part 3) can contain `siAttributeList`, which

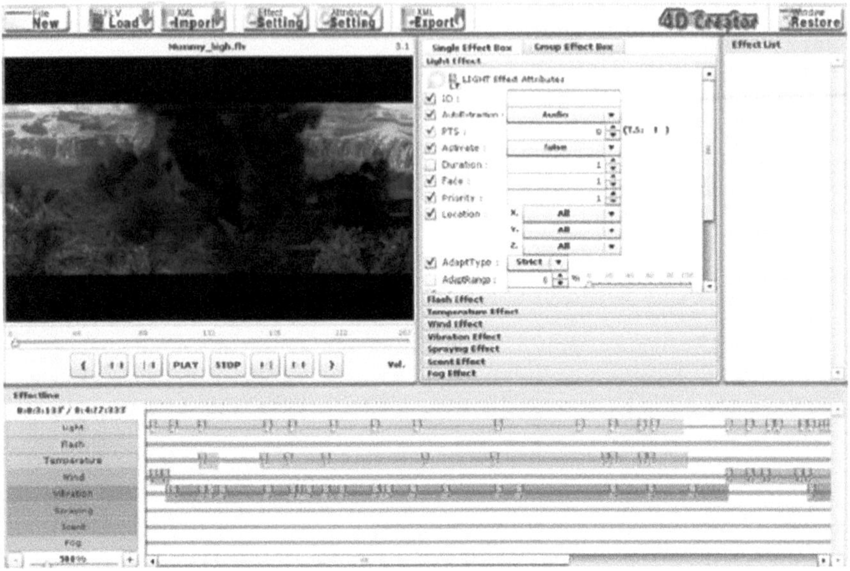

Figure 2.32 GUI of an SE authoring tool (SMURF [5]).

is the XML streaming instruction specified in MPEG-21, Part 7 (ISO/IEC 21000-7). The XML streaming instructions first allow identification of the process units in an XML document, and second, assign the time information to the process units. Table 2.8 shows an XML instance of sensory effect metadata with XML streaming instructions.

A fragmenter (Figure 2.33) parses an XML document with XSI attributes, shown in Table 2.8, in a depth-first order. An element with the `anchorElement` property set to true indicates an anchor element and a new process unit. The process unit then comprises the connected elements according to the `puMode` property of the anchor element.

The XSI attributes of the `SEM` root element, `puMode` and `timeScale`, are inherited to its child anchor elements. The `timeScale` attribute from the `SEM` root element and `pts` can designate the time information of each processing unit.

The following instances (Table 2.9) are examples of processing units generated by the fragmenter. Because the `puMode` of the `SEM` root element is `sequential`, the first processing unit includes the following elements until the next element is flagged as an anchor element. Therefore, the first processing unit contains the `SEM` root, `DescriptionMetadata`, and `Declarations`. Because `puMode` of the second, third, and fourth

Table 2.8 Example instance of SEM root element with several SEs

```
<?xml version="1.0" encoding="UTF-8" standalone="yes"?>
<SEM
xmlns:xsi="http://www.w3.org/2001/XMLSchema-instance"
xmlns="urn:mpeg:mpeg-v:2010:01-SEDL-NS"
xmlns:sev="urn:mpeg:mpeg-v:2010:01-SEV-NS"
xmlns:mpeg7="urn:mpeg:mpeg7:schema:2004"
xmlns:ct="urn:mpeg:mpeg-v:2010:01-CT-NS"
xmlns:si="urn:mpeg:mpeg21:2003:01-DIA-XSI-NS"
xsi:schemaLocation="urn:mpeg:mpeg-v:2010:01-SEV-NS MPEG-V-SEV.xsd"
si:puMode="sequential"
si:anchorElement="true"
si:timeScale="1000">
  <DescriptionMetadata>
    <ClassificationSchemeAlias href="urn:mpeg:mpeg-v:01-SI-ColorCS-NS"
alias="COLOR"/>
  </DescriptionMetadata>

  <Declarations>
    <Parameter xsi:type="ColorCorrectionParameterType" id="ccpt001">
      <ToneReproductionCurves>
        <ct:DAC_Value>0</ct:DAC_Value>
        <ct:RGB_Value>0 0 0</ct:RGB_Value>
        <ct:DAC_Value>255</ct:DAC_Value>
        <ct:RGB_Value>255 255 255</ct:RGB_Value>
      </ToneReproductionCurves>
      <ConversionLUT>
        <ct:RGB2XYZ_LUT mpeg7:dim="3 3">
          86.60 67.60 38.0
          46.00 137.0 16.5
          2.365 19.41 203.9
        </ct:RGB2XYZ_LUT>
        <ct:RGBScalar_Max>
          1.0 1.0 1.0
        </ct:RGBScalar_Max>
        <ct:Offset_Value>
          0.2150 0.2050 0.4250
        </ct:Offset_Value>
        <ct:Gain_Offset_Gamma mpeg7:dim="3 3">
          1.0228 -0.0228 1.6222
          1.0242 -0.0242 1.5624
          1.0220 -0.0220 1.6180
        </ct:Gain_Offset_Gamma>
        <ct:InverseLUT mpeg7:dim="3 3">
          0.0155 -0.0073 -0.0023
          -0.0052 0.0099 0.0002
          0.0003 -0.0009 0.0049
        </ct:InverseLUT>
      </ConversionLUT>
```

(Continued)

Table 2.8 Continued

```
      <ColorTemperature>
        <ct:xy_Value x="0.1" y="0.8"/>
        <ct:Y_Value>100</ct:Y_Value>
      </ColorTemperature>
      <InputDeviceColorGamut>
        <ct:IDCG_Type>BARCO</ct:IDCG_Type>
        <ct:IDCG_Value mpeg7:dim="3 2">
          0.2835 0.6043
          0.1509 0.0624
          0.6244 0.3410
        </ct:IDCG_Value>
      </InputDeviceColorGamut>
      <IlluminanceOfSurround>500</IlluminanceOfSurround>
    </Parameter>
</Declarations>

  <Effect xsi:type="sev:LightType" si:puMode="ancestorsDescendants"
si:anchorElement="true" activate="true" color=":COLOR:white" intensity-
value="50" intensity-range="0.0 100.0" duration="5000" si:pts="1000"/>
  <Effect xsi:type="sev:SprayingType" si:puMode="ancestorsDescendants"
si:anchorElement="true" activate="true" intensity-value="0.7" intensity-
range="0.0 10.0" duration="2000" si:pts="3000"/>

  <GroupOfEffects si:puMode="ancestorsDescendants" si:anchorElement=
"true" id="explosion_effect" si:pts="20000">
    <Effect xsi:type="sev:FlashType" intensity-range="0.0 100.0"
intensity-value="65.0" color=":COLOR:white" duration="5000"
activate="true" si:ptsDelta="0"/>
    <Effect xsi:type="sev:TemperatureType" intensity-range="0.0
100.0" intensity-value="40.0" duration="5000" activate="true"
si:ptsDelta="0"/>
    <Effect xsi:type="sev:WindType" intensity-range="0.0
100.0" intensity-value="50.0" duration="5000" activate="true"
si:ptsDelta="0"/>
    <Effect xsi:type="sev:VibrationType" intensity-range="0.0 100.0"
intensity-value="60.0" duration="5000" activate="true" si:ptsDelta="0"/>
  </GroupOfEffects>
</SEM>
```

anchorElement are ancestorsDescedents, puMode of the SEM root element is overridden such that anchor elements include themselves with their ancestors (e.g., the SEM root element). The processing units generated by the fragmenter are well-formed documents, and thus each processing unit can be decoded validly on the decoder side.

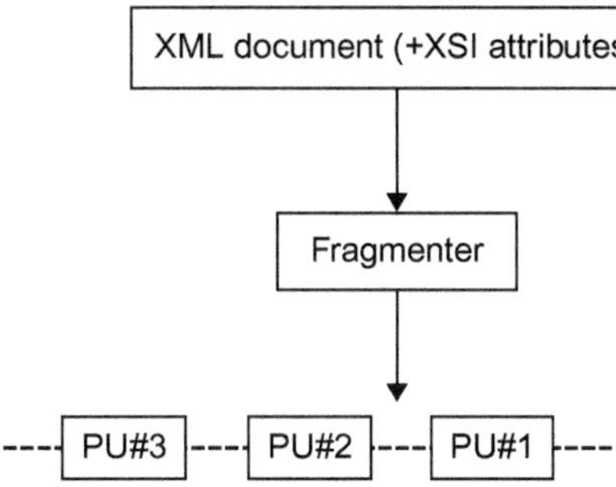

Figure 2.33 Generating processing units related to XML streaming instructions.

Table 2.9 Processing unit #1: instance of a `SEM` root element with `DescriptionMedata` and `Declaration`

```
<?xml version="1.0" encoding="UTF-8" standalone="yes"?>
<SEM
xmlns:xsi="http://www.w3.org/2001/XMLSchema-instance"
xmlns="urn:mpeg:mpeg-v:2010:01-SEDL-NS"
xmlns:sev="urn:mpeg:mpeg-v:2010:01-SEV-NS"
xmlns:mpeg7="urn:mpeg:mpeg7:schema:2004"
xmlns:ct="urn:mpeg:mpeg-v:2010:01-CT-NS"
xmlns:si="urn:mpeg:mpeg21:2003:01-DIA-XSI-NS"
xsi:schemaLocation="urn:mpeg:mpeg-v:2010:01-SEV-NS MPEG-V-SEV.xsd"
si:puMode="sequential"
si:anchorElement="true"
si:timeScale="1000">

  <DescriptionMetadata>
    <ClassificationSchemeAlias href="urn:mpeg:mpeg-v:01-SI-ColorCS-NS"
alias="COLOR"/>
  </DescriptionMetadata>

  <Declarations>
    <Parameter xsi:type="ColorCorrectionParameterType" id="ccpt001">
      ...
    </Parameter>
  </Declarations>
</SEM>
```

Table 2.9 shows a processing unit with an instance of a `SEM` root element with `DescriptionMedata` and `Declaration`. `DescriptionMedata` contains `ClassificationSchemeAlias` "COLOR" to abbreviate the URN of the color classification scheme.

Table 2.10 Processing unit #2: instance of a light effect

```
<?xml version="1.0" encoding="UTF-8" standalone="yes"?>
<SEM
xmlns:xsi="http://www.w3.org/2001/XMLSchema-instance"
xmlns="urn:mpeg:mpeg-v:2010:01-SEDL-NS"
xmlns:sev="urn:mpeg:mpeg-v:2010:01-SEV-NS"
xmlns:mpeg7="urn:mpeg:mpeg7:schema:2004"
xmlns:ct="urn:mpeg:mpeg-v:2010:01-CT-NS"
xmlns:si="urn:mpeg:mpeg21:2003:01-DIA-XSI-NS"
xsi:schemaLocation="urn:mpeg:mpeg-v:2010:01-SEV-NS MPEG-V-SEV.xsd"
si:puMode="sequential"
si:anchorElement="true"
si:timeScale="1000">

  <Effect xsi:type="sev:LightType" si:puMode="ancestorsDescendants"
si:anchorElement="true" activate="true" color=":COLOR:white" intensity-
value="50" intensity-range="0.0 100.0" duration="5000" si:pts="1000"/>
</SEM>
```

Table 2.11 Processing unit #3: instance of a spraying effect

```
<?xml version="1.0" encoding="UTF-8" standalone="yes"?>
<SEM
xmlns:xsi="http://www.w3.org/2001/XMLSchema-instance"
xmlns="urn:mpeg:mpeg-v:2010:01-SEDL-NS"
xmlns:sev="urn:mpeg:mpeg-v:2010:01-SEV-NS"
xmlns:mpeg7="urn:mpeg:mpeg7:schema:2004"
xmlns:ct="urn:mpeg:mpeg-v:2010:01-CT-NS"
xmlns:si="urn:mpeg:mpeg21:2003:01-DIA-XSI-NS"
xsi:schemaLocation="urn:mpeg:mpeg-v:2010:01-SEV-NS MPEG-V-SEV.xsd"
si:puMode="sequential"
si:anchorElement="true"
si:timeScale="1000">

  <Effect xsi:type="sev:SprayingType" si:puMode="ancestorsDescendants"
si:anchorElement="true" activate="true" intensity-value="0.7" intensity-
range="0.0 10.0" duration="2000" si:pts="3000"/>
</SEM>
```

Table 2.10 shows a processing unit with an instance of a SEM root element with a light effect. The color of the light is white, its intensity is 50 lux, and it lasts about 5 s at the presentation time of 5,000 clock ticks with a speed of 1,000 clock ticks per second.

Table 2.12 Processing unit #4: instance of a group of effects

```
<?xml version="1.0" encoding="UTF-8" standalone="yes"?>
<SEM
xmlns:xsi="http://www.w3.org/2001/XMLSchema-instance"
xmlns="urn:mpeg:mpeg-v:2010:01-SEDL-NS"
xmlns:sev="urn:mpeg:mpeg-v:2010:01-SEV-NS"
xmlns:mpeg7="urn:mpeg:mpeg7:schema:2004"
xmlns:ct="urn:mpeg:mpeg-v:2010:01-CT-NS"
xmlns:si="urn:mpeg:mpeg21:2003:01-DIA-XSI-NS"
xsi:schemaLocation="urn:mpeg:mpeg-v:2010:01-SEV-NS MPEG-V-SEV.xsd"
si:puMode="sequential"
si:anchorElement="true"
si:timeScale="1000">

  <GroupOfEffects si:puMode="ancestorsDescendants" si:anchorElement=
"true" id="explosion_effect" si:pts="20000">
    <Effect xsi:type="sev:FlashType" intensity-range="0.0 100.0"
intensity-value="65.0" color=":COLOR:white" duration="5000"
activate="true" si:ptsDelta="0"/>
   <Effect xsi:type="sev:TemperatureType" intensity-range="0.0 100.0"
intensity-value="40.0" duration="5000" activate="true" si:ptsDelta="0"/>
    <Effect xsi:type="sev:WindType" intensity-range="0.0
100.0" intensity-value="50.0" duration="5000" activate="true"
si:ptsDelta="0"/>
    <Effect xsi:type="sev:VibrationType" intensity-range="0.0
100.0" intensity-value="60.0" duration="5000" activate="true"
si:ptsDelta="0"/>
  </GroupOfEffects>
</SEM>
```

Table 2.11 shows a processing unit with an instance of a SEM root element with a spraying effect. The spraying intensity is 0.7 ml/h (within a range of [0.0,10.0] ml/h) with a duration of 2 s, and the effect starts at the presentation time of 3,000 clock ticks with a speed of 1,000 clock ticks per second.

Table 2.12 shows a processing unit with an instance of a SEM root element with a group of effects. The group of effects contains four individual effects, i.e., flash, temperature, wind, and vibration, to express an "explosion" effect. Each individual effect has a different rendering duration, and the group of effects starts at the presentation time of 20,000 clock ticks with a speed of 1,000 clock ticks per second.

2.5 CONCLUSION

This chapter provided a detailed explanation of the sensory effect metadata format, which was designed to describe SEs for AV content as defined in ISO/IEC 23005-3 (MPEG-V, Part 3: Sensory information). As the constructs for the data format, each element and attribute was given along with an explanation of its meaning and the intention of its design. The sensory effect metadata can be carried along with the AV transport stream as separate metadata packets. A method for combining these SEM data with AV content to stream or store the 4D content more effectively will be investigated in the future.

REFERENCES

[1] B.S. Choi, S.-K. Kim (Eds.), Text of ISO/IEC FDIS 23005-3 Second Edition Sensory Information, ISO/IEC JTC 1/SC 29/WG 11/N13059, Shanghai, China, October 20.
[2] M. Waltl, C. Timmerer, H. Hellwagner, A Test-bed for quality of multimedia experience evaluation of sensory effects, in: Proceedings of the First International Workshop on Quality of Multimedia Experience, San Diego, CA, July 2009.
[3] B. Choi, E.-S. Lee, K. Yoon, Streaming media with sensory effect, in: Proceeding of the International Conference on Information Science and Applications, April 2011, pp. 1–6.
[4] M. Waltl, C. Timmerer, H. Hellwagner, A test-bed for quality of multimedia experience evaluation of Sensory Effects, in: Proceeding of the International Workshop on Quality of Multimedia Experience, July 2009, pp. 145–150.
[5] S.-K. Kim, Authoring multisensorial content, Signal Process. Image Commun. 28 (2013) 162–167.

CHAPTER 3

Standard Interfacing Format for Actuators and Sensors

Contents

3.1 INTRODUCTION

Actuators are devices that can be used to generate or render various sensory effects for users in the real world. Sensors are devices that can be used to pick up information from the environment, or can be used to provide user inputs to connected virtual world objects by sensing the signals generated by users. When we deal with actuators for generating or render ing sensory effects, and with sensors for collecting information, it is very important to have a standardized and consistent format for the information going into the actuators and coming out of the sensors. MPEG-V, Part 5 (ISO/IEC 23005-5) [1] provides a standardized format for the interfacing information for the actuators and sensors by defining the Interaction Information Description Language (IIDL) with the Device Command Vocabulary (DCV) and Sensed Information Vocabulary (SIV).

3.2 INTERACTION INFORMATION DESCRIPTION LANGUAGE

3.2.1 IIDL Structure

IIDL is a language based on XML to provide foundations or a framework for instantiating device commands or sensed information using

MPEG-V.
DOI: http://dx.doi.org/10.1016/B978-0-12-420140-8.00003-2

the MPEG-V standard. There are three root elements, InteractionInfo, DeviceCommand, and SensedInfo, of their own specific types available in IIDL. In other words, the interaction information description XML instance can start with a tag of either InteractionInfo, DeviceCommand, or SensedInfo. By allowing three different types of elements for the root element of the IIDL, the structure of IIDL allows three different IIDL use cases. The first is used to create an instance document (XML document) of either a sequence of device commands or a sequence of sensed information. The second is used to allow the transport of a single device command for an individual actuator. The third is used to allow transport of a single sensed information from an individual sensor.

3.2.2 DeviceCommand Element

The DeviceCommand element is an element of an abstract DeviceCommandBaseType, and its structure is shown in Figure 3.1. This abstract type structure is a way to provide extensibility in the standard, and allows any device command with extended type of DeviceCommandBaseType to be used when the DeviceCommand element is instantiated. This element is only allowed to have a single device command instance, and was designed for sending a single command to drive an actuator in real-time.

The abstract type of DeviceCommandBaseType provides a common base for all device commands, which can be defined as an extension of DeviceCommandBaseType. Any attribute or element defined in the DeviceCommandBaseType is inherited to any device command, and only the attributes and elements common to any device command are included in this type.

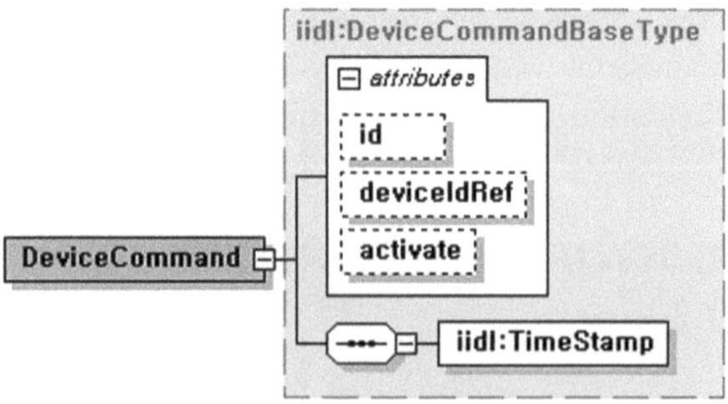

Figure 3.1 Definition of the DeviceCommand element.

Table 3.1 Schema definition of `DeviceCommandBaseType`

```
<complexType name="DeviceCommandBaseType" abstract="true">
  <sequence>
     <element name="TimeStamp" type="mpegvct:TimeStampType"/>
  </sequence>
  <attributeGroup ref="iidl:DeviceCmdBaseAttributes"/>
</complexType>
<attributeGroup name="DeviceCmdBaseAttributes">
  <attribute name="id" type="ID" use="optional"/>
  <attribute name="deviceIdRef" type="anyURI" use="optional"/>
  <attribute name="activate" type="boolean" use="optional" default="true"/>
</attributeGroup>
```

Table 3.1 shows the schema definition of `DeviceCommandBaseType`.

`DeviceCommandBaseType` contains a `TimeStamp` element, which is of the `TimeStampType` defined in Part 6 of the MPEG-V standard (ISO/IEC 23005-6) to provide timing information of the individual device command to be executed based on the media content time. The definition and use of `TimeStamp` is provided in Chapter 6. There are three optional attributes included in this base type as an attribute group of `DeviceCmdBaseAttributes`, which includes `ID`, `deviceIdRef`, and `activate`. The `ID` attribute is used to identify an individual device command instance. The `deviceIdRef` attribute refers to the identifier of the target device and is used to bind an individual device command to a specific actuator. The `activate` attribute, which is of a Boolean type, is used to signal the activation/deactivation (switch on/off) of the target actuator.

Table 3.2 shows an example instance of the `DeviceCommand` root element. When this element is used as a root element, there are several attributes used to identify the namespaces beyond those previously described. In this example, the `LightType` is used to instantiate the device command. The `LightType` extends the `DeviceCommandBaseType` by adding `color` and `intensity` attributes to denote the color and intensity of the light. This example shows a device command to activate a light with an id of Light01 at a time of 1 h 23 min and 45 s after the start of the media content with the color of red at an intensity of 7. The identifier of this instance itself is LT1.

3.2.3 `SensedInfo` Element

The `SensedInfo` element is an element of abstract `SensedInfoBaseType`, the structure of which is shown in Figure 3.2. This abstract type structure is

Table 3.2 Example instance of `DeviceCommand` root element

```
<iidl:DeviceCommand xmlns:iidl="urn:mpeg:mpeg-v:2010:01-IIDL-NS"
xmlns:mpegvct="urn:mpeg:mpeg-v:2010:01-CT-NS" xmlns:mpegdcv="urn:mpeg:
mpeg-v:2010:01-DCV-NS" xmlns:mpegsiv="urn:mpeg:mpeg-v:2010:01-SIV-NS"
xmlns:si="urn:mpeg:mpeg21:2003:01-DIA-XSI-NS"
xmlns:mpeg7="urn:mpeg:mpeg7:schema:2004"
xmlns:xsi="http://www.w3.org/2001/XMLSchema-instance"
xsi:schemaLocation="urn:mpeg:mpeg-v:2010:01-IIDL-NSV-IIDL.xsd"
xsi:type="mpegdcv:LightType" id="LT1" deviceIdRef="Light01"
color="urn:mpeg:mpeg-v:01-SI-ColorCS-NS:red" intensity="7">
  <iidl:TimeStamp xsi:type="mpegvct:AbsoluteTimeType" absTime="1:23:45"/>
</iidl:DeviceCommand>
```

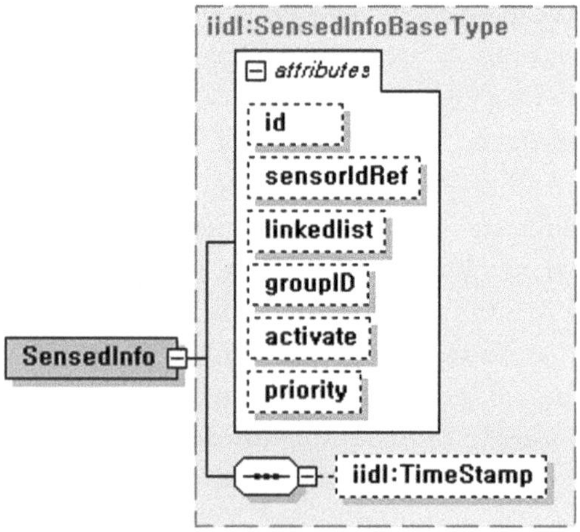

Figure 3.2 Definition of the `SensedInfo` element.

also a way to provide extensibility in the standard, and allows any sensor with an extended `SensedInfoBaseType` to be used when the `SensedInfo` element is instantiated, just as in the case of the `DeviceCommand` element. This element also only allows a single sensed information instance and was designed for acquiring a single instance of information from the sensor in real-time.

Table 3.3 shows a schema definition of the `SensedInfoBaseType`.

The `SensedInfoBaseType` contains a `TimeStamp` element, which is of `TimeStampType` defined in Part 6 of the MPEG-V standard (ISO/IEC 23005-6) to provide temporal information of the individual information acquired by a sensor device. The definition and use of `TimeStamp` is provided in Chapter 6. There are six optional attributes included in this

Table 3.3 Schema definition of `SensedInfoBaseType`

```
<complexType name="SensedInfoBaseType" abstract="true">
  <sequence>
    <element name="TimeStamp" type="mpegvct:TimeStampType" minOccurs="0"/>
  </sequence>
  <attributeGroup ref="iidl:sensedInfoBaseAttributes"/>
</complexType>
<attributeGroup name="sensedInfoBaseAttributes">
  <attribute name="id" type="ID" use="optional"/>
  <attribute name="sensorIdRef" type="anyURI" use="optional"/>
  <attribute name="linkedlist" type="anyURI" use="optional"/>
  <attribute name="groupID" type="anyURI" use="optional"/>
  <attribute name="activate" type="boolean" use="optional"/>
  <attribute name="priority" type="nonNegativeInteger" use="optional"
default="0"/>
</attributeGroup>
```

base type as an attribute group of `sensedInfoBaseAttributes`, which are `id`, `sensorIdRef`, `linkedlist`, `groupID`, `activate`, and `priority`. The `id` attribute is used to identify individual information acquired by a sensor. The `sensorIdRef` attribute refers to the identifier of the sensor from which the information is acquired. The `linkedlist` attribute is used to refer to the information acquired from the next sensor of the multisensor structure, when a group of sensors consists of a multisensor structure. The `groupID` attribute is used for identifying the group of sensors consisting of a multisensor structure to which this specific sensor, referenced by the `sensorIdRef`, belongs. The `activate` attribute, which is a Boolean type, is used to signal the activation/deactivation (switch on/off) of the referring sensor. The `priority` attribute designates the priority/importance of the sensed information among multiple types of sensed information at the same temporal point. A value of 1 implies the highest priority, and the processing occurs before the other sensed information with a lower priority (with larger values), when the sensed information is processed or adapted.

Table 3.4 shows an example instance of the `SensedInfo` root element. When this element is used as a root element, in addition to the previously described attributes, there are several other attributes used to identify the namespaces. In this example, `DistanceSensorType` is used to instantiate the sensed information. `DistanceSensorType` extends `SensedInfoBaseType` by adding an optional value and unit attributes to denote the distance measured. This example shows information with the identifier "DS1" acquired by a distance sensor with the identifier of "LSID001." This distance sensor

Table 3.4 Example instance of `SensedInfo` root element

```
<iidl:SensedInfo xmlns:iidl="urn:mpeg:mpeg-v:2010:01-IIDL-NS"
xmlns:mpegvct="urn:mpeg:mpeg-v:2010:01-CT-NS" xmlns:mpegdcv="urn:mpeg:
mpeg-v:2010:01-DCV-NS" xmlns:mpegsiv="urn:mpeg:mpeg-v:2010:01-SIV-NS"
xmlns:si="urn:mpeg:mpeg21:2003:01-DIA-XSI-NS"
xmlns:mpeg7="urn:mpeg:mpeg7:schema:2004"
xmlns:xsi="http://www.w3.org/2001/XMLSchema-instance"
xsi:schemaLocation="urn:mpeg:mpeg-v:2010:01-IIDL-NS MPEG-V-IIDL.xsd"
xsi:type="mpegsiv:DistanceSensorType" id="DS1" sensorIdRef="LSID001"
groupID="SG01" linkedlist="LSID002" priority="1" value="23">
  <iidl:TimeStamp xsi:type="mpegvct:AbsoluteTimeType" absTime="0:12:34"/>
</iidl:SensedInfo>
```

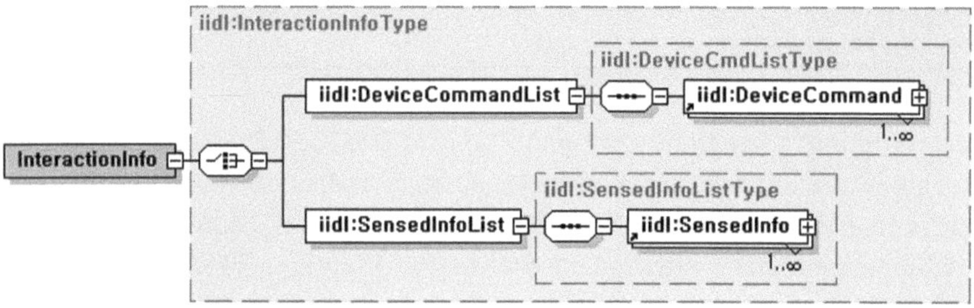

Figure 3.3 Definition of the `InteractionInfo` element.

belongs to a group of sensors identified by the `groupID` "SG01," and the next sensor in the group has the identifier "LSID002." This information with the `id` "DS1" has the highest priority and must be processed first when the information is acquired by the group of sensors. The acquired value is "23" in m, which is the default unit of the distance sensor because the unit is not specified in this instance.

3.2.4 `InteractionInfo` Element

The `InteractionInfo` is of `InteractionInfoType` and has a choice of `DeviceCommandList` or `SensedInfoList`, as shown in Figure 3.3.

`DeviceCommandList` is designed to contain a sequence of `DeviceCommand` elements, each of which represents an individual command for the actuators. By instantiating a sequence of commands, which may cover a certain period of time or even an entire play period of certain media content, `InteractionInfo` can be used to transport device commands generated offline and to activate actuators at a later time in synchronization

Table 3.5 Schema definition of InteractionInfoType

```
<complexType name="InteractionInfoType">
   <choice>
      <element name="DeviceCommandList" type="iidl:DeviceCmdListType"/>
      <element name="SensedInfoList" type="iidl:SensedInfoListType"/>
   </choice>
</complexType>
<complexType name="SensedInfoListType">
   <sequence>
      <element ref="iidl:SensedInfo" maxOccurs="unbounded"/>
   </sequence>
</complexType>
<complexType name="DeviceCmdListType">
   <sequence>
      <element ref="iidl:DeviceCommand" maxOccurs="unbounded"/>
   </sequence>
</complexType>
```

Table 3.6 Example instance of InteractionInfo root element with DeviceCommandList

```
<iidl:InteractionInfo xmlns:iidl="urn:mpeg:mpeg-v:2010:01-IIDL-NS"
xmlns:mpegvct="urn:mpeg:mpeg-v:2010:01-CT-NS" xmlns:mpegdcv="urn:mpeg:
mpeg-v:2010:01-DCV-NS" xmlns:mpegsiv="urn:mpeg:mpeg-v:2010:01-SIV-NS"
xmlns:si="urn:mpeg:mpeg21:2003:01-DIA-XSI-NS"
xmlns:mpeg7="urn:mpeg:mpeg7:schema:2004"
xmlns:xsi="http://www.w3.org/2001/XMLSchema-instance"
xsi:schemaLocation="urn:mpeg:mpeg-v:2010:01-IIDL-NS MPEG-V-IIDL.xsd">
  <iidl:DeviceCommandList>
    <iidl:DeviceCommand xsi:type="dcv:FogType" activate="true"
                        deviceIdRef="fdc1" id="command1" intensity="20">
      <iidl:TimeStamp xsi:type="mpegvct:AbsoluteTimeType"
                        absTime="0:12:34"/>
    <iidl:DeviceCommand/>
...
    <iidl:DeviceCommand xsi:type="dcv:..." .../>
...
  </iidl:DeviceCommandList>
</iidl:InteractionInfo>
```

with the media content. The details of each DeviceCommand element are described further in this chapter. Table 3.5 shows the schema definition of InteractionInfoType.

Table 3.6 shows an example instance of the InteractionInfo root element with DeviceCommandList. In this example, DeviceCommandList

Table 3.7 Example instance of `InteractionInfo` root element with `SensedInfoList`

```
<iidl:InteractionInfo xmlns:iidl="urn:mpeg:mpeg-v:2010:01-IIDL-NS"
xmlns:mpegvct="urn:mpeg:mpeg-v:2010:01-CT-NS" xmlns:mpegdcv="urn:mpeg:
mpeg-v:2010:01-DCV-NS" xmlns:mpegsiv="urn:mpeg:mpeg-v:2010:01-SIV-NS"
xmlns:si="urn:mpeg:mpeg21:2003:01-DIA-XSI-NS"
xmlns:mpeg7="urn:mpeg:mpeg7:schema:2004"
xmlns:xsi="http://www.w3.org/2001/XMLSchema-instance"
xsi:schemaLocation="urn:mpeg:mpeg-v:2010:01-IIDL-NS MPEG-V-IIDL.xsd">
  <iidl:SensedInfoList>
    <iidl:SensedInfo xsi:type="mpegsiv:DistanceSensorType" id="DS1"
     sensorIdRef="LSID001" groupID="SG01" linkedlist="LSID002" priority="1"
     activate="true" value="23">
      <iidl:TimeStamp xsi:type="mpegvct:AbsoluteTimeType"
                      absTime="0:12:34"/>
    </iidl:SensedInfo>
    <iidl:SensedInfo xsi:type="siv:..." .../>
...
  </iidl:SensedInfoList>
</iidl:InteractionInfo>
```

is chosen from the choice of `DeviceCommandList` and `SensedInfoList`. `DeviceCommandList` contains one or more `DeviceCommand` elements, and one `DeviceCommand` element instance is shown in this example. The `DeviceCommand` element shown in this example is of `FogType` with the id "*command1*" and is used to activate the device (actuator) identified by the id "*fdc1*" at a media time of 12 min and 34 s with an intensity of "*20*." Other possible instances of the `DeviceCommand` elements are not shown in this example for the sake of simplicity.

The `SensedInfoList` element is designed to contain a sequence of `SensedInfo` elements, each of which represents information acquired from a sensor at a certain moment in time. By instantiating a sequence of sensed information, which may be acquired from multiple sensors over a certain duration of time, `InteractionInfo` can be used to save environment information or capture a sequence of user interactions for reproducing the real world within a virtual world.

Table 3.7 shows an example instance of the `InteractionInfo` root element with `SensedInfoList`. In this example, `SensedInfoList` is chosen from between `DeviceCommandList` and `SensedInfoList`. `SensedInfoList` contains one or more `SensedInfo` elements, and one instance of the `SensedInfo` element is shown in this example. The `SensedInfo` element shown in this example is of `DistanceSensorType` with the `id` "*DS1*" received from the sensor identified by the `id` "*LSID001*" at a media time of 12 min and 34 s. The value received by this sensor is "*23*," and this identified sensor belongs to the sensor group with the `id` "*SG01*," with the next sensor in this group having the `id` "*LSID002*." For simplicity, other possible instances of `SensedInfo` elements are not shown in this example.

3.3 DCV: DATA FORMAT FOR CREATING EFFECTS USING ACTUATORS

The IIDL provides a high-level structure, and as explained in this chapter, only provides abstract elements through which an extended type of individual device command can be instantiated. In this standard, the data format for each individual device command is defined as a DCV. Table 3.8 shows the list of device commands defined in ISO/IEC 23005-5:2013. There are 14 device commands currently defined, each of which, with the exception of `FlashType`, is defined as an extension of `DeviceCommandBaseType`. `FlashType` is defined as an extension of `LightType` because a flash device is a special variation of a light device and inherits all characteristics of a light device.

Among these 15 device command types, `HeatingType`, `CoolingType`, `WindType`, `VibrationType`, and `FogType` have only the `intensity` attribute and the element and attributes inherited from `DeviceCommandBaseType`, as shown in Figure 3.4, which provides the structure of `HeatingType` as a representative of the four above types, which are identical except for their semantics. The `intensity` attribute of the device commands expresses the relative intensity of the device in percentage with respect to the maximum intensity that the specific device is capable of generating.

In addition to the `intensity` attribute, `SprayerType` and `ScentType` have another attribute, `mpeg7:termReferenceType`. `sprayingType` is used in `SprayerType` to identify the material sprayed by the sprayer, and `scent` is used in `ScentType` to identify the specific scent generated by the scent generator. `mpeg7:termReferenceType` provides a mechanism for referencing a specific term from a predefined classification scheme using a URI-like addressing mechanism. Figure 3.5 shows the structure of `SprayerType`.

`ColorCorrectionType` and `InitializeColorCorrectionParameterType` are more complex types of device commands. `ColorCorrectionType` specifies a device command type that can generate a color correction effect. In addition to the elements and attributes inherited from `DeviceCommandBaseType`, `ColorCorrectionType` can optionally designate

Table 3.8 DCV defined in ISO/IEC 23005-5:2013

Type name	Base type	Corresponding effect
LightType	DeviceCommandBaseType	Light effect
FlashType	LightType	Flash effect
HeatingType	DeviceCommandBaseType	Temperature effect
CoolingType	DeviceCommandBaseType	Temperature effect
WindType	DeviceCommandBaseType	Wind effect
VibrationType	DeviceCommandBaseType	Vibration effect
SprayerType	DeviceCommandBaseType	Spraying effect
ScentType	DeviceCommandBaseType	Scent effect
FogType	DeviceCommandBaseType	Fog effect
ColorCorrectionType	DeviceCommandBaseType	Color correction effect
InitializeColorCorrectionParameterType	DeviceCommandBaseType	Color correction effect
RigidBodyMotionType	DeviceCommandBaseType	Rigid body motion effect
TactileType	DeviceCommandBaseType	Tactile effect
KinestheticType	DeviceCommandBaseType	Active/passive kinesthetic effect
GlobalPositionCommandType	DeviceCommandBaseType	NA

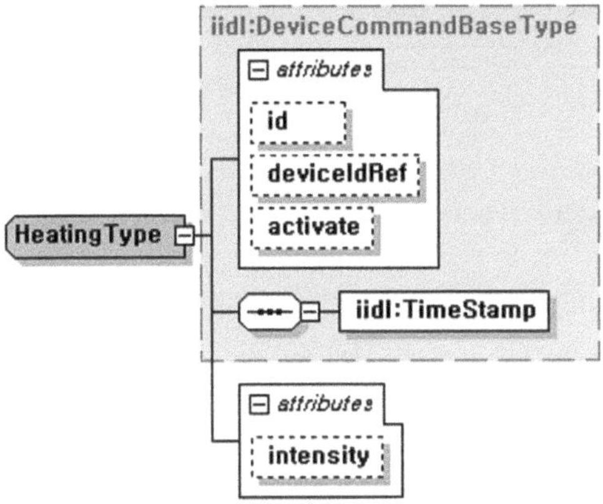

Figure 3.4 Structure of `HeatingType`.

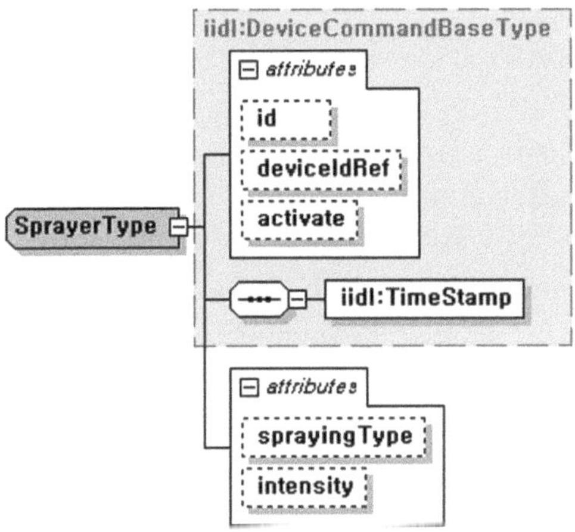

Figure 3.5 Structure of `SprayerType`.

the regions (i.e., SpatialLocator) within a video segment where the color correction effect is applied. If no regions are specified, the color correction effect is applied to the entire scene. Figure 3.6 shows the structure of `ColorCorrectionType`.

`InitializeColorCorrectionParameterType` is a command used to deliver the parameters supporting the color correction effect. These parameters define the color characteristics of the content provider's display device along with the lighting conditions of the provider's surroundings. The parameters passing through this command enable the display colors to be reproduced on the consumer side exactly as they were

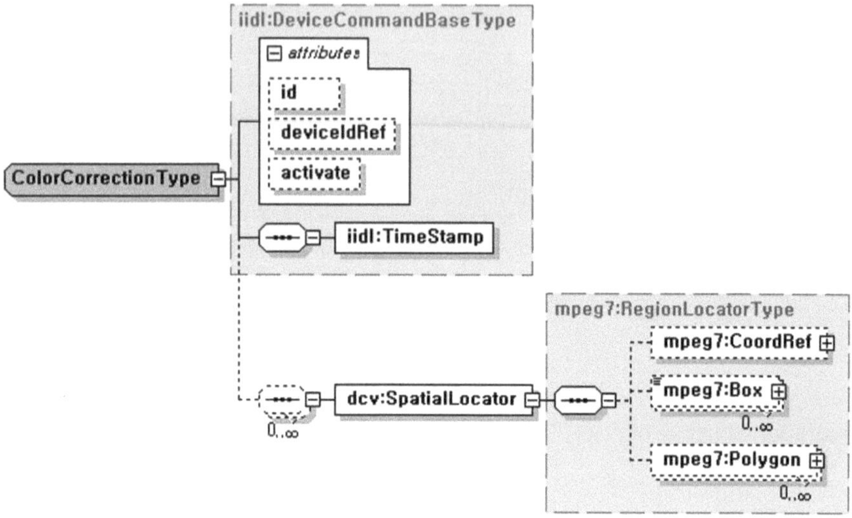

Figure 3.6 Structure of ColorCorrectionType.

created by the content provider. InitializeColorCorrectionParameterType contains five elements: ToneReproductionCurves, ConversionLUT, ColorTemperature, InputDeviceColorGamut, and IlluminanceOfSurround. The ToneReproductionCurves element represents the characteristics (e.g., gamma curves for the R, G, and B channels) of the provider's display device. The ConversionLUT element is a look-up table (matrix) that converts an image between an image color space (e.g., RGB) and a standard connection space (e.g., CIE XYZ). The ColorTemperature element describes the white point setting (e.g., D65, D93) of the provider's display device. The InputDeviceColorGamut element describes the color gamut of an input display device, which is represented by the chromaticity values of the R, G, and B channels with maximum Digital-to-Analog (DAC) values. The IlluminanceOfSurround element describes the illuminance level of the provider's viewing environment. The illuminance is represented in lux. Figure 3.7 shows the structure of InitializeColorCorrectionParameterType.

RigidBodyMotionType is one of the most complex types of device commands. In addition to the elements and attributes inherited from DeviceCommandBaseType, it includes MoveTowards and Incline elements, as well as a duration attribute to specify the motion of a rigid object such as a motion chair. The MoveTowards element has nine attributes to describe a motion. The three attributes directionX, directionY, and directionZ

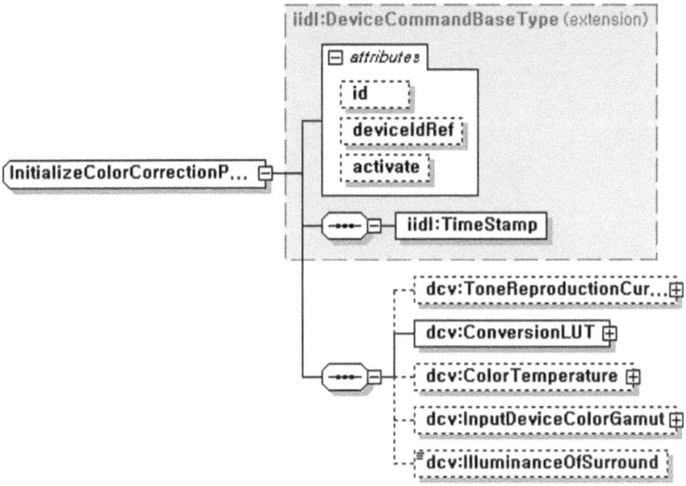

Figure 3.7 Structure of `InitializeColorCorrectionParameterType`.

provide the displacement of the object to be moved with respect to its current position in the *X*, *Y*, and *Z* directions, respectively, in cm. The three attributes `speedX`, `speedY`, and `speedZ` provide the desired speed of the object in the *X*, *Y*, and *Z* directions, respectively, as a percentage of the maximum speed that the device can generate. The three attributes `accelerationX`, `accelerationY`, and `accelerationZ` provide the desired acceleration of an object in the *X*, *Y*, and *Z* directions, respectively, as a percentage of the maximum acceleration of the device.

The `Incline` element also has nine attributes, of which, `pitchAngle`, `yawAngle`, and `rollAngle`, respectively describe the rotating angle along the *X*, *Y*, and *Z* axes counterclockwise; `pitchSpeed`, `yawSpeed`, and `rollSpeed` describe the desired rotating speed of the device along the *X*, *Y*, and *Z* axes, counterclockwise as a percentage of its maximum angular speed; and `pitchAcceleration`, `yawAcceleration`, and `rollAcceleration` describe the desired rotating acceleration of the device along the *X*, *Y*, and *Z* axes counterclockwise as a percentage of its maximum angular acceleration.

The *X*, *Y*, and *Z* directions for any actuator defined in this section are commonly defined by adapting a right-hand coordinate system, as shown in Figure 3.8.

The *X*-axis is defined in the direction of the left-hand side of the user facing the screen. The *Y*-axis is defined in the reverse direction of gravity. The *Z*-axis is defined in the direction of the user's front when facing the screen. Figure 3.9 shows the structure of `RigidBodyMotionType`.

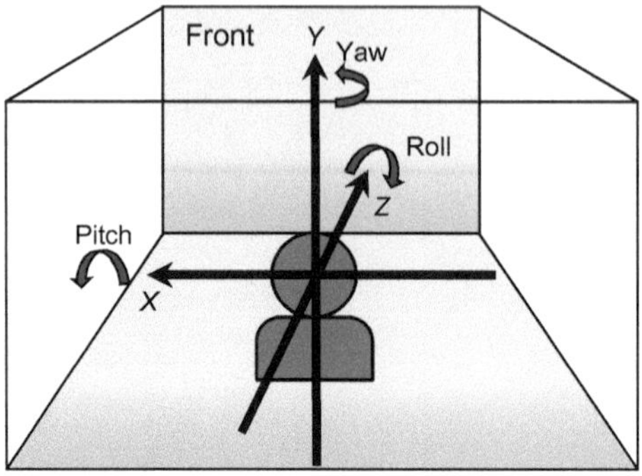

Figure 3.8 Reference coordinate system for actuators.

There are two other types defined to support haptic devices: `TactileType` and `KinestheticType`. `TactileType` is designed to support devices composed of an array of actuators, such as a tactile display, and users can feel senses similar to actually touching the surface of a certain object by touching the tactile device. By extending `DeviceCommandBaseType`, `TactileType` has an additional attribute of `tactileDisplay` and an element of `ArrayIntensity`. The `tactileDisplay` attribute describes the type of tactile display device, e.g., a vibrotactile display, an electrotactile display, a pneumatic tactile display, a piezoelectric tactile display, or a thermal display, as defined in Annex A.2.11 of Part 6 [2]. The `ArrayIntensity` element provides the intensity value of an individual actuator in the array. Figure 3.10 shows the structure of `TactileType`. `KinestheticType` is designed to command kinesthetic devices by specifying certain combinations of the four elements `Position`, `Orientation`, `Force`, and `Torque`. The `Position` element is used to provide the coordinates of the expected position with respect to the home position of the device in mm along the *X*, *Y*, and *Z* axes. The `Orientation` element is used to provide the orientation of the device in degrees along the *X*, *Y*, and *Z* axes with respect to the home position of the device. By combining `Position` and `Orientation`, any movement of a rigid object can be expressed as a combination of 6 DoF. The `Force` and `Torque` elements are defined to specify the force and torque in percentage of the object's maximum force or torque in the *X*, *Y*, and *Z* directions when the device/actuator is moving. When these elements are not specified, it is assumed that the device is moving with maximum force and torque. Figure 3.11 shows the structure of `KinestheticType`.

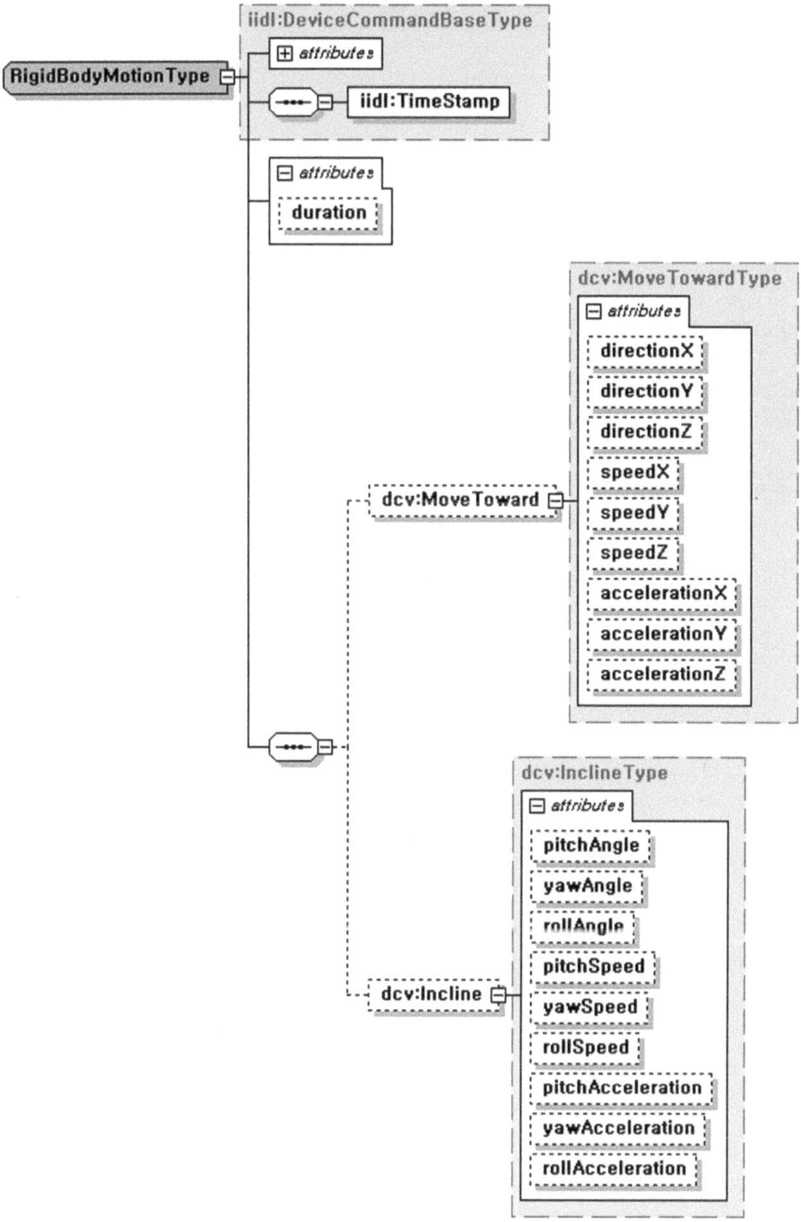

Figure 3.9 Structure of `RigidBodyMotionType`.

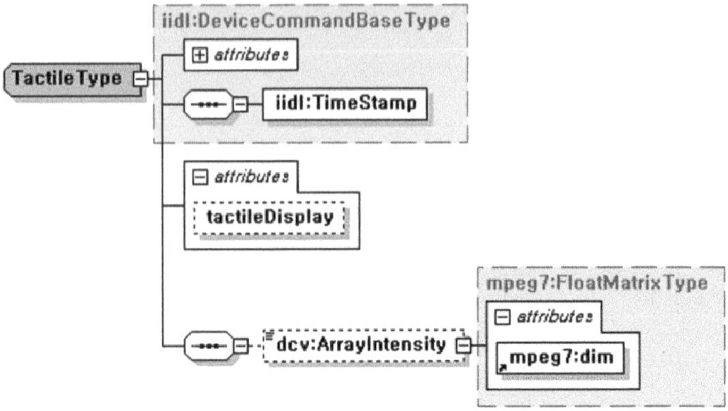

Figure 3.10 Structure of `TactileType`.

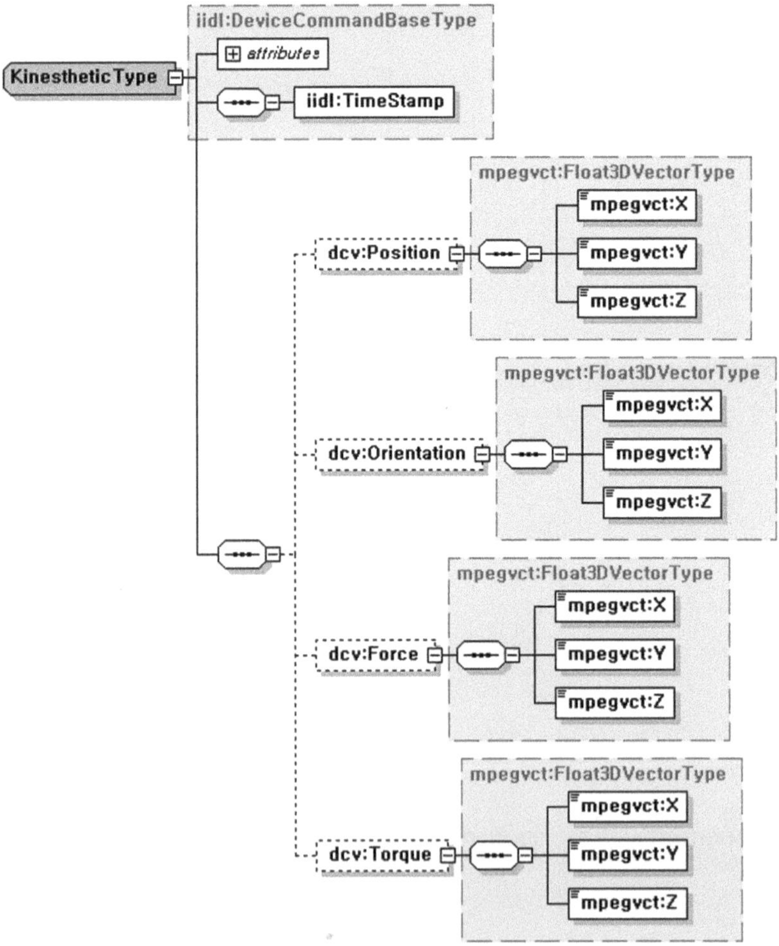

Figure 3.11 Structure of `KinestheticType`.

Unlike other device command vocabularies, GlobalPositionCommandType does not have a matching sensory effect. This type is designed to control an unmanned mobile vehicle and synchronize the positions of mobile objects in both the real and virtual worlds. By providing the intended position of a mobile object in longitude, latitude, and altitude, the designated mobile object should move to the described position.

3.4 SIV: DATA FORMAT FOR SENSING INFORMATION USING SENSORS

For the data format of the sensor inputs, the IIDL provides an abstract element called SensedInfoBaseType, through which the extended types defining the data formats of an individual sensor can be instantiated. In this standard, the extended types defining the data format for each individual sensor are defined as an SIV. Table 3.9 shows a list of sensor formats defined in ISO/IEC 23005-5:2013. There are 48 sensors or sensed information types currently defined, and all of them are defined as either a direct or indirect extension of SensedInfoBaseType.

LightSensorType describes information on the light intensity and color as acquired by a sensor. In addition to the TimeStamp element and the basic attributes inherited from SensedInfoBaseType, it has five other attributes: value, unit, color, colorValue, and model. When a light sensor senses a particular color, it should use the model attribute to specify the color space by selecting CIE XYZ, Yxy, CIE Lab, CIE Lch, CIE LUV, or Hunter Lab. Once the color space is selected, the sensed color can be specified by giving three values of double precision in the colorValue attribute, in which the three values are given in order of the variables specified in the color model. Another alternative to specifying the color is using the color attribute, through which either the colors specified in the color classification scheme given in Annex 2.1 of the ISO/IEC 23005-6 should be referenced, or a two-digit hexadecimal notation of the R, G, and B colors should be given to specify a color in an RGB space. The sensed intensity of the light can be described using the value attribute, which is able to take a float value to specify the intensity of light in lux, or take a colorWType value specifying the luminance of the light in a two-digit hexadecimal value to denote the grayscale brightness within 256 levels from black (#00) to white (#FF). When this intensity of light is measured in units other than lux, it should be specified through the unit attribute by referencing one of the values specified in the unit type classification scheme specified in Annex 2.1 of ISO/IEC 23005-6.

Table 3.9 Information acquired from a temperature sensor

```
<iidl:InteractionInfo>
      <iidl:SensedInfoList>
            <iidl:SensedInfo xsi:type="siv:TemperatureSensorType"
id="TS001" sensorIdRef="TSID001" activate="true" value="26.5">
                  <iidl:TimeStamp xsi:type="mpegvct:ClockTickTime
Type" timeScale="100" pts="60000"/>
            </iidl:SensedInfo>
      </iidl:SensedInfoList>
</iidl:InteractionInfo>
```

AmbientNoiseSensorType is defined to support sensors that sense ambient noise for a certain duration of time. It has the specially defined lifespan attribute. The lifespan attribute is as a float type used to specify the number of clock ticks to indicate the time period during which the ambient noise is measured. For this purpose, the frequency of the internal clock tick must be specified in the Timestamp element. The average noise during the given time period in dB is specified in the value attribute. If the value is given in units other than dB, it should be specified by the unit attribute by referencing one of the values specified in the unit-type classification scheme specified in Annex 2.1 of ISO/IEC 23005-6.

TemperatureSensorType is one of the simplest SIV types, and in addition to the base attributes of SensedInfoBaseType, has only value and unit attributes defined. Any temperature sensed can be expressed using a float-type value attribute. By default (if not specified by the unit attribute), the value is given in degrees Celsius, or should be specified by referencing the unit type specified in the unit type classification scheme in Annex 2.1 of ISO/IEC 23005-6. BodyTemperatureSensorType is defined as a simple extension of TemperatureSensorType by adding the optional location attribute to specify the body location, at which the temperature is measured. The location information is specified by selecting a non-negative number identifying a specific body location given through the following: (i) general body temperature; (ii) axillary (armpit); (iii) ear (usually earlobe); (iv) finger; (v) gastrointestinal tract; (vi) mouth; (vii) rectum; (viii) toe; and (ix) tympanum (ear drum).

HumiditySensorType, DistanceSensorType, AtmosphericPressureSensorType, PressureSensorType, DustSensorType, BodyHeightSensorType, BodyWeightSensorType, BodyFatSensorType, BloodSugarSensorType, BloodOxygenSensorType, and HeartRateSensorType are simpler sensor types that, in

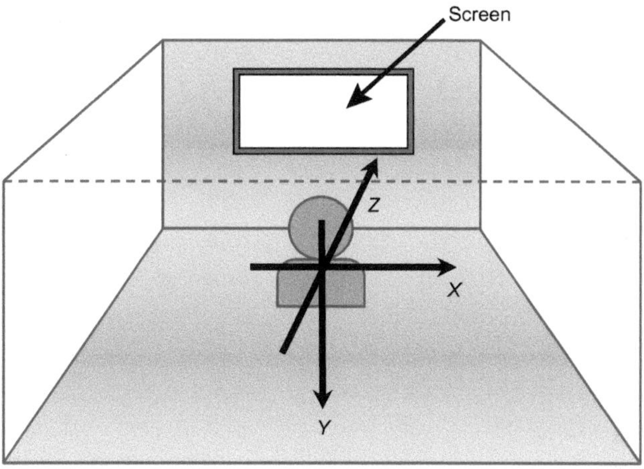

Figure 3.12 Reference coordinate system for sensors.

addition to the elements and attributes inherited from `SensedInfoBaseType`, have only value and unit attributes. Although all of these sensor types have the same float-type `value` attribute to specify the intensity of the sensed information, the semantics of the `value` attribute differ for each sensor type, percentage of humidity for `HumiditySensorType`, distance in m for `DistanceSensorType`, atmospheric pressure in hectopascal (hPa) for `AtmosphericPressureSensorType`, pressure in N-mm^2 for `PressureSensorType`, amount of dust in μg/m^3 for `DustSensorType`, height in cm for `BodyHeightSensorType`, weight in kg for `BodyWeightSensorType`, percentage of body fat for `BodyFatSensorType`, density of sugar in the blood in mg/dl for `BloodSugarSensorType`, blood oxygen saturation in percentage for `BloodOxygenSensorType`, and the heart BPM for `HeartRateSensorType`, to be specific. The default unit for each type is specified in the semantics of the value attribute as given, and if any unit other than the specified default unit is used, it is specified in the unit attribute.

`PositionSensorType` has an optional element of the 3D float position vector to denote the position (offset) of the object from the coordinate origin. The general reference coordinate system for the sensors is given in Figure 3.12. In this case, the coordinate origin is defined as the position of the sensor when it is either first activated or calibrated. The offset from the origin is given by the distance in the unit given in the `unit` attribute or in m in the *X*, *Y*, and *Z* directions, as defined in the coordinate system. `VelocitySensorType` also has an optional element of a 3D float velocity vector to denote the velocity in a 3D vector of the *X*, *Y*, and *Z* directions. The default unit of velocity is m/s. `AccelerationSensorType`, in addition to the elements and attributes inherited from `SensedInfoBaseType`, has an optional element of `Acceleration` with a 3D float vector to express the acceleration in three directions, an optional `axis` attribute, and an optional `unit` attribute. The default unit is m/s^2. When the acceleration in only one or two directions is specified, the `axis` attribute should be set to either 1 or 2. When `axis` is set to 1, only the acceleration in the *X* direction can be specified. When `axis` is set to 2, only the acceleration in *X* and *Y* directions can be specified. `OrientationSensorType` also has an optional element of `Orientation` with three float values denoting orientations along the *X*, *Y*, and *Z* directions (pitch, yaw, and roll) in degrees, with respect to the original pose. The original pose is the pose of the object sensed either at the time of sensor activation, or right after the calibration.

`AngularVelocitySensorType` and `AngularAccelerationSensorType` are very similar in their structure and semantics, except that `AngularVelocitySensor` is designed for the velocity and `AngularAccelerationSensory` is designed for the acceleration. The `AngularVelocity` element with a 3D float vector in `AngluarVelocitySensorType` denotes the angular velocity along the three axes (pitch along the *X*-axis, yaw along the *Y*-axis, and roll along the *Z*-axis) in degrees/s. The `AngularAcceleration` element with a 3D float vector in `AngularAccelerationSensorType` denotes the angular acceleration along the three axes (pitch along the *X*-axis, yaw along the *Y*-axis, and roll along the *Z*-axis) in degrees/s^2.

`ForceSensorType` and `TorqueSensorType` are also very similar in their structure and semantics, just as in the cases of `AngularVelocitySensorType` and `AngularAccelerationSensorType`. `ForceSensorType` has a 3D float vector of the force element to specify the force in three directions in *N*, by default. If the force is to be specified in units other than *N*, it can be specified in the `unit` attribute. `TorqueSensorType` also has a 3D float vector of the `Torque` element to specify the torque in three directions in N-mm. If the torque is to be specified in units other than N-mm, it can also be specified in the `unit` attribute.

`MotionSensorType` is an aggregation of six sensor types: `PositionSensorType`, `OrientationSensorType`, `VelocitySensorType`, `AngularVelocitySensorType`, `AccelerationSensorType`, and `AngularAccelerationSensorType`. By specifying any combination of these six types of sensed information, any motion of an object can be described without losing the generality of the description.

IntelligentCameraType is used to describe the sensed information by a camera-type sensor, which can sense information such as facial expressions, body gestures, and facial and body feature points. There are control facial-feature points defined in clause 5.2.8.7 of ISO/IEC 23005-4, and control body-feature points defined in clause 5.2.8.5 of ISO/IEC 23005-4. There can be up to 255 FaceFeature elements and 255 BodyFeature elements defined in IntelligentCameraType. FaceFeature elements are given in order of the face-feature points defined in clause 5.2.8.7 of ISO/IEC 23005-4. Each FaceFeature element is of a 3D float vector type denoting a sensed position of a specific face-feature point by giving the offset from the center of the camera position in m. BodyFeature elements are also given in order of the body-feature points defined in clause 5.2.8.5 of ISO/IEC 23005-4. Each BodyFeature element is of a 3D float-vector type denoting a sensed position of a specific body-feature point by giving the offset from the center position of the camera in m. By referencing a specific animation clip using FacialAnimationID or BodyAnimationID, the captured face-feature point positions and/or body-feature point positions can be synchronized with the face or body of the linked animation by controlling the feature points in the animation. FacialAnimationID and BodyAnimationID can also be used to reference a facial or body expression term from FacialExpressionAnimationCS or BodyExpressionAnimationCS defined in A.2.3.12 and A.2.3.13 of ISO/IEC 23005-4.

FacialExpressionSensorType is a special case of IntelligentCameraType, which senses the relative displacement of the facial feature points. By extending IntelligentCameraType, FacialExpressionSensorType can have up to 66 optional elements of FacialExpressionBasis with the three attributes facialExpressionBasisID, facialExpressionBasisValue, and facialExpressionBasisUnit. For identifying the basis of the displacement measurements, 119 bases are defined in FacialExpressionBasisIDCS in Annex B.9 of ISO/IEC 23005-5 for reference by the facialExpressionBasisID attribute. The percentage of displacement is given in facialExpressionBasisValue with respect to the maximum displacement value, by default. If any other unit is used, it is identified in facialExpressionBasisUnit by referencing one of the terms specified in UnitTypeCS specified in Annex 2.1 of ISO/IEC 23005-6.

FacialMorphologySensorType is used to acquire the initialization parameters for supporting the facial expression sensors. It has four float-type elements, IrisDiameter, EyeSeparation, EyeNoseSeparation, and MouthWidth. The IrisDiameter element describes the percentage of distance between the upper and lower eyelids. The EyeSeparation element describes the distance between the left- and right-center of the eyes. EyeNoseSeparation describes the shortest distance between the line connecting the center of the two eyes and the bottom line of the nose. MouthWidth describes the distance between the left and right ends of the mouth.

FacialExpressionCharacteristicsSensorType is used to acquire the initialization parameters for supporting the facial expression sensors. By adding a maximum of 66 optional FacialExpressionBasisRange elements, FacialExpressionCharacteristicsSensorType extends SensedInfoBaseType. The FacialExpressionBasisRange element has five optional attributes: facialExpressionBasisID, maxValueFacialExpressionBasis, minValueFacialExpressionBasis, neutralValueFacialExpressionBasis, and facialExpressionBasisUnit. By referencing a term (i.e., based on a facial expression) in FacialExpressionBasisIDCS specified in Annex B.9, a specific displacement measuring point is selected. For the selected displacement point, the maximum displacement (or maximum value of this parameter) minimum displacement (or minimum value of this parameter), and neutral displacement (or value of this parameter in a neutral face) can be specified in maxValueFacialExpressionBasis, minValueFacialExpressionBasis, and neutralValueFacialExpressionBasis, respectively. The unit used to describe these parameters is specified in facialExpressionBasisUnit. When the percentage is used in FacialExpressionSensorType based on a specific facial expression, 100% is given when the measured parameter value is the same as maxValueFacialExpressionBasis, and 0% is given when the measured parameter value is the same as minValueFacialExpressionBasis.

MultiInteractionPointSensorType is designed to capture the user interactions through touch-based user inputs using the InteractionPoint element, which has two attributes, interactionPointId and interactionPointStatus. When a certain number of interaction points of an interaction device are identified, each interaction point is assigned with an InteractionPoint element with a unique identifier (interactionPointId). For each interaction point, the interactionPointStatus is either set to true or false depending on whether it receives a user interaction or not.

GazeTrackingSensorType is designed to capture and track the blinking and position of the user's eyes based on the orientation of the user's gaze. Therefore, GazeTrackingSensorType contains the personIdx attribute to identify the user, and one Gaze element to capture the blinking, position, and gaze of each eye. The Gaze element, defined for each eye, has

Position and Orientation elements, and gazeIdx and blinkStatus attributes. The Position element provides the position of the eye in a 3D float vector as defined in PositionSensorType. The origin of the coordinate is the eye position at the time of the sensor activation, or after calibration. The Orientation element provides the orientation of the gaze direction in a 3D float vector as defined in OrientationSensorType. The origin of the coordinate is the gaze direction at the time of the sensor activation, or the gaze direction right after the calibration. The blinkStatus attribute is a Boolean-type attribute used to show whether the eye is blinking or not at the time of measurement.

WindSensorType is exactly the same as VelocitySensorType, with only the semantics modified for the measurement of the wind velocity. The Velocity element of a 3D float vector specifies the sensed speed of the wind in the *X*, *Y*, and *Z* directions in m/s.

In addition to SensedInfoBaseType, GlobalPositionSensorType has three attributes, i.e., crs, longitude, and latitude. The crs attribute, by giving the URI, specifies the coordinate reference system based upon which the values of the longitude, latitude, and altitude are given. The default coordinate reference system is specified using code 4326 in the EPSG database, available at http://www.epsg.org/, and the URI is specified as urn:ogc:def:crs:EPSG::4326. The longitude of a position is given based on a double precision number ranging from −180.0 to +180.0, where western longitudes are represented in negative degrees and eastern longitudes in positive degrees. The latitude of a position is given by a double precision number ranging from −90.0 to +90.0, where northern latitudes are represented in positive degrees and southern latitudes in negative degrees.

AltitudeSensorType also has two new attributes, crs and altitude, and unit is added to SensedInfoBaseType. Even though most global position sensors have altitude sensors included, AltitudeSensorType is separately defined here, as there are separate types of altitude sensors available. The crs attribute is the same as the one in GlobalPositionSensor, specifying the coordinate reference system, and altitude is the double precision number specifying the measured altitude in the default unit of m or in the unit specified by the unit attribute.

BendSensorType specifies a sensor that senses the angles bent at each sensing point. BendSensorType can have multiple channels, where each channel can have multiple sensing points. At each sensing point, bending angles of up to three axes can be measured. Therefore, as many occurrences of ArrayBendValue as the number of channels can be instantiated, and each occurrence of ArrayBendValue can be an $m \times n$ matrix float value where m is the number of axes at the sensing points and n is the number of sensing points at the given channel. Therefore, if there is a two-channel bending sensor that senses the degree of bending of three axes at four measuring points, there will be two occurrences of the ArrayBendValue element in an instantiation of BendSensorType, and each ArrayBendValue element will have 3×4 float numbers specifying the bending degrees.

GasSensorType represents a sensor that senses the type of gas and/or its concentration. The GasType element is used to represent the detected gas type by referencing a term in GasTypeCS defined in Annex B.6. Two additional attributes, value and unit, are used to specify the gas concentration through a float number with respect to the default unit ppm, or the unit specified in the unit attribute by referencing UnitTypeCS defined in Annex 2.1 of ISO/IEC 23005-6.

DustSensorType is a specific type of gas sensor, in which only the concentration of dust is measured without identifying the type of dust or gas. The default unit is also ppm, and the value is given as a float type.

BloodTypeSensorType has two additional elements, ABOType and RhType. The ABOType element takes A, B, AB, or O to represent the blood type in ABO type. The RhType element takes a + or −, representing the blood type in the Rh blood group system.

In addition to the attributes inherited from the SensedInfoBaseType, BloodPressureSensorType has the four attributes systolicBP, diastolicBP, MAP, and unit. The systolic blood pressure measured in mmHg is recorded in the systolicBP attribute, and the diastolic blood pressure measured in mmHg is recorded in the diastolicBP attribute. The MAP attribute describes the mean arterial pressure in mmHg. When the default unit of mmHg is not used in measuring the blood pressure, it should be specified in the unit attribute by referencing one of the terms defined in UnitTypeCS specified in Annex 2.1 of ISO/IEC 23005-6.

ElectrographSensorType, which also extends SensedInfoBaseType, is a base type for any electrograph-related biosensors, such as electroencephalogram (EEG), electrocardiogram (ECG), electromyogram (EMG), and electro-oculogram (EOG) sensors. It has an optional element of WaveValue in a float-matrix type for describing the sensed values in the time series in μV. If any unit other than the default μV unit is used in describing the values, the unit of choice should be specified in the unit attribute by referencing the unit type defined in UnitTypeCS specified in Annex 2.1 of ISO/IEC 23005-6. The waveformLabel attribute is used to specify the label of the waveform by referencing a term listed in the classification scheme of waveformLabelCS of EEG, ECG, EMG, and EOG defined in Annex B.1, B.2, B.3, and B.4, respectively. Each waveform label is used to identify the location of the electrodes used to depict a specific wave or a time series of values, and waveformLabelCS maintains a list of electrode locations for each type of electrograph-related sensor. The maxAmplitude attribute is used to specify the maximum amplitude of the values given in the time series in μV or in the unit defined by the unit attribute.

EEGSensorType is defined for the EEG sensor by extending the electrograph sensor. An EEG sensor is designed to detect the brain waves in various positions of the human scalp. It has an additional attribute, wavePattern, to denote one of five EEG patterns of delta, theta, alpha, beta, and gamma. The mapping between the electrode locations and waveform labels is provided in the semantics table of the EEG sensor type. The waveform labels for the EEG sensors are provided in EEG_waveformLabelCS defined in Annex B.1 of ISO/IEC 23005-5.

ECGSensorType is defined for an electrocardiography sensor to produce an ECG by extending the electrograph sensor. The default unit for measuring the heart wave is also μV. The waveform labels for the ECG are given in ECG_waveformLabelCS defined in Annex B.2, and mapped to each of 12 leads as described in the semantics table of ECG Sensor Type.

EMGSensorType is defined for an electromyography sensor to produce an EMG, and records the electrical activity produced by the muscles by extending an electrograph sensor. The default measurement unit here is also μV. The waveform labels for an EMG are given in EMG_waveformLabelCS defined in Annex B.3, and mapped to each of the 65 measurement points on the body.

EOGSensorType is defined for the electro-oculograph sensor to produce an EOG, and record the electrical activity caused by eye movements by extending an electrograph sensor. The μV unit is also used for this measurement. The waveform labels for an EOG are given in EOG_waveformLabelCS defined in Annex B.4, and are mapped to each of the six measurement points around the eyes.

GSRSensorType is defined for galvanic skin response sensors that measure a set of electrical conductance waves of the skin, which vary with the moisture level. GSRSensorType is based on SensedInfoBaseType and is extended by adding an optional Array_Value element of a float-matrix type and the unit attribute. Array_Value records the sensed value in the unit of micromho, which is the unit of electrical conductance with the reciprocal in ohm.

BioSensorType is a sensor type aggregating all 14 human-body or bio-related sensor types: BodyHeightSensorType, BodyWeightSensorType, BodyTemperatureSensorType, BodyFatSensorType, BloodTypeSensorType, BloodPressureSensorType, BloodSugarSensorType, BloodOxygenSensorType, HeartRateSensorType, EEGSensorType, ECGSensorType, EMGSensorType, EOGSensorType, and GSRSensorType. However, this does not mean that all 14 sensed information elements should be present at an instance of the BioSensorType element because all of these element types are optional.

WeatherSensorType is a complex sensor type designed to record various weather-related information. There may be no physical sensors that map with this type of sensor exactly, and this type of sensor may be considered a virtual sensor in which various weather-related information collected from various sources, including Web sites, can be aggregated. There are seven main elements, WeatherDescription, Temperature, Precipitation, Snow, Wind, Humidity, and Place, defined in this sensor. WeatherDescription provides a textual description of the weather, such as sunny, cloudy, rainy, snowy, windy, or partly cloudy, by referencing a term in WeatherCS defined in Annex B.7 of ISO/IEC 23005-5. The Temperature element is of TemperatureSensorType to provide the temperature information. The Precipitation element has four attributes: value, valueUnit, duration, and durationUnit. The precipitation during the period of time specified by the duration and durationUnit attributes is specified in the value attribute in the default mm unit, or in the unit specified by the valueUnit attribute. The Snow element is in a similar structure as the Precipitation element with the value, valueUnit, duration, and durationUnit attributes. The amount of snow measured during the time period specified by the duration and durationUnit is specified in the value attribute in either the default unit of cm, or in the unit specified by the valueUnit attribute. The Wind element has three attributes: velocity, unit, and direction. The speed of the wind is recorded in the velocity attribute in m/s by default, or in the unit given in the unit attribute. The direction the wind is blowing from is specified in the direction attribute by referencing a term defined in WindDirectionTypeCS of Annex B.8. The Humidity element of HumiditySensorType is used to specify the humidity. The Place element of the MPEG-7 PlaceType is used to specify the location where the weather is measured. The point in time at which the weather is measured is given in the time attribute.

GeomagneticSensorType is used to describe the absolute direction that the sensor or device is pointing toward. GeomagneticSensorType is an extension of SensedInfoBaseType, and has a float-type attribute of azimuth ranging from 0 to 360 and the unit attribute. When the value of the azimuth attribute is 0, it indicates magnetic north. When the value of the azimuth attribute is 90, it indicates an eastward direction.

3.5 CREATING COMMANDS AND ACCEPTING SENSOR INPUTS

There are various use cases of standardized interfaces for actuators and sensors. The command formats for the actuators, and sensed information formats for the sensors, can be used separately or together depending on the use cases.

One use case can be a virtualized world, which is a regenerated version of the real world and is synchronized with the real world. In this use case, various sensors can be used to gather environmental and/or surrounding data from the real world using the standardized interfaces provided in this chapter. The gathered information can be fed to the Real-to-Virtual adaptation engine, which generates commands to control the virtual world, synchronizing this virtual world to the target real world. For example, we can build a replica of a street with buildings in Seoul within a virtual world, and synchronize it with the real world by reproducing environmental elements such as the weather, temperature, lighting, and the opening of doors. In such applications, the information acquired by each individual sensor can be fed to the Real-to-Virtual adaptation engine either as a sequence of separate control information if the real-time synchronization is of high priority, or as a packaged control information if the real-time synchronization requirement can be somewhat relaxed. The following three tables (Tables 3.9–3.11) show example sequences of information acquired from independent sensors as separate XML files.

In these three example instances, a temperature of 26.5°C is sensed by the sensor with a sensor id of TSID001, at a time of 60,000 clock ticks with a speed of 100 clock ticks per second.

Depending on the situation, these three instances of sensed information can be integrated as a single instance, as shown in Table 3.12, and sent to the Real-to-Virtual adaptation engine.

This example shows a Real-to-Virtual adaptation. An example of a Virtual-to-Real adaptation can be a 4-D theater or multisensorial media. In a 4-D theater or multisensorial media applications, the media content

Table 3.10 Information acquired from a weather sensor

```
<iidl:InteractionInfo>
      <iidl:SensedInfoList>
            <iidl:SensedInfo xsi:type="siv:WeatherSensorType"
id="Weather01" sensorIdRef="WeatherSensor01" activate="true">
                  <iidl:TimeStamp xsi:type="mpegvct:ClockTickTime
Type" timeScale="1000" pts="600000"/>
                  <siv:WeatherDescription>urn:mpeg:mpeg-v:01-CI-
WeatherCS-NS:snow</siv:WeatherDescription>
                        <siv:Snow value="100" valueUnit="urn:mpeg:
mpeg-v:01-CI-UnitTypeCS-NS:cm" duration="1"/>
                        <siv:Place>
                              <mpeg7:GeographicPosition>
                                    <mpeg7:Point latitude="37"
longitude="127"/>
                              </mpeg7:GeographicPosition>
                  </siv:Place>
            </iidl:SensedInfo>
      </iidl:SensedInfoList>
</iidl:InteractionInfo>
```

Table 3.11 Information acquired from a light sensor

```
<iidl:InteractionInfo>
      <iidl:SensedInfoList>
            <iidl:SensedInfo xsi:type="siv:LightSensorType" id="LS001"
                  sensorIdRef="LSID001" activate="true" value="200"
color="#FF0000">
                  <iidl:TimeStamp xsi:type="mpegvct:ClockTickTimeType"
timeScale="1000" pts="600000"/>
            </iidl:SensedInfo>
      </iidl:SensedInfoList>
</iidl:InteractionInfo>
```

may have information regarding multisensorial effects or descriptions of multisensorial effects. These descriptions can be transformed into a sequence of commands to generate multisensorial effects using various actuators. These commands can be expressed using the device commands described in this chapter. Table 3.13 gives an example of a command sequence for driving the actuators.

In this example, there are four devices controlled with respective identifiers of `light01`, `heater001`, `wind001`, and `sprayer001`. The first device with an ID of `light01` is a light-type device activated at 1 h, 30 min, and

Table 3.12 Integrated information acquired from three different sensors

```
<iidl:InteractionInfo>
      <iidl:SensedInfoList>
            <iidl:SensedInfo xsi:type="siv:TemperatureSensorType"
id="TS001" sensorIdRef="TSID001" activate="true" value="26.5">
                  <iidl:TimeStamp xsi:type="mpegvct:ClockTickTime
Type" timeScale="100" pts="60000"/>
            </iidl:SensedInfo>
            <iidl:SensedInfo xsi:type="siv:WeatherSensorType"
id="Weather01" sensorIdRef="WeatherSensor01" activate="true">
                  <iidl:TimeStamp xsi:type="mpegvct:ClockTickTime
Type" timeScale="1000" pts="600000"/>
                  <siv:WeatherDescription>urn:mpeg:mpeg-v:01-CI-
WeatherCS-NS:snow</siv:WeatherDescription>
                  <siv:Snow value="100" valueUnit="urn:mpeg:mpeg-
v:01-CI-UnitTypeCS-NS:cm" duration="1"/>
                  <siv:Place>
                        <mpeg7:GeographicPosition>
                              <mpeg7:Point latitude="37"
longitude="127"/>
                        </mpeg7:GeographicPosition>
                  </siv:Place>
            </iidl:SensedInfo>
            <iidl:SensedInfo xsi:type="siv:LightSensorType" id="LS001"
                  sensorIdRef="LSID001" activate="true" value="200"
                  color="#FF0000">
                  <iidl:TimeStamp xsi:type="mpegvct:ClockTickTime
Type" timeScale="1000" pts="600000"/>
            </iidl:SensedInfo>
      </iidl:SensedInfoList>
</iidl:InteractionInfo>
```

23 s, generating a red-colored light at 30% of its maximum intensity, and deactivated at 1 h, 32 min, and 23 s after the start point of the media content. The second device is a heater-type device with an ID of `heater001`, which is activated at 1 h, 31 min, and 10 s generating heat at 60% intensity, and deactivated at 1 h, 31 min, and 35 s, meaning that the heater is on for 25 s. The third device is a wind-type device with an ID of `wind001`, which is activated at 1 h, 31 min, and 33 s, with 30% of its maximum intensity, and deactivated at 1 h, 32 min, and 20 s. The fourth device is a sprayer-type device with a device ID of `sprayer001`. This device is commanded to be activated at 1 h, 32 min, and 20 s, spraying water at 50% of its maximum intensity, and deactivated at 1 h, 32 min, and 21 s.

Table 3.13 Example instance of controlling four devices

```
<iidl:InteractionInfo>
      <iidl:DeviceCommandList>
            <iidl:DeviceCommand xsi:type="dcv:LightType" id="light1"
            deviceIdRef="light01"
            color="urn:mpeg:mpeg-v:01-SI-ColorCS-NS:red" activate="true"
            intensity="30">
                  <iidl:TimeStamp xsi:type="mpegvct:AbsoluteTimeType"
                  absTime="1:30:23"/>
            </iidl:DeviceCommand>
            <iidl:DeviceCommand xsi:type="dcv:HeatingType" id="heater1"
                  deviceIdRef="heater001" activate="true" intensity="60">
                  <iidl:TimeStamp xsi:type="mpegvct:AbsoluteTimeType"
                  absTime="1:31:10"/>
            </iidl:DeviceCommand>
            <iidl:DeviceCommand xsi:type="dcv:WindType" id="wind01"
                  deviceIdRef="wind001" activate="true" intensity="30">
                  <iidl:TimeStamp xsi:type="mpegvct:AbsoluteTimeType"
                  absTime="1:31:33"/>
            </iidl:DeviceCommand>
            <iidl:DeviceCommand xsi:type="dcv:HeatingType" id="heater2"
                  deviceIdRef="heater001" activate="false">
                  <iidl:TimeStamp xsi:type="mpegvct:AbsoluteTimeType"
                  absTime="1:31:35"/>
            </iidl:DeviceCommand>
            <iidl:DeviceCommand xsi:type="dcv:SprayerType" id="sprayer01"
                  deviceIdRef="sprayer001" activate="true" intensity="50"
                  sprayingType="urn:mpeg:mpeg-v:01-SI-SprayingTypeCS-
NS:water">

                  <iidl:TimeStamp xsi:type="mpegvct:AbsoluteTimeType"
                  absTime="1:32:20"/>
            </iidl:DeviceCommand>
            <iidl:DeviceCommand xsi:type="dcv:WindType" id="wind02"
                  deviceIdRef="wind001" activate="false">
                  <iidl:TimeStamp xsi:type="mpegvct:AbsoluteTimeType"
                  absTime="1:32:20"/>
            </iidl:DeviceCommand>
            <iidl:DeviceCommand xsi:type="dcv:SprayerType" id="sprayer02"
                  deviceIdRef="sprayer001" activate="false">
                  <iidl:TimeStamp xsi:type="mpegvct:AbsoluteTimeType"
                  absTime="1:32:21"/>
            </iidl:DeviceCommand>
            <iidl:DeviceCommand xsi:type="dcv:LightType" id="light2"
            deviceIdRef="light01"
            color="urn:mpeg:mpeg-v:01-SI-ColorCS-NS:red"
            activate="false">
                  <iidl:TimeStamp xsi:type="mpegvct:AbsoluteTimeType"
                  absTime="1:32:23"/>
            </iidl:DeviceCommand>
      </iidl:DeviceCommandList>
</iidl:InteractionInfo>
```

3.6 CONCLUSION

This chapter provided a detailed explanation of the device commands and sensed information format designed to control the actuators and gather information through the sensors, as defined in ISO/IEC 23005-5 MPEG-V, Part 5: Data Format for Interaction Devices. Each element and attribute as a construct for the data format was given along with an explanation of its meaning and the intention of its design. Some integrated examples using these specifications were also provided. These device commands or sensed information can be instantiated as a long sequence of commands or sensed information as a group for storage or transfer. They can also be instantiated as a single command or single sensed information as a way for controlling the actuators or retrieving real-time information from a sensor.

REFERENCES

[1] ISO/IEC 23005-5:2013 Information technology—Media context and control—Part 5 Data formats for interaction devices.
[2] ISO/IEC 23005-6:2013 Information technology—Media context and control—Part 6 Common types and tools.

CHAPTER 4

Adapting Sensory Effects and Adapted Control of Devices

Contents

4.1 INTRODUCTION

All devices (actuators) used to render the sensory effects, and the sensors collecting information from the user and/or environment, have different capabilities and a different range of operating parameters. To control a device, or interpret information received from a sensor, knowing the capabilities or characteristics of the device or sensor can greatly help enhance the accuracy of the control or interpretation. In addition, for personalized adaptation of the commands or sensed information, it is very critical to know the preferences of the users. MPEG-V, Part 2 (ISO/IEC 23005-5) [1] provides a standardized format for the precise control or adaptation of such devices by defining the Control Information Description Language (CIDL) using the Device Capability Description Vocabulary (DCDV), Sensor Capability Description Vocabulary (SCDV), User's Sensory Preference Vocabulary (USPV), and Sensor Adaptation Preference Vocabulary (SAPV). Without the tools provided in this chapter (or in MPEG-V, Part 2), users can still issue commands for the actuators or receive information from the sensors, but a personal adaptation, detailed

MPEG-V.
DOI: http://dx.doi.org/10.1016/B978-0-12-420140-8.00004-4

control of the actuators, or detailed understanding of the received information may not be possible.

4.2 CONTROL INFORMATION DESCRIPTION LANGUAGE

4.2.1 CIDL Structure

CIDL is an XML-based language used to provide the foundation or framework for instantiating capability descriptions of the actuators and sensors, or the user's preferences regarding certain sensory effects and sensors, using the MPEG-V standard.

Unlike Interaction Information Description Language (IIDL), there is only one root element in CIDL, called `ControlInfo`, meaning that the XML instance of a control information description can only begin with a `ControlInfo` tag. The `ControlInfo` root element can have a sequence of optional elements, i.e., `SensoryDeviceCapabilityList`, `SensorDeviceCapabilityList`, `UserSensoryPreferenceList`, and `SensorAdapatationPreferenceList`, as shown in Figure 4.1. These four elements are optional, meaning that we can have any combination of them. `SensoryDeviceCapabilityList` is a list of one or more `SensoryDeviceCapability` elements of `SensoryDeviceCapabilityBaseType`; `SensorDeviceCapabilityList` is a list of one or more `SensorDeviceCapability` of `SensorCapabilityBaseType`; `UserSensoryPreferenceList` is a list of one or more `USPreference` elements of `UserSensoryPreferenceBaseType`; and `SensorAdapationPreferenceList` is a list of one or more `SAPreference` elements of `SensorAdaptationPreferenceBaseType`.

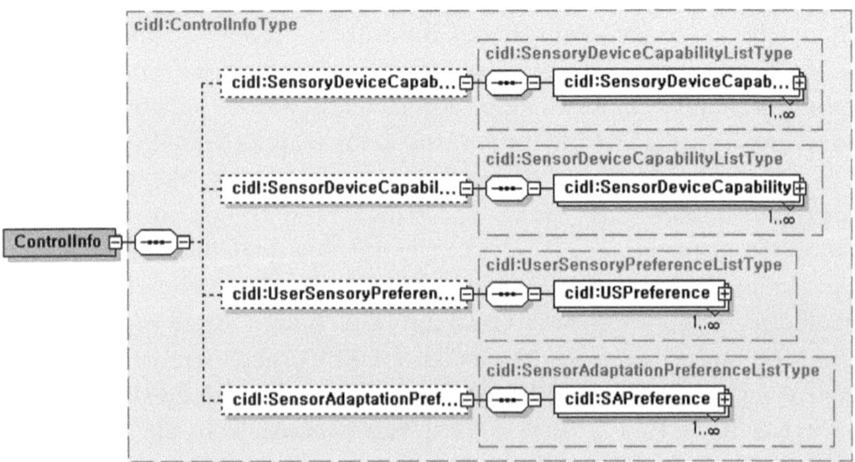

Figure 4.1 Structure of `ControlInfo` root element of CIDL.

4.2.2 SensoryDeviceCapability Element

The SensoryDeviceCapability element, whose structure is given in Figure 4.1, is of the abstract SensoryDeviceCapabilityBaseType type. This abstract-type structure provides extensibility in the standard and allows any sensory device capability description with an extended SensoryDeviceCapabilityBaseType to be used when the SensoryDeviceCapability element is instantiated (Figure 4.2).

As shown in Table 4.1, SensoryDeviceCapabilityBaseType is defined as an extension of dia:TerminalCapabilityBaseType, which is defined in ISO/IEC 21000-7 MPEG-21, Part 7: Digital Item Adaptation [2], by adding the sensoryDeviceCapabilityAttributes attribute group. This group of attributes, which are zerothOrderDelayTime, firstOrderDelayTime, and locator, are intended to be included in any capability description of a sensory device because they are believed to be commonly needed descriptions of any sensory device capability. zerothOrderDelayTime represents the time in ms needed for a device to be activated or start performing its intended functionality. For example, there is a delay or certain period of time before a cooling system starts working once it receives a turn-on signal, if it started in a turned-off state; this delay is call a zeroth-order delay. firstOrderDelayTime represents the time in ms needed for a device to reach the commanded intensity after it receives a command when the device is operating. For example, when we change the target temperature of a cooling system from 75°F to 70°F, it takes some time for the cooler to adjust the temperature of the air blowing out of the cooling system. The locator represents the position of the device from the user's perspective, by pointing to

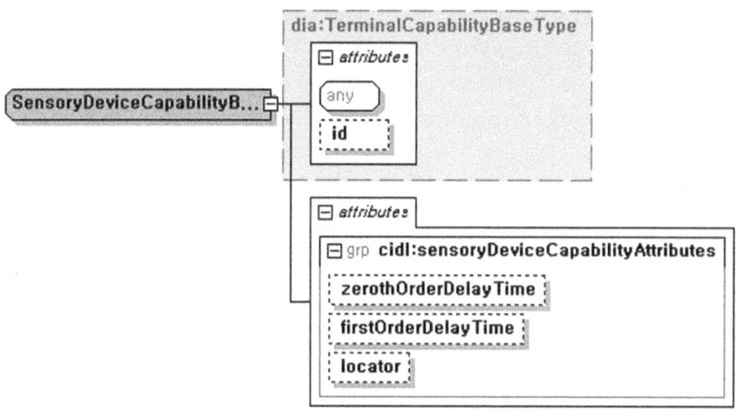

Figure 4.2 Structure of SensoryDeviceCapabilityBaseType.

Table 4.1 Schema definition of `SensoryDeviceCapabilityBaseType`

```
<!-- ################################################################-->
<!--  Sensory Device capability base type                         -->
<!-- ################################################################-->
<complexType name="SensoryDeviceCapabilityBaseType" abstract="true">
       <complexContent>
              <extension base="dia:TerminalCapabilityBaseType">
                     <attributeGroup
                       ref="cidl:sensoryDeviceCapabilityAttributes"/>
              </extension>
       </complexContent>
</complexType>
<!-- ######################################################     -->
<!--  Sensory Device Capability Attributes                      -->
<!-- ######################################################     -->
<attributeGroup name="sensoryDeviceCapabilityAttributes">
      <attribute name="zerothOrderDelayTime" type="nonNegativeInteger"
        use="optional"/>
      <attribute name="firstOrderDelayTime" type="nonNegativeInteger"
        use="optional"/>
      <attribute name="locator" type="mpeg7:termReferenceType"
        use="optional"/>
</attributeGroup>
```

one of 11 predefined positions in the *X*, *Y*, and *Z* directions. The predefined positions in `LocationCS` of Annex 2.3 of ISO/IEC 23005-6 [3] are left, center-left, center, center-right, and right in the *X* direction; bottom, middle, and top in the *Y* direction; and back, midway, and front in the *Z* direction. The `id` attribute inherited from `dia:TerminalCapabilityBaseType` specifies the sensory device (actuator) to which this capability description is bound.

The coordinate system for the sensory device is shown in Figure 4.3. The origin of the coordinate is the position of the user, and the direction of the *Z*-axis is the direction of the user when facing the screen.

4.2.3 `SensorDeviceCapability` Element

The `SensorDeviceCapability` element, whose structure is shown in Figure 4.4, is an element of an abstract `SensorCapabilityBaseType` type. This abstract-type structure provides extensibility in the standard and allows any sensory device capability description with an extended `SensorCapabilityBaseType` to be used when the `SensorDeviceCapability` element is instantiated.

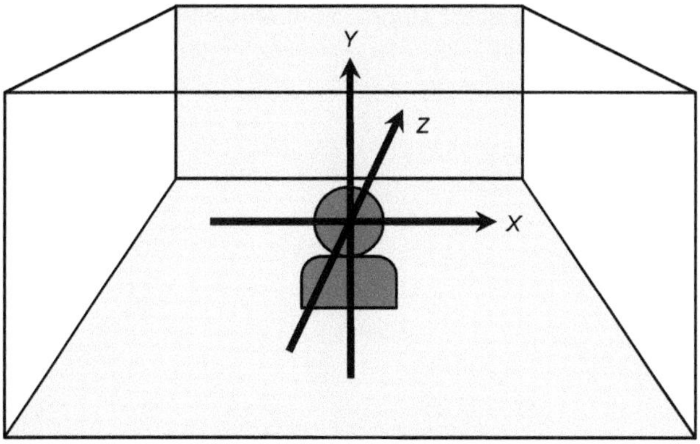

Figure 4.3 Reference coordinate system for sensory devices.

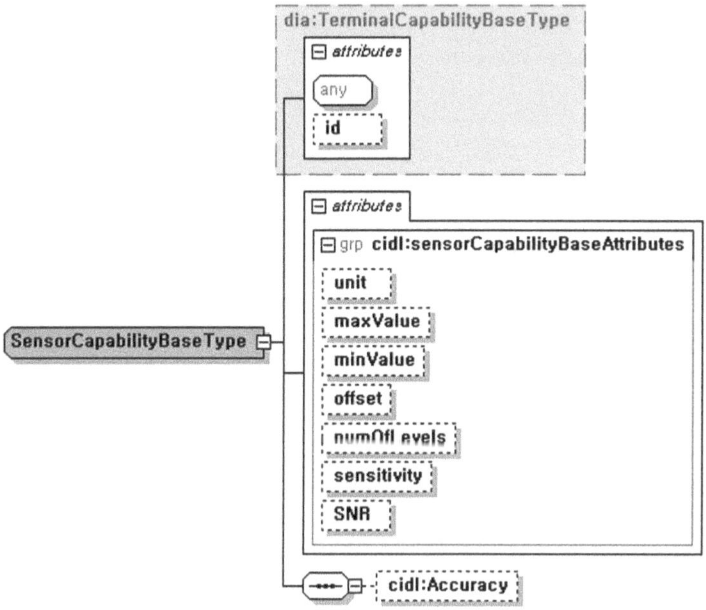

Figure 4.4 Structure of `SensorCapabilityBaseType`.

As shown in Table 4.2, it is also defined as an extension of `dia:TerminalCapabilityBaseType` by adding an `Accuracy` element and a group of attributes called the `sensorCapabilityBaseAttributes` attribute group. This group of attributes, which are `unit`, `maxValue`, `minValue`, `offset`, `numOfLevels`, `sensitivity`, and `SNR`, are designed to be included in any definition of a sensor capability description. The `Accuracy` element is

Table 4.2 Schema definition of SensorCapabilityBaseType

```
<!-- ################################################## -->
<!--  Sensor Capability base type                        -->
<!-- ################################################## -->
<complexType name="SensorCapabilityBaseType" abstract="true">
        <complexContent>
                <extension base="dia:TerminalCapabilityBaseType">
                        <sequence>
                                <element name="Accuracy"
                                  type="cidl:AccuracyType" minOccurs="0"/>
                        </sequence>
                        <attributeGroup
                            ref="cidl:sensorCapabilityBaseAttributes"/>
                </extension>
        </complexContent>
</complexType>
<complexType name="AccuracyType" abstract="true"/>
<complexType name="PercentAccuracy">
        <complexContent>
                <extension base="cidl:AccuracyType">
                        <attribute name="value" type="mpeg7:zeroToOneType"/>
                </extension>
        </complexContent>
</complexType>
<complexType name="ValueAccuracy">
        <complexContent>
                <extension base="cidl:AccuracyType">
                        <attribute name="value" type="float"/>
                </extension>
        </complexContent>
</complexType>
<!-- ################################################## -->
<!-- Sensor Capability Base Attributes                   -->
<!-- ################################################## -->
<attributeGroup name="sensorCapabilityBaseAttributes">
        <attribute name="unit" type="mpegvct:unitType" use="optional"/>
        <attribute name="maxValue" type="float" use="optional"/>
        <attribute name="minValue" type="float" use="optional"/>
        <attribute name="offset" type="float" use="optional"/>
        <attribute name="numOfLevels" type="nonNegativeInteger"
         use="optional"/>
        <attribute name="sensitivity" type="float" use="optional"/>
        <attribute name="SNR" type="float" use="optional"/>
</attributeGroup>
```

designed to provide the accuracy of the sensor either in the percentage of possible error range using a value of 0 to 1, or in the actual value with a range of error of (− Value, + Value) for the given unit. The unit attribute is defined to describe the unit of measurement for the sensor's value, and references a classification scheme term provided by UnitTypeCS defined in A.2.1 of ISO/IEC 23005-6. The maxValue and minValue attributes are introduced to describe the maximum and minimum values that a sensor can perceive, respectively. The offset attribute specifies the value added to the base value to provide an adjusted value reading appropriate for the specific sensor. The numOfLevels attribute specifies the number of levels that the sensor can perceive if the sensor describes a perceived value within a discrete number of levels instead of presenting the perceived value itself. For example, if a sensor presents the perceived value in one of five levels, e.g., XS, S, M, L, and XL, the numOfLevels attribute has a value of 5. The sensitivity attribute specifies the minimum magnitude of the sensed signal required to produce a meaningful output value by the sensor. SNR describes signal-to-noise power ratio in the received signal.

The reference coordinate system for sensors is given in Chapter 3.

4.2.4 USPreference Element

The USPreference element, whose structure is defined in Figure 4.5, is also an abstract UserSensoryPreferenceBaseType element. This abstract type structure was explained in the previous sections on the DeviceCommand element.

The abstract type UserSensoryPreferenceBaseType provides a common base for any kind of user preference regarding a sensory effect, and

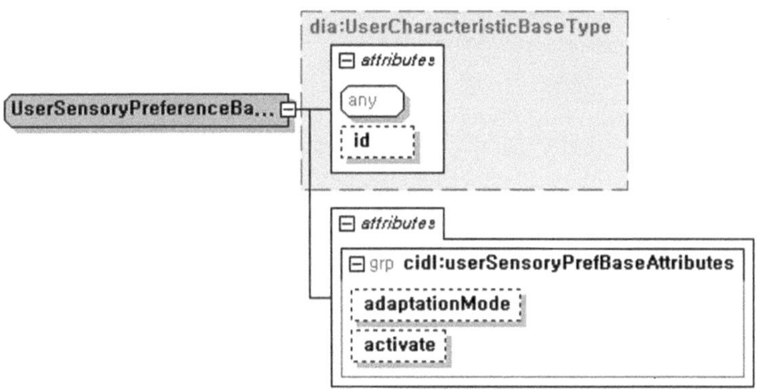

Figure 4.5 Structure of UserSensoryPreferenceBaseType.

thus any specific description of a user's preference toward a sensory effect should inherit this structure. As shown in Table 4.3, this type is defined as an extension of `UserCharacteristicBaseType` defined in MPEG-21, Part 7, by adding a group of attributes called `userSensoryPrefBaseAttributes`. This group of attributes includes the two attributes `adaptationMode` and `activate`. The `adaptationMode` attribute describes the user's choice of adaptation method for sensory effects. The `strict` mode indicates that the user wants the sensory effect to be adapted strictly, such that when the effect is given a degree of intensity higher than what the device can generate, the effect intensity should be adapted to generate the maximum intensity that the device can generate. The `scalable` mode means that the user wants the sensory effect to be linearly scaled to the operational range of intensity. The `activate` attribute determines whether a certain specific effect should be generated if possible. If the `activate` attribute

Table 4.3 Schema definition of `UserSensoryPreferenceBaseType`

```
<!-- ############################################################-->
<!--  User Sensory Preference base type                          -->
<!-- ############################################################-->
<complexType name="UserSensoryPreferenceBaseType" abstract="true">
        <complexContent>
                <extension base="dia:UserCharacteristicBaseType">
                        <attributeGroup
                          ref="cidl:userSensoryPrefBaseAttributes"/>
                </extension>
        </complexContent>
</complexType>
<!-- ############################################################-->
<!--  User Sensory Preference Base Attributes     -->
<!-- ############################################################-->
<attributeGroup name="userSensoryPrefBaseAttributes">
        <attribute name="adaptationMode" type="cidl:adaptationModeType"
use="optional"/>
        <attribute name="activate" type="boolean" use="optional"/>
</attributeGroup>
<!--  User Preference of Adaptation Mode Types      -->
<simpleType name="adaptationModeType">
        <restriction base="string">
                <enumeration value="strict"/>
                <enumeration value="scalable"/>
        </restriction>
</simpleType>
```

value is false, then the user does not want this specific effect to be generated, regardless of what the author of the effect requests.

4.2.5 SAPreference Element

The SAPreference element, the structure of which is shown in Figure 4.6, is an abstract SensorAdaptationPreferenceBaseType element (Table 4.4).

The abstract SensorAdaptationPreferenceBaseType type provides a common base for any specific description of user preferences regarding the adaptation of the sensors. As shown in Table 4.5, this type is defined by extending UserCharacteristicBaseType defined in MPEG-21, Part 7. There is a group of seven attributes called sensorAdaptationPrefBaseAttributes, i.e., sensorIdRef, sensorAdaptationMode, activate, unit, maxValue, minValue, and numOfLevels. The sensorIdRef refers to the identifier of the specific sensor for which this sensor adaptation preference is generated. sensorAdaptationMode describes the user's preference regarding the adaptation method of the sensed information by designating one of the two values, strict and scalable. The value of strict indicates that the user wants to transmit the sensed data to the virtual world exactly as described, whereas the value of scalable indicates that the user wishes to allow the virtual world to adjust the sensed data using the scaled value

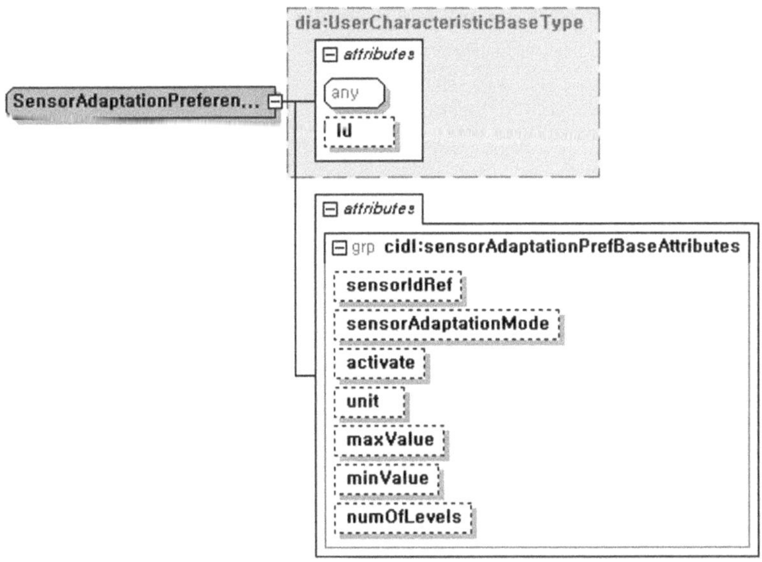

Figure 4.6 Structure of SensorAdaptationPreferenceBaseType.

Table 4.4 Schema definition of SensorAdaptationPreferenceBaseType

```
<!-- ################################################ -->
<!--  Sensor Adaptation Preference base type           -->
<!-- ################################################ -->
<complexType name="SensorAdaptationPreferenceBaseType" abstract="true">
        <complexContent>
                <extension base="dia:UserCharacteristicBaseType">
                        <attributeGroup
                        ref="cidl:sensorAdaptationPrefBaseAttributes"/>
                </extension>
        </complexContent>
</complexType>
<!-- ################################################ -->
<!--  Sensor Adaptation Preference Base Attributes     -->
<!-- ################################################ -->
<attributeGroup name="sensorAdaptationPrefBaseAttributes">
        <attribute name="sensorIdRef" type="anyURI" use="optional"/>
        <attribute name="sensorAdaptationMode"
         type="cidl:sensorAdaptationModeType" use="optional"/>
        <attribute name="activate" type="boolean" use="optional"/>
        <attribute name="unit" type="mpegvct:unitType" use="optional"/>
        <attribute name="maxValue" type="float" use="optional"/>
        <attribute name="minValue" type="float" use="optional"/>
        <attribute name="numOfLevels" type="nonNegativeInteger"
         use="optional"/>
</attributeGroup>
<!--  Adaptation Preference of Sensor Adaptation Mode Types       -->
<simpleType name="sensorAdaptationModeType">
        <restriction base="string">
                <enumeration value="strict"/>
                <enumeration value="scalable"/>
        </restriction>
</simpleType>
```

according to the user's intention. The activate attribute describes whether the user wants the specific sensed information to be used. The unit attribute describes the unit of the value that the user wants to be adapted. The maxValue and minValue attributes describe the maximum and minimum values of the sensed information to be used in units as specified in the unit attribute, respectively. For example, when sensorAdaptationMode is set to scalable, maxValue and minValue are mapped to the maximum and minimum sensed values, respectively, and the values in between are scaled accordingly. The numOfLevels attribute specifies the desired number of value levels in between the maximum and minimum values if the sensed information is mapped into discrete numbers.

4.3 DEVICE CAPABILITY DESCRIPTION VOCABULARY

SensoryDeviceCapabilityList, contained in the ControlInfo root element, can have one or more SensoryDeviceCapability elements. However, the SensoryDeviceCapability element is of an abstract SensoryDeviceCapabilityBaseType element. Therefore, when instantiating the SensoryDeviceCapability element, other nonabstract types extending SensoryDeviceCapabilityBaseType should be used. A DCDV provides these extended types for a capability description of each sensory device. The current version of MPEG-V, Part 2, includes 14 types for the DCDV, i.e., LightCapabilityType, FlashCapabilityType, HeatingCapabilityType, CoolingCapabilityType, WindCapabilityType, VibrationCapabilityType, ScentCapabilityType, FogCapabilityType, SprayerCapabilityType, ColorCorrectionCapabilityType, TactileCapabilityType, Kinesthetic CapabilityType, RigidBodyMotionCapabilityType, and 7MobileDevice PositionCapabilityType. Among these 14 DCDV types, the simplest is the ColorCorrectionCapabilityType which, in addition to those attributes inherited from SensoryDeviceCapabilityBaseType, only has a flag attribute to denote whether this device can perform a color correction or not. WindCapabilityType for wind-generating actuators, Vibration CapabilityType for devices generating vibration effects, and FogCapability Type for fog effect generators are the next simplest types, and have the same structure as shown in Figure 4.7. These types have three additional attributes, maxIntensity (or maxWindSpeed for WindCapabilityType), unit, and numOfLevels. The maxIntensity attribute specifies the maximum intensity that the device can generate. The maxIntensity attribute has a default unit for the intensity, and if it is specified using a unit other than the default, this can be specified by the unit attribute by referring to the classification scheme terms provided by UnitTypeCS defined in A.2.1 of ISO/IEC 23005-6. The numOfLevels attribute provides the number of possible intensity levels between zero and the maximum intensity.

The structure of LightCapabilityType for lighting devices is similar to that of the simplest types, except that it has an additional Color element to specify the color of light, as shown in Figure 4.8. The Color element is defined as colorType, which is specified in MPEG-V, Part 6. The colorType provides two ways of specifying the color: one is to reference

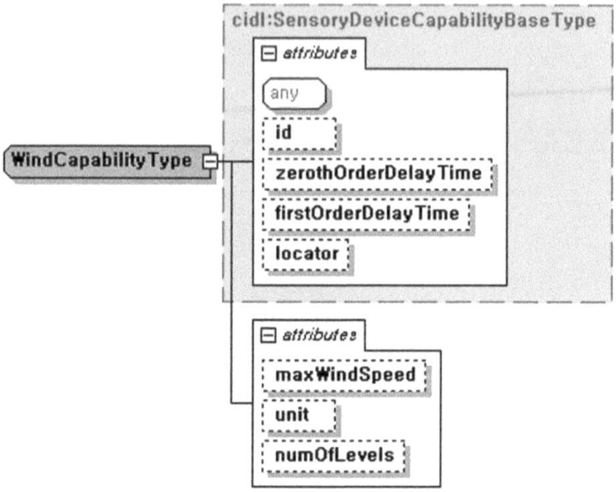

Figure 4.7 Structure of `WindCapabilityType`.

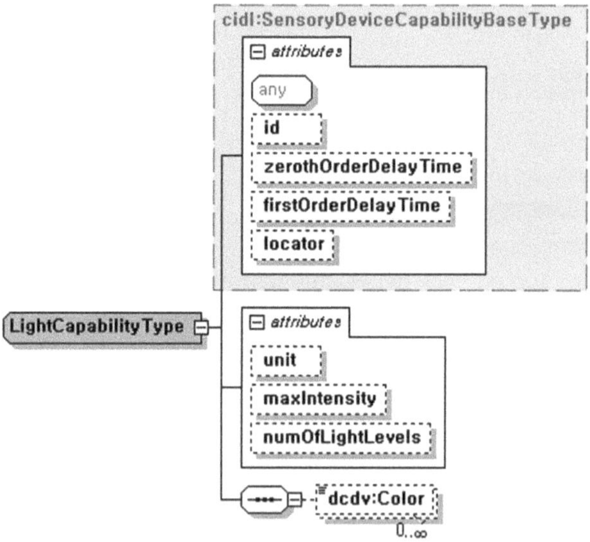

Figure 4.8 Structure of `LightCapabilityType`.

the terms defined in `ColorCS` of A.2.2 of ISO/IEC 23005-6, and the other is to directly give a hexadecimal representation of a 24-bit RGB color. A flash device is a special kind of lighting device, and generates a sequence of short impulses of light.

`FlashCapabilityType` is defined to specify the capability of the flash device and is specified as an extension of `LightCapabilityType` instead of

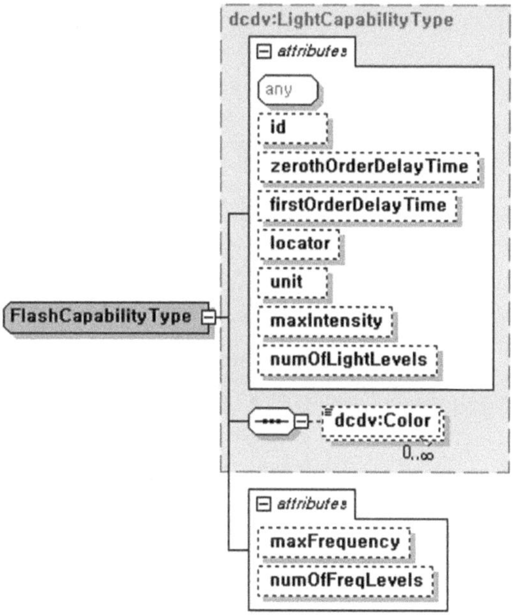

Figure 4.9 Structure of `FlashCapabilityType`.

extending `SensoryDeviceCapabilityBaseType` because it inherits all characteristics of a light device. The structure of `FlashCapabilityType` is shown in Figure 4.9. The two additional attributes of `FlashCapabilityType` are `maxFrequency` and `numOfFreqLevels`. The `maxFrequency` attribute is used to denote the maximum amount of flickering that the flash device can generate. The `numOfFreqLevels` attribute is used to denote the number of frequency levels that the flash device can provide, if it can provide multiple flickering frequency settings.

Similar to `LightCapabilityType` is `ScentCapabilityType`, which has additional occurrences of the `Scent` element of zero or more, instead of the `Color` element in `LightCapabilityType`. As shown in Figure 4.10, `ScentCapabilityType` has an identical structure as `LightCapabilityType` except for the difference in the `Color` and `Scent` elements. The `Scent` element is defined to describe a scent that the perfume device can generate by referencing the terms defined in `ScentCS` of A.2.4 of ISO/IEC 23005-6.

In addition, `SprayerCapabilityType` is very similar to `ScentCapabilityType`, but the description of the sprayed material is given as an attribute of `sprayingType`, as shown in Figure 4.11, by providing a reference to the terms defined in `SprayingTypeCS` in A.2.7 of ISO/IEC 23005-6.

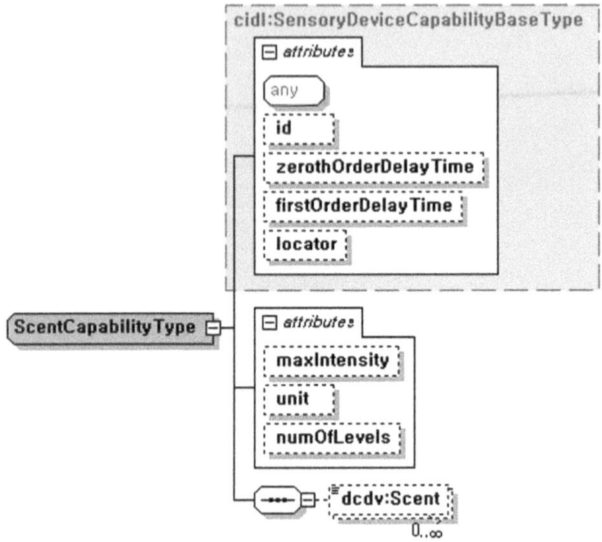

Figure 4.10 Structure of `ScentCapabilityType`.

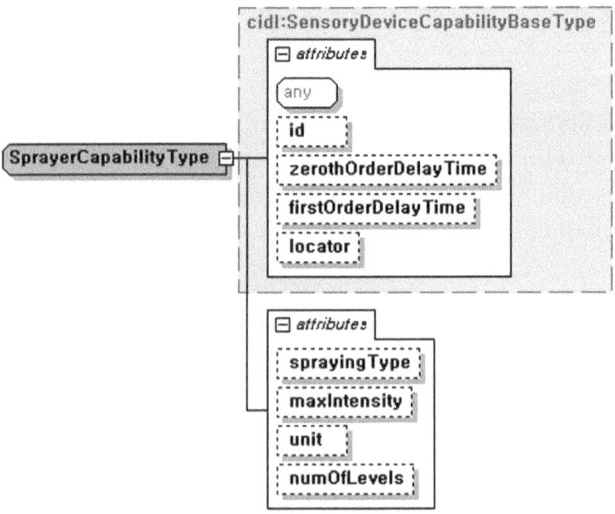

Figure 4.11 Structure of `SprayerCapabilityType`.

`HeatingCapabilityType` and `CoolingCapabilityType` are two capability descriptions that are very similar to `LightCapabilityDescription`, but with an additional description of the minimum intensity of the device, as shown in Figure 4.12.

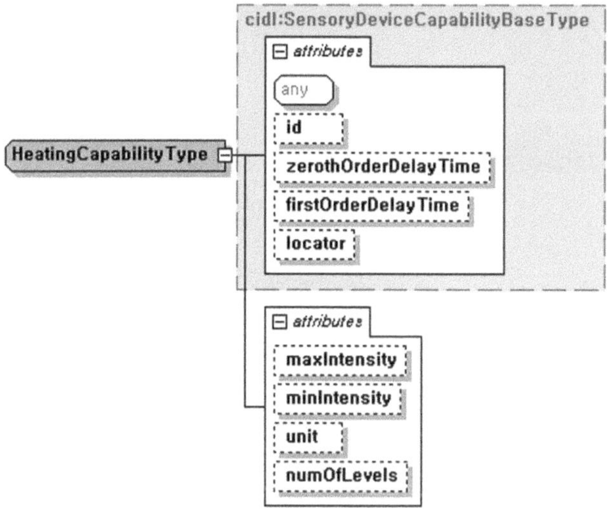

Figure 4.12 Structure of `HeatingCapabilityType`.

The types defined for the capability description of the remaining sensory devices (or actuators) are more complex than the previous described types. `TactileCapabilityType`, shown in Figure 4.13, is one of the more complex types.

There are 12 attributes added in `TactileCapabilityType`. The `intensityUnit` attribute is used to specify the unit of the `maxValue` and `minValue` attribute values by referencing the terms specified in `UnitTypeCS` in A.2.1 of ISO/IEC 23005-6. Because there are various types of tactile devices in which the intensity values are specified in different units, no default units are provided in this specification. The `maxValue` and `minValue` attributes are used to specify the maximum and minimum intensities that the specified tactile device can generate. The tactile devices are formed by positioning the actuators in *m* x *n* array types, and the `arraysizeX` and `arraysizeY` attributes specify the number of actuators in the *X* (horizontal) and *Y* (vertical) directions. The `gapX` and `gapY` attributes specify the space between actuators in the *X* and *Y* directions for a tactile device. The `gapUnit` attribute specifies the unit for the value given in the `gapX` and `gapY` attributes. The `maxUpdateRate` attribute is used to specify the maximum updated rate that the tactile device can generate for a new intensity level. The `updateRateUnit` attribute specifies the unit of `maxUpdateRate`. The `actuatorType` attribute specifies the type of actuator embedded in the tactile device by referencing the terms (or actuator types) defined in `TactileDisplayCS` of

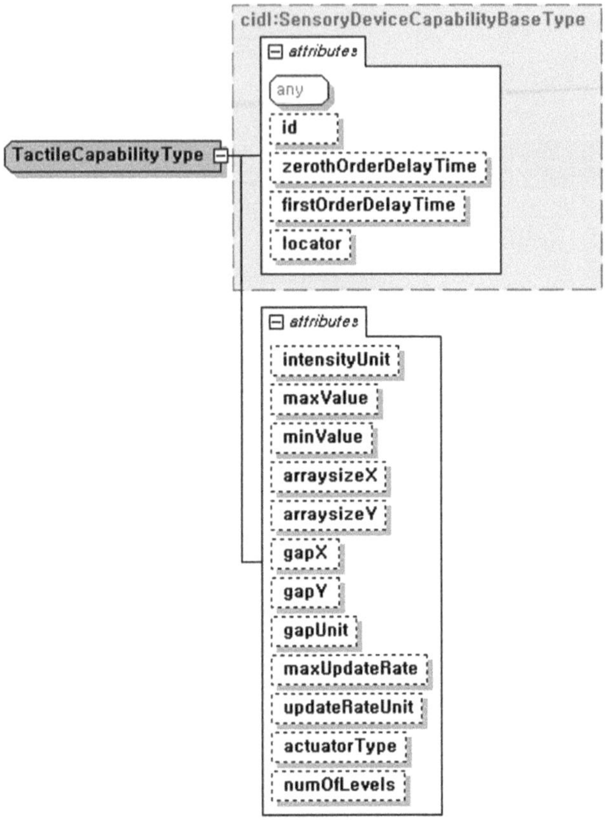

Figure 4.13 Structure of `TactileCapabilityType`.

A.2.11 of ISO/IEC 23005-6. Currently, there are five different types of actuators, i.e., vibrotactile, electrotactile, pneumatictactile, piezoelectrictactile, and thermal actuators, defined in the specifications. Finally, the `numOfLevels` attribute is defined to specify the number of intensity levels that the tactile device can generate.

Figure 4.14 specifies the structure of `KinestheticCapabilityType`, which is used to describe the kinesthetic capability of a haptic device.

The `KinestheticCapabilityType` type has six new attributes and five new elements added. The `MaximumForce`, `MaximumTorque`, and `MaximumStiffness` elements share the same structure with 3D-vector type float numbers. Each number of the three dimensions represents the maximum force, torque, and stiffness in the *X*, *Y*, and *Z* directions, respectively, that the device can generate. The units for these numbers are given in the

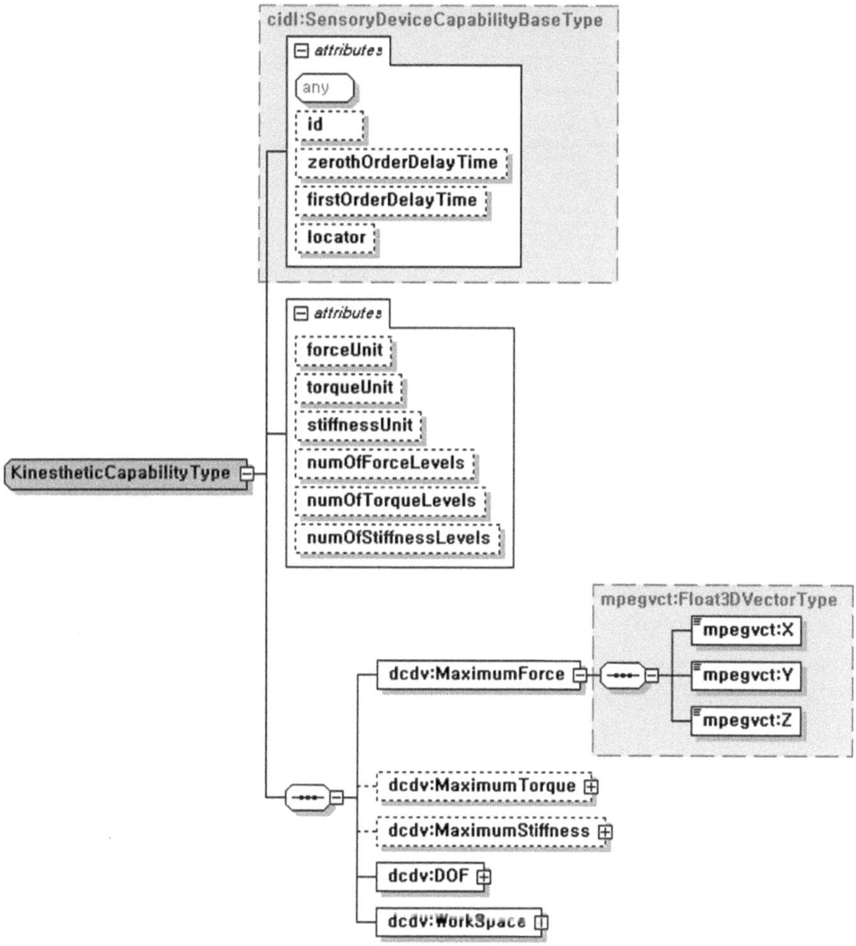

Figure 4.14 Structure of `KinestheticCapabilityType`.

`forceUnit`, `torqueUnit`, and `stiffnessUnit` attributes. `numOfForceLevels`, `numOfTorqueLevels`, and `numOfStiffnessLevels` describe the number of intensity levels of the force, torque, and stiffness, respectively, that the device can generate. The `DOF` element has six elements of a Boolean value used to specify whether the device has 6 DoF capability. To be specific, the `Tx`, `Ty`, and `Tz` elements are used to represent with a Boolean value whether the given device has the freedom of movement or translation in the *X*, *Y*, and *Z* directions, respectively. The `Rx`, `Ry`, and `Rz` elements are used to represent when the given device is allowed to rotate along the *X*, *Y*, and *Z* axes, respectively. The `WorkSpace` element is of `WorkSpaceType` and has six

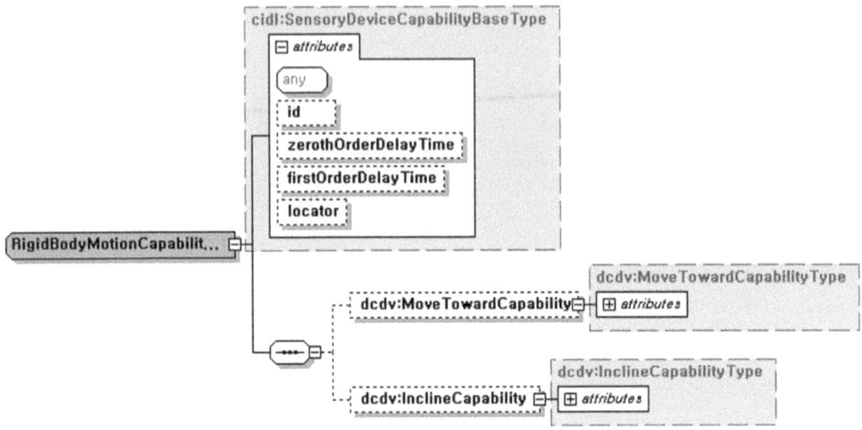

Figure 4.15 Structure of `RigidBodyMotionCapabilityType`.

elements, i.e., `Width`, `Height`, `Depth`, `RotationX`, `RotationY`, and `RotationZ`, representing the space within which the kinesthetic device can move by specifying the maximum range of movement in the *X*, *Y*, and *Z* directions in mm, and can rotate by specifying the maximum range of rotation in the *X* (pitch), *Y* (yaw), and *Z* (roll) axes, respectively (Figure 4.15).

Another complex capability description is `RigidBodyMotionCapabilityType`, which is designed to describe the movement capability of a rigid object. In addition to the `SensoryDeviceCapabilityBaseType` extension, `RigidBodyMotionCapabilityType` has two additional elements, `MoveTowardCapability` and `InclineCapability`. `MoveTowardCapability` of `MoveTowardCapabilityType`, and `InclineCapability` of `InclineCapabilityType`, each describe the capability of motion in terms of translation and rotation for three perpendicular axes, respectively. The schema definition of `MoveTowardCapabilityType` is given in Table 4.5, and that of `InclineCapabilityType` is given in Table 4.6.

The three attributes `maxXDistance`, `maxYDistance`, and `maxZDistance` provide the maximum distance of movement in the *X* (`maxXDistance`), *Y* (`maxYDistance`), and *Z* (`maxZDistance`) directions that the device can provide, respectively, with the unit provided by the `distanceUnit` attribute of the `MoveTowardCapability` element. The speed of movement is described by `maxXSpeed`, `maxYSpeed`, and `maxZSpeed` in the three perpendicular axes, *X*, *Y*, and *Z*, with the unit described in the `speedUnit` attribute. The acceleration of the movement is also described by `maxXAccel`, `maxYAccel`, and `maxZAccel` in the three perpendicular axes, *X*, *Y*, and *Z*, with the unit described in the `accelUnit` attribute. The `xDistanceLevels`,

Table 4.5 Schema definition of `MoveTowardCapabilityType`

```
<!-- ################################################ -->
<!--  MoveToward Capability type                      -->
<!-- ################################################ -->
<complexType name="MoveTowardCapabilityType">
        <attribute name="maxXDistance" type="float" use="optional"/>
        <attribute name="maxYDistance" type="float" use="optional"/>
        <attribute name="maxZDistance" type="float" use="optional"/>
        <attribute name="distanceUnit" type="mpegvct:unitType"
                    use="optional"/>
        <attribute name="maxXSpeed" type="float" use="optional"/>
        <attribute name="maxYSpeed" type="float" use="optional"/>
        <attribute name="maxZSpeed" type="float" use="optional"/>
        <attribute name="speedUnit" type="mpegvct:unitType" use="optional"/>
        <attribute name="maxXAccel" type="float" use="optional"/>
        <attribute name="maxYAccel" type="float" use="optional"/>
        <attribute name="maxZAccel" type="float" use="optional"/>
        <attribute name="accelUnit" type="mpegvct:unitType" use="optional"/>
        <attribute name="xDistanceLevels" type="nonNegativeInteger"
                    use="optional"/>
        <attribute name="yDistanceLevels" type="nonNegativeInteger"
                    use="optional"/>
        <attribute name="zDistanceLevels" type="nonNegativeInteger"
                    use="optional"/>
        <attribute name="xSpeedLevels" type="nonNegativeInteger"
                    use="optional"/>
        <attribute name="ySpeedLevels" type="nonNegativeInteger"
                    use="optional"/>
        <attribute name="zSpeedLevels" type="nonNegativeInteger"
                    use="optional"/>
        <attribute name="xAccelLevels" type="nonNegativeInteger"
                    use="optional"/>
        <attribute name="yAccelLevels" type="nonNegativeInteger"
                    use="optional"/>
        <attribute name="zAccelLevels" type="nonNegativeInteger"
                    use="optional"/>
</complexType>
```

`yDistanceLevels`, `zDistanceLevels`, `xSpeedLevels`, `ySpeedLevels`, `zSpeedLevels`, `xAccelLevels`, `yAccelLevels`, and `zAccelLevels` attributes are defined to provide the discrete levels for the *X*, *Y*, and *Z* directional distance, speed, and acceleration that the device can provide.

`InclineCapabilityType` provides rotational capability of a rigid device for the three perpendicular axes. The `maxPitchAngle`, `maxYawAngle`, and `maxRollAngle` attributes describe the maximum rotational angle of the device along the *X*, *Y*, and *Z* axes in degrees, respectively. `maxPitchSpeed`, `maxYawSpeed`, and `maxRollSpeed` specify the maximum rotational speed of a device along the *X*, *Y*, and *Z* axes in degrees/s if the unit is not specified by the `speedUnit` attribute. `maxPitchAccel`, `maxYawAccel`, and `maxRollAccel` specify the maximum rotational acceleration of a device along the *X*, *Y*, and *Z* axes in degrees/s^2 if

Table 4.6 Schema definition of `InclineCapabilityType`

```
<!-- ################################################ -->
<!--  Incline Capability type                          -->
<!-- ################################################ -->
<complexType name="InclineCapabilityType">
        <attribute name="maxPitchAngle" type="mpegvct:InclineAngleType"
                   use="optional"/>
        <attribute name="maxYawAngle" type="mpegvct:InclineAngleType"
                   use="optional"/>
        <attribute name="maxRollAngle" type="mpegvct:InclineAngleType"
                   use="optional"/>
        <attribute name="maxPitchSpeed" type="float" use="optional"/>
        <attribute name="maxYawSpeed" type="float" use="optional"/>
        <attribute name="maxRollSpeed" type="float" use="optional"/>
        <attribute name="speedUnit" type="mpegvct:unitType" use="optional"/>
        <attribute name="maxPitchAccel" type="float" use="optional"/>
        <attribute name="maxYawAccel" type="float" use="optional"/>
        <attribute name="maxRollAccel" type="float" use="optional"/>
        <attribute name="accelUnit" type="mpegvct:unitType" use="optional"/>
        <attribute name="pitchAngleLevels" type="nonNegativeInteger"
                   use="optional"/>
        <attribute name="yawAngleLevels" type="nonNegativeInteger"
                   use="optional"/>
        <attribute name="rollAngleLevels" type="nonNegativeInteger"
                   use="optional"/>
        <attribute name="pitchSpeedLevels" type="nonNegativeInteger"
                   use="optional"/>
        <attribute name="yawSpeedLevels" type="nonNegativeInteger"
                   use="optional"/>
        <attribute name="rollSpeedLevels" type="nonNegativeInteger"
                   use="optional"/>
        <attribute name="pitchAccelLevels" type="nonNegativeInteger"
                   use="optional"/>
        <attribute name="yawAccelLevels" type="nonNegativeInteger"
                   use="optional"/>
        <attribute name="rollAccelLevels" type="nonNegativeInteger"
                   use="optional"/>
</complexType>
```

the unit is not specified by the `accelUnit` attribute. The attributes specifying the level of degree or intensity are defined in `pitchAngleLevels`, `yawAngleLevels`, `rollAngleLevels`, `pitchSpeedLevels`, `yawSpeedLevels`, `rollSpeedLevels`, `pitchAccelLevels`, `yawAccelLevels`, and `rollAccelLevels` for the angle, speed, and acceleration of a device along the *X*, *Y*, and *Z* axes, respectively.

The final device-capability description provided by the second edition of ISO/IEC 23005-2 is `MobileDevicePositionCapabilityType`, which does not describe the capability of a mobile phone but rather the capability of a mobile device such as an unmanned aerial vehicle. The structure of `MobileDevicePositionCapabilityType` is shown in Figure 4.16. `MobileDevicePositionCapabilityType` provides device capability by defining the area that a device can reach through the specifications of the lower and upper bounds of the longitude, latitude, and altitude in the `Boundary` element of `PhysicalSpaceBoundingBoxType`. The longitude is given between −180°

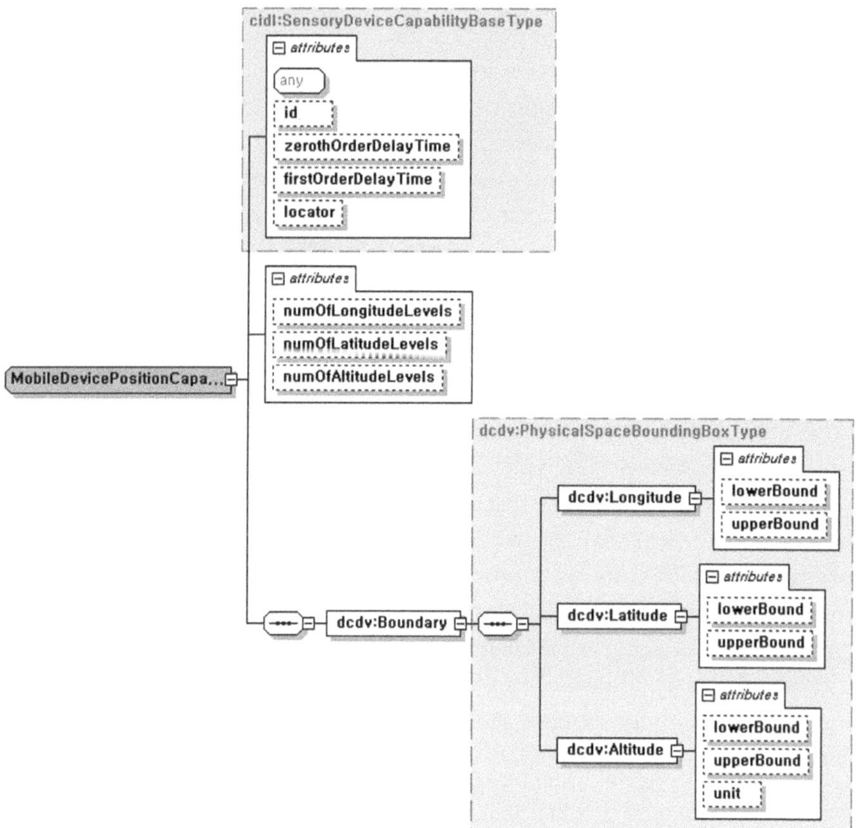

Figure 4.16 Structure of `MobileDevicePositionCapabilityType`.

and 180°, where a negative value indicates a western longitude and a positive value indicates an eastern longitude. The latitude is given between − 90° and 90°, where a negative value indicates a southern latitude and a positive value indicates a northern latitude. The altitude is given in m above sea level by default; otherwise, the unit should be specified in the `unit` attribute of the `Boundary` element. The `numOfLongitudeLevels`, `numOfLatitudeLevels`, and `numOfAltitudeLevels` attributes of `MobileDevicePositionCapabilityType` describe the possible number of levels provided by the device for controlling the longitude, latitude, and altitude, respectively.

4.4 SENSOR CAPABILITY DESCRIPTION VOCABULARY

`SensorDeviceCapabilityList`, contained in the `ControlInfo` root element, can have one or more `SensorDeviceCapability` elements. However, the `SensorDeviceCapability` element is of an abstract `SensorCapabilityBaseType`, which has a similar structure. Therefore, when instantiating the `SensorDeviceCapability` element, other nonabstract types extending `SensorCapabilityBaseType` should be used. The SCDV provides these extended types for a capability description of each sensor device. The current version of MPEG-V, Part 2, includes 25 extended types for the SCDV. Among these 25 SCDVs, eight sensor capability descriptions, i.e., `VelocitySensorCapabilityType` for a 3D velocity sensor, `AccelerationSensorCapabilityType` for a 3D acceleration sensor, `AngularVelocitySensorCapabilityType` for an angular velocity sensor, `AngularAccelerationSensorCapabilityType` for an angular acceleration sensor, `ForceSensorCapabilityType` for a force sensor, `TorqueSensorCapabilityType` for a torque sensor, `PressureSensorCapabilityType` for a pressure sensor, and `DustSensorCapabilityType` for a dust sensor, are the simplest and have exactly the same structure as `SensorCapabilityBaseType` without an extension, as shown in Figure 4.17.

There are several SCDVs that extend the base type through the addition of a single element, five of which are `AmbientNoiseSensorCapabilityType` for an ambient noise sensor, `TemperatureSensorCapabilityType` for a temperature sensor, `HumiditySensorCapabilityType` for a humidity sensor, `DistanceSensorCapabilityType` for a distance sensor, and `AtmosphericPressureSensorCapabilityType` for an atmospheric pressure sensor, which simply extends the base type by adding only the `Location` element, as shown in Figure 4.18.

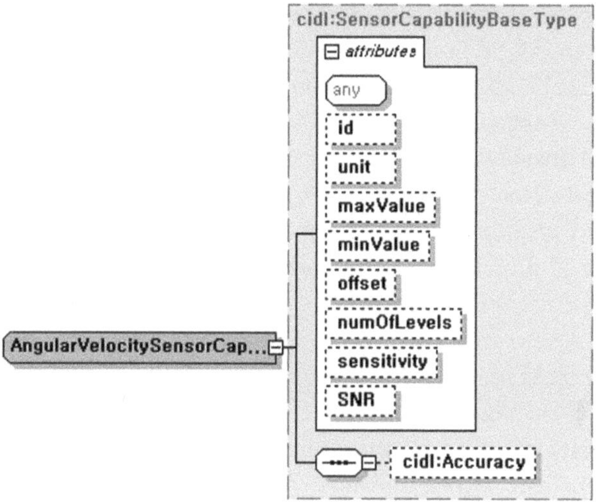

Figure 4.17 Structure of `AngularVelocitySensorCapabilityType`.

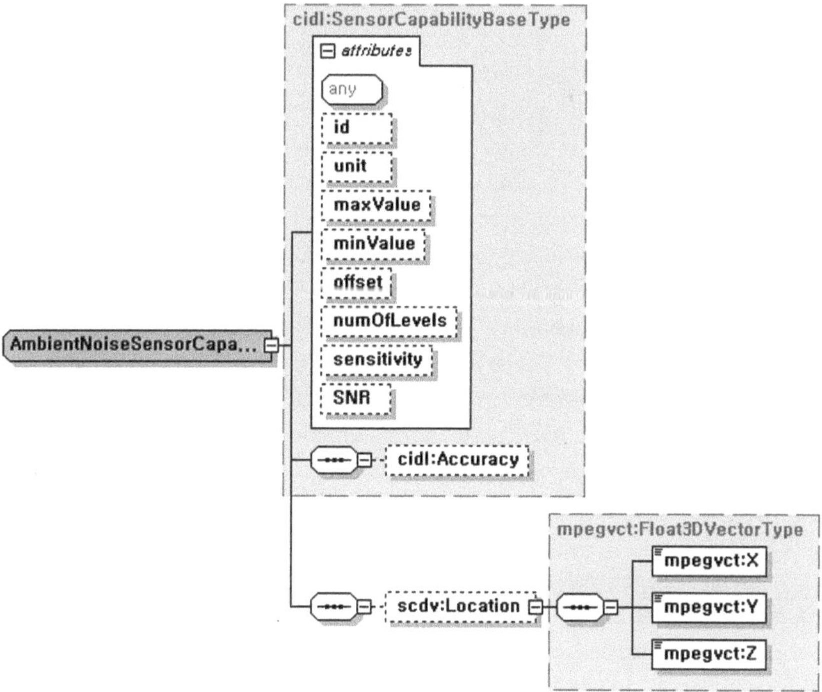

Figure 4.18 Structure of `AmbientNoiseSensorCapabilityType`.

The Location element provides the location information of the sensor by providing the *X*, *Y*, and *Z* coordinates using the global coordinate system of the sensors described in Chapter 3.

PositionSensorCapabilityType is similar to these types of sensors with the exception that PositionSensorCapabilityType has a Range element of RangeType instead of a Location element. The Range element provides the minimum and maximum displacement that the sensor can recognize in the *X*, *Y*, and *Z* directions of the global coordinate system relative to the idle position of the sensor.

OrientationSensorCapabilityType has the OrientationRange element of OrientationRangeType instead of the Location element. The OrientationRange element provides the minimum and maximum sensible degrees of rotation in terms of the pitch, yaw, and roll.

GasSensorCapabilityType provides a description of a gas sensor and has an additional GasType element for the extension of the base type. GasType can specify the type of gas that the gas sensor can detect by referencing a term in GasTypeCS defined in ISO/IEC 23005-6.

AltitudeSensorCapabilityType is used to describe the capability of an altitude sensor and has the crs attribute, which is the only extension to SensoryCapabilityBaseType, for specifying the URI of the reference coordinate system based upon which the altitude is given.

MultiInteractionPointSensorCapabilityType describes the capability of multi-interaction point sensing devices such as a touch pad and has the numOfInteractionPoints attribute as an extension of SensoryCapabilityBaseType to specify the maximum acceptable number of interaction points of a multi-interaction point sensor.

The LightSensorCapabilityType type is also relatively simple because it is an extension of SensorCapabilityBaseType through the addition of the Location and Color elements, as shown in Figure 4.19. The Color element of colorType defined in MPEG-V, Part 6, enables a description of the color of the sensed light either by a hexadecimal representation of a 24-bit RGB color or by referencing a color name defined in ColorCS of A.2.2 of ISO/IEC 23005-6.

BendSensorCapabilityType, the structure of which is given in Figure 4.20, describes the capability of a bend sensor. As described in Chapter 3, a bend sensor assumes the existence of multiple channels with multiple bending points, and a capability description is given for each channel. BendSensorCapabilityType has the numOfChannels attribute describing the number of channels that the given bend sensor provides, and zero or

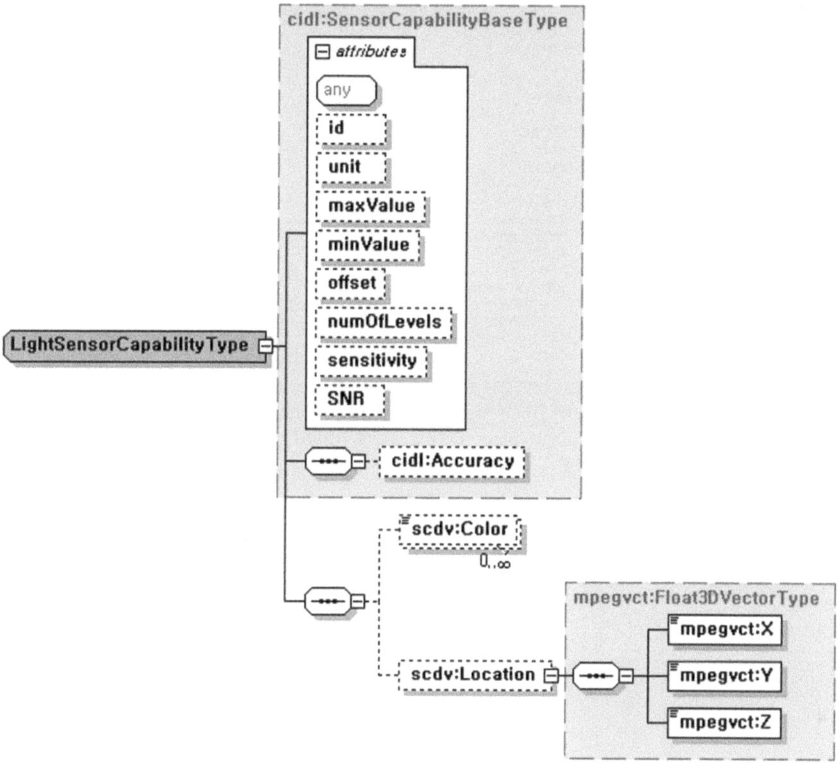

Figure 4.19 Structure of `LightSensorCapabilityType`.

more occurrences of the `Channels` element are assigned for the description of each channel. Each `Channels` element is defined as an extension of `SensorCapabilityBaseType` and has the optional elements of `NumOfLocations`, `DistanceBtwnLocations`, and `NumOfAxes`. The `NumOfLocations` element can have a non-negative integer number for describing a possible number of sensing points at which the sensor can measure the bend angles. The `DistanceBtwnLocations` element using a float number describes the distance between the adjacent sensing locations in m. The `NumOfAxes` element in a non-negative integer can describe the number of axes for which the sensor can measure the bend angles.

`GazeTrackingSensorCapabilityType` is complex in the sense that it has the `PositionCapability` element of `PositionSensorCapabilityType` and the `OrientationCapability` element of `OrientationSensorCapabilityType` embedded in it with two additional attributes added to `SensorCapabilityBaseType`. These two additional attributes are `gazeTrackingOn` and `blink`

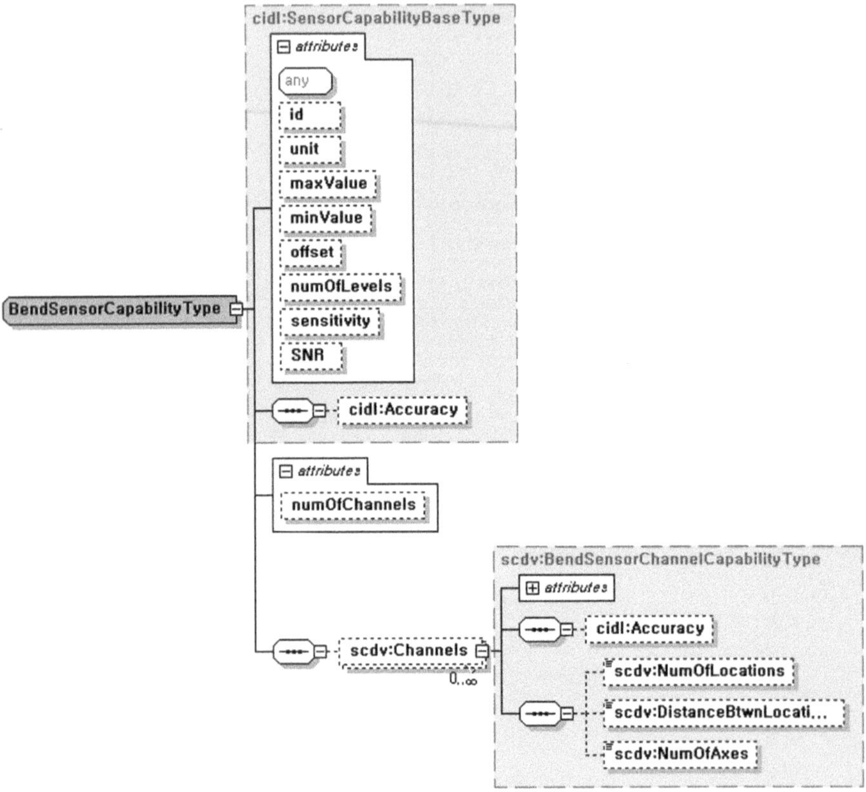

Figure 4.20 Structure of `BendSensorCapabilityType`.

`TrackingOn`, which specify whether this sensor is activated for gaze tracking or blinking detection.

`MotionSensorCapabilityType` is defined for the description of a motion sensor designed for the detection of various movements of an object, including translational and rotational movements. For this purpose, it is defined as a composition of the SCDV and includes the `PositionCapability` element of `PositionSensorCapabilityType`, the `OrientationCapability` element of `OrientationSensorCapabilityType`, the `VelocityCapability` element of `VelocitySensorCapabilityType`, the `AngularVelocityCapability` element of `AngularVelocitySensorCapabilityType`, the `AccelerationCapability` element of `AccelerationSensorCapabilityType`, and the `AngularAcceleration Capability` element of `AngularAccelerationSensorCapabilityType`.

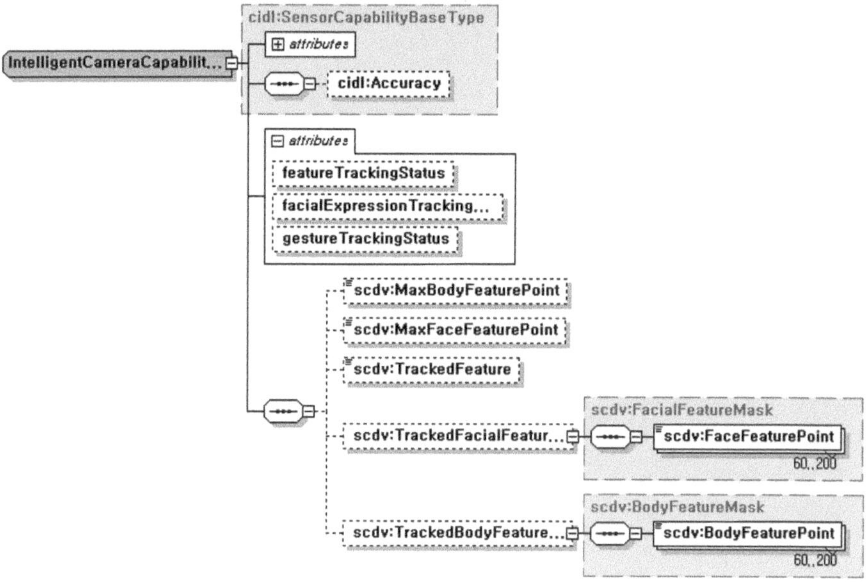

Figure 4.21 Structure of `IntelligentCameraCapabilityType`.

`IntelligentCameraCapabilityType` is defined for the description of an intelligent camera sensor, which is designed for the detection of feature points on the human face or body. As shown in Figure 4.21, it has three Boolean-type attributes, `featureTrackingStatus`, `facialExpressionTrackingStatus`, and `gestureTrackingStatus`, to describe whether the sensor can track the features, extract a facial animation, and extract a body animation, respectively. The `MaxBodyFeaturePoint` and `MaxFaceFeaturePoint` elements describe the number of body and facial feature points that the camera sensor can track, respectively. `TrackedFeature` describes the type of feature points that can be tracked, i.e., it describes whether the feature points that can be tracked are facial feature points, body feature points, or both.

`GlobalPositionSensorCapabilityType` has five additional attributes, i.e., `crs`, `latitudeOffset`, `longitudeOffset`, `maxOperatingTemp`, and `minOperationTemp` and one more additional element, `VariousAccuracy`, with three attributes, `accuracyType`, `value`, and `accuracyUnit`, as shown in Figure 4.22.

The `crs` attribute specifies the URI for the reference coordinate system based on which global position (longitude, latitude, or altitude) is calculated. The `latitudeOffset` and `longitudeOffset` attributes provide the values added to the base value to obtain the specified absolute value based

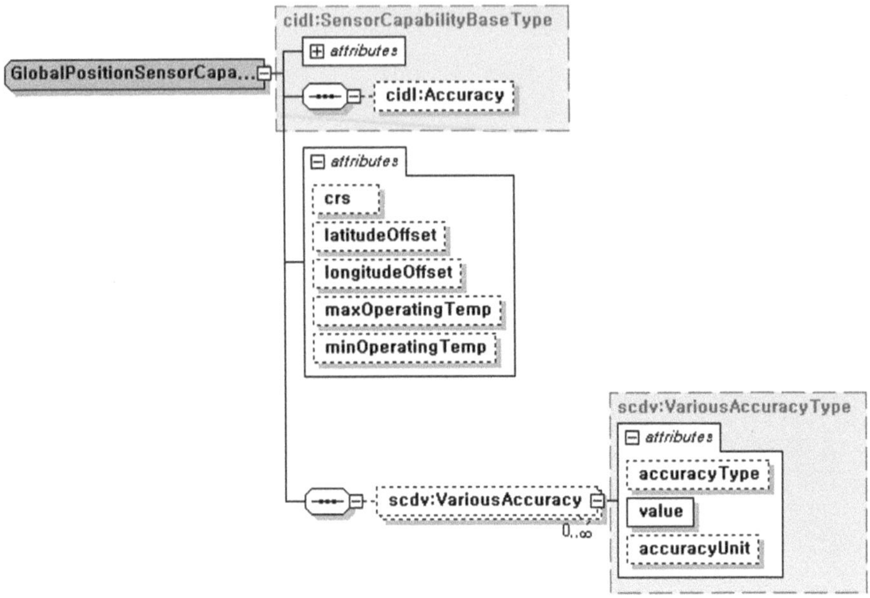

Figure 4.22 Structure of `GlobalPositionSensorCapabilityType`.

on the given reference coordinate system. The `maxOperatingTemp` and `minOperatingTemp` attributes give the range of temperature within which the normal operation of the sensor is intended by providing the maximum and minimum temperatures. The `VariousAccuracy` element provides a way to specify various types of accuracy by specifying the `variousType` attribute with a term defined in `AccuracyTypeCS`. Currently, there are seven types defined in the classification scheme, i.e., the reacquisition time, cold acquisition time, warm acquisition time, hot acquisition time, update rate, position accuracy, and velocity accuracy. The value and unit of the value are given by the `value` and `accuracyUnit` attributes.

`WeatherSensorCapabilityType` is defined as shown in Table 4.7, and contains multiple SCDVs. It has the `TemperatureCapability` element of `TemperatureSensorCapabilityType` and the `HumidityCapability` element of `HumiditySensorCapabilityType`. In addition, it has the `PrecipitationCapability` element based on `SensorCapabilityBaseType` to describe the sensor's capability of measuring the amount of raindrops, and the `SnowCapability` element based on `SensorCapabilityBaseType` to describe the sensor capability measuring the amount of snowfall. The `WindCapability` element is also based on `SensorCapabilityBaseType` for describing the sensor's wind-measuring capability.

Table 4.7 **Schema definition of** `WeatherSensorCapabilityType`

```
<!-- ################################################ -->
<!-- Weather Sensor capability type                   -->
<!-- ################################################ -->
<complexType name="WeatherSensorCapabilityType">
        <complexContent>
                <extension base="cidl:SensorCapabilityBaseType">
                        <sequence>
                                <element name="TemperatureCapability"
                                 type="scdv:TemperatureSensorCapabilityType"
                                 minOccurs="0"/>
                                <element name="PrecipitationCapability"
                                 minOccurs="0">
                                        <complexType>
                                                <complexContent>
                                                        <extension
                                   base="cidl:SensorCapabilityBaseType"/>
                                                </complexContent>
                                        </complexType>
                                </element>
                                <element name="SnowCapability" minOccurs="0">
                                        <complexType>
                                                <complexContent>
                                                        <extension
                                   base="cidl:SensorCapabilityBaseType"/>
                                                </complexContent>
                                        </complexType>
                                </element>
                                <element name="WindCapability" minOccurs="0">
                                        <complexType>
                                                <complexContent>
                                                        <extension
                                   base="cidl:SensorCapabilityBaseType"/>
                                                </complexContent>
                                        </complexType>
                                </element>
                                <element name="HumidityCapability"
                                 type="scdv:HumiditySensorCapabilityType"
                                 minOccurs="0"/>
                        </sequence>
                </extension>
        </complexContent>
</complexType>
```

4.5 USER'S SENSORY EFFECT PREFERENCE VOCABULARY

Another important part of the control information is the description of the user's preference regarding the sensory effects. The UserSensoryPreferenceList element contained in the ControlInfo root element can have one or more USPreference elements. However, the USPreference element is of abstract UserSensoryPreferenceBaseType. Therefore, when instantiating the USPreference element, other nonabstract types extending UserSensoryPreferenceBaseType should be used. The Sensory Effect Preference Vocabulary (SEPV) provides these extended types for describing the user's preference for each sensory effect. The current version of MPEG-V, Part 2, includes 13 preference types.

Among them, the simplest type is ColorCorrectionPrefType, which only has those attributes provided by UserSensoryPreferenceBaseType, and specifies whether the color correction is preferred. The next simplest types having a structure similar to WindPrefType, as shown in Figure 4.23, specify the user's preference regarding the intensity of the wind effect.

WindPrefType extends UserSensoryPreferenceBaseType by adding only two attributes, maxIntensity and unit. maxIntensity provides information on the maximum intensity of the effect that the user can tolerate or allow to be given, in either the default unit or that specified in the unit attribute. VibrationPrefType, specifying the user's preference regarding the vibration effect, and FogPrefType, specifying the user's preference for a fog effect, both have the same structure and specify the maximum desirable intensity by providing the maxIntensity attribute. The default unit for WindPrefType

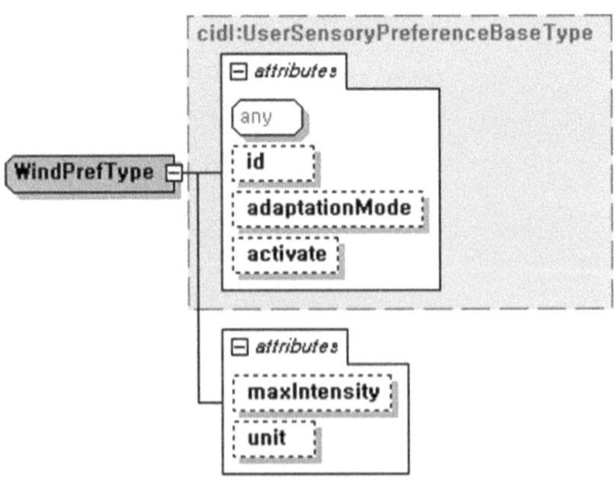

Figure 4.23 Structure of WindPrefType.

is the Beaufort scale, the default unit for `VibrationPrefType` is Hz, and the default unit for `FogPrefType` is ml/h.

By adding one more attribute, `minIntensity`, specifying the minimum intensity that the user can recognize, to the `WindPrefType` structure, we can create the structure of the `HeatingPrefType` type as shown in Figure 4.24, specifying the user's preference regarding the heating effect. `CoolingPrefType`, specifying the user's preference regarding the cooling effect, also has the same structure.

Other simple-structured SEPVs similar to these include `LightPrefType`, `FlashPrefType`, `ScentPrefType`, and `SprayingPrefType`. `LightPrefType` has an `UnfavorableColor` element of `colorType` in addition to the `maxIntensity` and `unit` attributes extending `UserSensoryPreferenceBaseType`. `UnfavorableColor` of `colorType` is used to point out the user's disliked colors for the light effect using `colorType`, which allows the specification of a color by either referencing the `ColorCS` or the hexadecimal representation of a 24-bit RGB color. `FlashPrefType` extends `LightPrefType` instead of `UserSensoryPreferenceBaseType` because a flash effect device is a kind of light effect device. In addition to the attributes and elements of `LightPrefType`, `FlashPrefType` has the `maxFrequency` and `freqUnit` attributes to specify the preferred maximum flashing frequency. `ScentPrefType` describes the user's preference toward particular scent effects, and has the `HedonicScent` element to reference undesirable scents from the list of `ScentCS` specified in A.2.4 of ISO/IEC 23005-6. `SprayingPrefType` describes the user's preference toward a particular spraying effect and has the

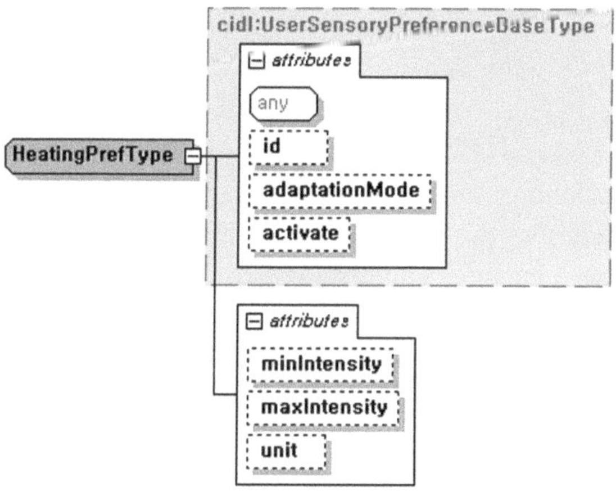

Figure 4.24 Structure of `HeatingPrefType`.

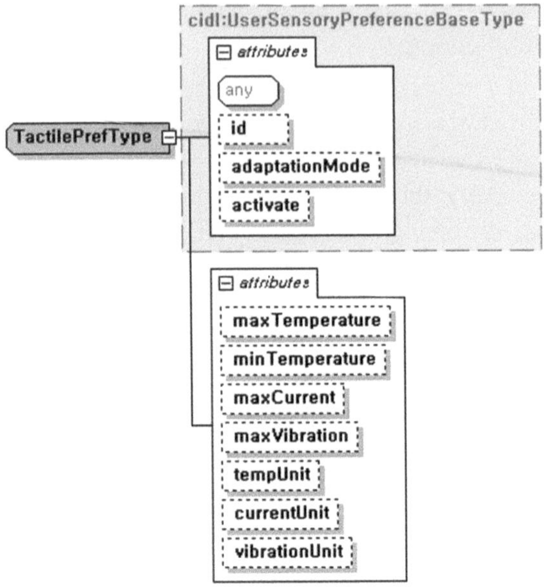

Figure 4.25 Structure of `TactilePrefType`.

additional `sprayingType` attribute to specify a single spray material that this preference is referring to, which is described as a reference to a term defined in the `SprayingTypeCS` of A.2.7 of ISO/IEC 23005-6.

More complex-structured preference types are `TactilePrefType`, `KinestheticPrefType`, and `RigidBodyMotionPrefType`. The structure of `TactilePrefType` is given in Figure 4.25.

`TactilePrefType`, which describes the user's preferences regarding tactile effects, has the additional attributes, `maxTemperature`, `minTemperature`, `maxCurrent`, `maxVibration`, `tempUnit`, `currentUnit`, and `vibrationUnit`. `maxTemperature` and `minTemperature` describe the maximum (hot) and minimum (cold) temperatures in Celsius that the tactile device can generate. `maxCurrent` describes the maximum current in mA that the tactile device can generate. `maxVibration` describes the maximum amplitude of vibration in mm that the tactile device can generate. The `tempUnit`, `currentUnit`, and `vibrationUnit` attributes provide information on the unit of temperature, current, and vibration amplitude if the default units are not used in the description.

Figure 4.26 shows the structure of `KinestheticPrefType`. `KinestheticPrefType` uses two additional attributes and elements to extend `UserSensoryPreferenceBaseType`. The `MaxForce` element provides the desirable maximum force in the *X*, *Y*, and *Z* directions in N. If any unit other

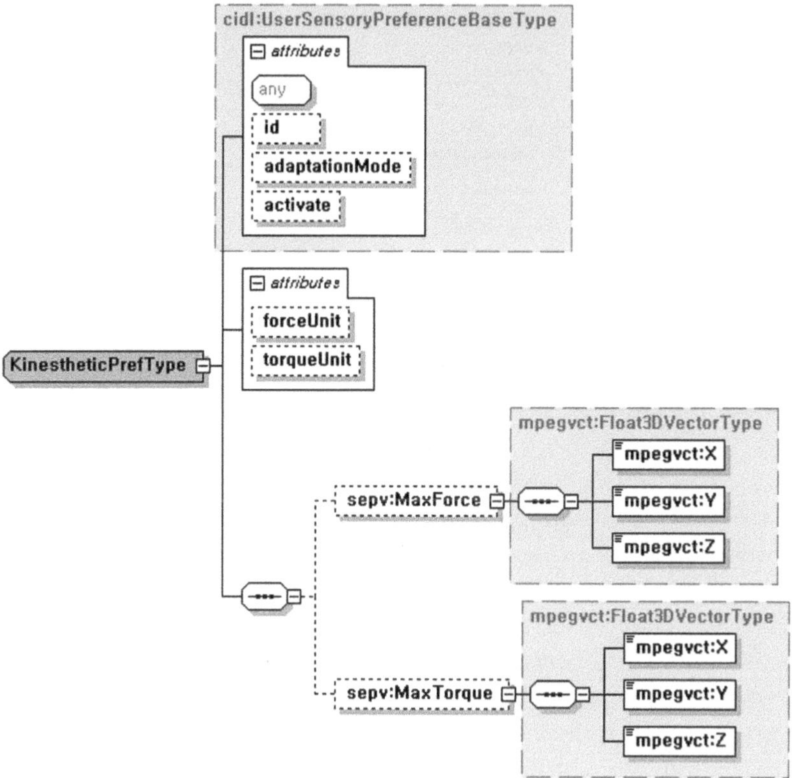

Figure 4.26 Structure of `KinestheticPrefType`.

than N is used, the `forceUnit` attribute should be used to specify this unit by referencing one of the terms specified in `UnitTypeCS` in A.2.1 of ISO/IEC 23005-6. The `MaxTorque` element provides the desirable maximum torque in the *X*, *Y*, and *Z* directions in N-mm. If any unit other than N-mm is used, the `torqueUnit` attribute should be used to specify the unit by referencing one of the terms specified in `UnitTypeCS` in A.2.1 of ISO/IEC 23005-6.

As shown in Figure 4.27, the structure of `RigidBodyMotionPrefType` itself is relatively simple, but `MotionPreferenceBaseType` is of an abstract type, and concrete types extending `MotionPreferenceBaseType` should replace the `MotionPreference` elements in the actual instantiation. Like other preference descriptions, each preference description type for a specific motion type describes the preferred maximum or minimum level of intensity. If the user does not like a specific type of motion effect to be generated, they

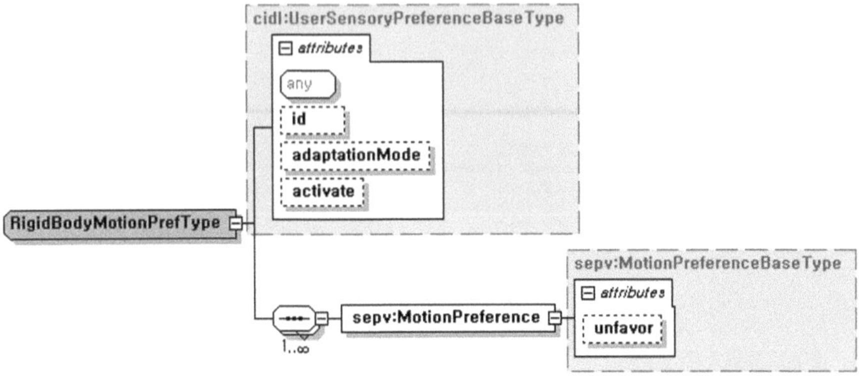

Figure 4.27 Structure of `RigidBodyMotionPrefType`.

can use the `unfavor` attribute given in the `MotionPreferenceBaseType` itself to specify so. There are seven new types defined for a specific type of motion achieved by extending `MotionPreferenceBaseType` in the current specifications, as shown in Table 4.8. These seven specific motion-oriented preference description types are `MoveTowardPreferenceType`, `InclinePreferenceType`, `WavePreferenceType`, `CollidePreferenceType`, `TurnPreferenceType`, `ShakePreferenceType`, and `SpinPreferenceType`. `MoveTowardPreferenceType` describes the preference for linear movements by giving the maximum allowable distance (`maxMoveDistance`), maximum allowable speed (`maxMoveSpeed`), and maximum allowable acceleration (`maxMoveAccel`) using three attributes. The corresponding units are specified by the `distanceUnit`, `speedUnit`, and `accelUnit` attributes using `UnitTypeCS`. `InclinePreferenceType` describes the preference for rotational movements by giving the maximum allowable rotational angle (`maxRotationAngle`), maximum allowable rotational speed (`maxRotationSpeed`), and maximum allowable rotational acceleration (`maxRotationAccel`) using three attributes. The corresponding units for the values of these attributes are specified by `angleUnit`, `speedUnit`, and `accelUnit` by referencing the terms defined in `UnitTypeCS`. `WavePreferenceType` describes the preference for wave type effects by providing the maximum allowable wave distance using the `maxWaveDistance` attribute, and the maximum allowable wave speed using the `maxWaveSpeed` attribute. The corresponding units are provided by the `distanceUnit` and `speedUnit` attributes. `CollidePreferenceType` describes the preference regarding a collision effect by providing the maximum allowable collision speed using the `maxCollideSpeed` attribute with the unit specified by the `speedUnit` attribute. `TurnPreferenceType` describes the preference

Table 4.8 Schema definition of `RigidBodyMotionPrefType`

```
<!-- ################################################ -->
<!-- RigidBodyMotion Preference type                      -->
<!-- ################################################ -->
<complexType name="RigidBodyMotionPrefType">
        <complexContent>
                <extension base="cidl:UserSensoryPreferenceBaseType">
                        <sequence maxOccurs="unbounded">
                                <element name="MotionPreference"
                                        type="sepv:MotionPreferenceBaseType"/>
                        </sequence>
                </extension>
        </complexContent>
</complexType>
<!-- ################################################ -->
<!--  Motion Preference base type                            -->
<!-- ################################################ -->
<complexType name="MotionPreferenceBaseType" abstract="true">
        <attribute name="unfavor" type="boolean" use="optional" default="0"/>
</complexType>
<!-- ################################################ -->
<!--  Move Toward Preference type                        -->
<!-- ################################################ -->
<complexType name="MoveTowardPreferenceType">
        <complexContent>
                <extension base="sepv:MotionPreferenceBaseType">
                        <attribute name="maxMoveDistance" type="unsignedInt"
use="optional"/>
                        <attribute name="maxMoveSpeed" type="float"
use="optional"/>
                        <attribute name="maxMoveAccel" type="float"
use="optional"/>
                        <attribute name="distanceUnit" type="mpegvct:unitType"
use="optional"/>
                        <attribute name="speedUnit" type="mpegvct:unitType"
use="optional"/>
                        <attribute name="accelUnit" type="mpegvct:unitType"
use="optional"/>
                </extension>
        </complexContent>
</complexType>
<!-- ################################################ -->
<!--  Incline Preference type                            -->
<!-- ################################################ -->
```

Table 4.8 Schema definition of `RigidBodyMotionPrefType`

```
<complexType name="InclinePreferenceType">
	<complexContent>
		<extension base="sepv:MotionPreferenceBaseType">
			<attribute name="maxRotationAngle" type="float"
use="optional"/>
			<attribute name="maxRotationSpeed" type="float"
use="optional"/>
			<attribute name="maxRotationAccel" type="float"
use="optional"/>
			<attribute name="angleUnit" type="mpegvct:unitType"
use="optional"/>
			<attribute name="speedUnit" type="mpegvct:unitType"
use="optional"/>
			<attribute name="accelUnit" type="mpegvct:unitType"
use="optional"/>
		</extension>
	</complexContent>
</complexType>
<!-- ################################################ -->
<!--  Wave Preference type                            -->
<!-- ################################################ -->
<complexType name="WavePreferenceType">
	<complexContent>
		<extension base="sepv:MotionPreferenceBaseType">
			<attribute name="maxWaveDistance" type="float"
use="optional"/>
			<attribute name="maxWaveSpeed" type="float"
use="optional"/>
			<attribute name="distanceUnit" type="mpegvct:unitType"
use="optional"/>
			<attribute name="speedUnit" type="mpegvct:unitType"
use="optional"/>
		</extension>
	</complexContent>
</complexType>
<!-- ################################################ -->
<!--  Collide Preference type                         -->
<!-- ################################################ -->
<complexType name="CollidePreferenceType">
	<complexContent>
		<extension base="sepv:MotionPreferenceBaseType">
			<attribute name="maxCollideSpeed" type="float"
use="optional"/>
			<attribute name="speedUnit" type="mpegvct:unitType"
use="optional"/>
		</extension>
	</complexContent>
</complexType>
```

Table 4.8 Schema definition of `RigidBodyMotionPrefType`

```
<!-- ################################################ -->
<!--  Turn Preference type                              -->
<!-- ################################################ -->
<complexType name="TurnPreferenceType">
        <complexContent>
                <extension base="sepv:MotionPreferenceBaseType">
                        <attribute name="maxTurnSpeed" type="float"
use="optional"/>
                        <attribute name="speedUnit" type="mpegvct:unitType"
use="optional"/>
                </extension>
        </complexContent>
</complexType>
<!-- ################################################ -->
<!--  Shake Preference type                             -->
<!-- ################################################ -->
<complexType name="ShakePreferenceType">
        <complexContent>
                <extension base="sepv:MotionPreferenceBaseType">
                        <attribute name="maxShakeDistance" type="float"
use="optional"/>
                        <attribute name="maxShakeSpeed" type="float"
use="optional"/>
                        <attribute name="distanceUnit" type="mpegvct:unitType"
use="optional"/>
                        <attribute name="speedUnit" type="mpegvct:unitType"
use="optional"/>
                </extension>
        </complexContent>
</complexType>
<!-- ################################################ -->
<!--  Spin Preference type                              -->
<!-- ################################################ -->
<complexType name="SpinPreferenceType">
        <complexContent>
                <extension base="sepv:MotionPreferenceBaseType">
                        <attribute name="maxSpinSpeed" type="float"
use="optional"/>
                        <attribute name="speedUnit" type="mpegvct:unitType"
use="optional"/>
                </extension>
        </complexContent>
</complexType>
```

for a turning effect by providing the maximum allowable turning speed in degrees/s using the maxTurnSpeed attribute. If any unit other than the default unit of degrees/s is used in describing the maximum turning speed, the speedUnit attribute is used to specify the unit by referencing the terms defined in UnitTypeCS. ShakePreferenceType describes the user's preference for a shaking effect, which is usually provided by a device such as a motion chair, by providing the maximum allowable shaking distance or the maximum displacement of the position in the shaking effect using the maxShake-Distance attribute, and the maximum allowable shaking speed or maximum allowable number of shakes per second using the maxShakeSpeed attribute. If any unit other than cm is used for the value of maxShakeDistance, the distanceUnit attribute is used to specify this unit by referencing the terms in UnitTypeCS. If any unit other than cycles per second (Hz) is used for the value of maxShakeSpeed, the speedUnit attribute is used to specify the unit by referencing the terms in UnitTypeCS. SpinPreferenceType describes the preference regarding a spin effect by providing the maximum spin speed in cycles per second using the maxSpinSpeed attribute. If any unit other than cycles per second is used for the maxSpinSpeed attribute, the speedUnit attribute is used to specify the unit by referencing the terms in UnitTypeCS.

4.6 SENSOR ADAPTATION PREFERENCE VOCABULARY

The final vocabulary for the control information is the description of the user's preference regarding the adaptation of individual sensed information. The SAPV is defined for each and every sensor defined in ISO/IEC 23005-5. There are 17 types defined in the current version of the SAPV standard, and 12 of them have a simple structure inherited from SensorAdapatationPreferenceBaseType, i.e., AmbientNoise AdaptationPrefType, TemperatureAdaptationPrefType, HumidityAdaptation PrefType, DistanceAdaptationPrefType, AtmosphericPressureAdaptation PrefType, VelocityAdaptationPrefType, AccelerationAdaptationPrefType, AngularVelocityAdaptationPrefType, AngularAccelerationAdaptationPref Type, ForceAdaptationPrefType, TorqueAdaptationPrefType, and Pressure AdaptationPrefType, which describe the user's preference regarding the adaptation of the input from the ambient-noise, temperature, humidity, distance, atmospheric-pressure, velocity, acceleration, angular-velocity, angular-acceleration, force, torque, and pressure sensors, which are simple types having only attributes inherited from SensorAdaptationPreferenceBaseType, as shown in Figure 4.28.

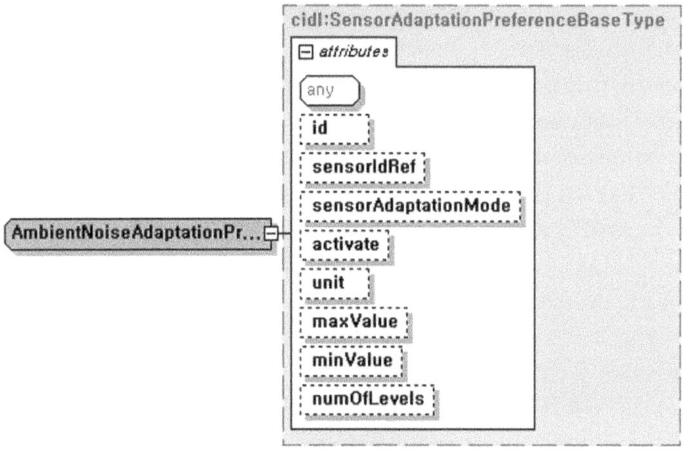

Figure 4.28 Structure of `AmbientNoiseAdaptationPrefType`.

Table 4.9 Example instance of `AmbientNoiseAdaptationPrefType`

```
<cidl:SAPreference xsi:type="sapv:AmbientNoiseAdaptationPrefType"
id="ANSAP001" sensorIdRef="AN011" activate="true" minValue="20"
maxValue="110" sensorAdaptationMode="strict" numOfLevels="10"/>
```

Because the main use case of sensor adaptation is the adapted control of a virtual world, the interpretation of an instance of the SAPV is very similar to the case of the SEPV. For example, the instance shown in Table 4.9 can be interpreted as follows. The identifier for this preference description is "ANSAP001." The user wants to receive sensor input from the ambient noise sensor, which is identified by the sensor ID of "AN011." When receiving the sensor input, the user wants to adapt the sensor input to a range between 20 and 110 dB in 10 levels. Any sensed value smaller than 20 dB should be denoted as 20 dB, and any sensed value larger than 110 dB should be clipped to 110 dB.

`LightSensorAdaptationPrefType`, describing the preference regarding the adaptation of light sensor input, has zero or more `UnfavorableColor` elements to denote those colors that the user does not want to receive or sense, in addition to the attributes inherited from the `SensorAdaptationPreferenceBaseType`. `OrientationAdaptationPrefType`, which describes the preference toward the adaptation of the orientation sensor input, has one `OrientationRange` element to describe the minimum and maximum allowable degrees of yaw, pitch, and roll using six float-type elements of `YawMin`, `YawMax`, `PitchMin`, `PitchMax`, `RollMin`, and RollMax. Similar to OrientationAdaptationPrefType in structure is PositionAdaptationPrefType, which describes the user's preference for an adaptation of the position sensor input. PositionAdaptationPrefType has an additional element of Range to describe the minimum and maximum allowable values of the position in the *X*, *Y*, and *Z* axes directions using XMinValue, XMaxValue, YMinValue, YMaxValue, ZMinValue, and ZMaxValue elements defined in the Range element.

MotionAdaptationPrefType, describing the user's preference regarding the adaptation of the motion sensor input, is a complex type defined by combinations of the PositionPreference element of PositionAdaptationPrefType, the OrientationPreference element of OrientationAdaptationPrefType, the VelocityPreference element of VelocityAdaptationPrefType, the AngularVelocityPreference element of AngularVelocityAdaptationPrefType, the AccelerationPreference element of AccelerationAdaptationPrefType, and the AngularAccelerationPreference element of AngularAcceleration AdaptationPrefType.

IntelligentCameraAdaptationPrefType describes the user's preference toward the adaptation of an intelligent camera sensor input and has four Boolean-type elements and two elements having multiple Boolean subelements. FaceFeatureTrackingOn, BodyFeatureTrackingOn, FacialExpressionTrackingOn, and GestureTrackingOn, which are Boolean-type elements, are used to describe whether the facial feature tracking mode, body feature tracking mode, facial expressions for animation, and body gesture for animation should be extracted. The FacialFeatureMask element provides the selection of facial components to be tracked using Boolean-type elements of Eyes for the left and right eye outlines, Mouth for the mouth lip outline, Nose for the nose outline, and Ears for the left and right ear outlines. The BodyFeatureMask element provides the selection of body components to be tracked using the Boolean-type elements of Head for the head bones, Arms for the arms in upper-body bones, Hands for the left and right hands in the upper-body bones, Legs for left and right legs in the lower-body bones, Feet for the left and right feet in the lower-body bones, and MiddleBody for the mid-body bones.

4.7 CONCLUSION

This chapter provided a detailed description of the control information composed of a sensory device capability description, sensor capability description, and the user's preference regarding the sensory effects and the adaptation of the sensor inputs. This information was designed to be used for detailed control of the actuators and sensors defined in ISO/IEC 23005-5 MPEG-V, Part 5: Data Format for Interaction Devices [4].

The sensory device capability descriptions and sensor capability descriptions can be used not only for the adaptation of commands for the actuators and the information acquired by the sensors, but also for the recognition of the actuators and sensors available if the capability description is broadcasted by the device. The user preferences toward the sensory effects can be used to personalize the sensory effects for each user. The sensor adaptation preference can be used for the adaptation of the sensor input for each user, or for the purpose of the application.

REFERENCES

[1] ISO/IEC 23005-2:2013 Information technology—Media context and control—Part 2 Control Information.
[2] ISO/IEC 21000-7:2007 Information technology—Multimedia framework (MPEG-21)—Part 7: Digital Item Adaptation.
[3] ISO/IEC 23005-6:2013 Information technology—Media context and control—Part 6 Common types and tools.
[4] ISO/IEC 23005-2:2013 Information technology—Media context and control—Part 5 Data format for interaction devices.

CHAPTER 5

Interoperable Virtual World

Contents

5.1 INTRODUCTION

Virtual worlds integrate existing and emerging media technologies (e.g., instant messaging, video, 3D, VR, AI, chat, and voice) that allow the support of existing networks and the development of new kinds of social networks. The virtual worlds therefore provide users with an immersive experience that allows them to feel like they are living in a virtual world by simulating modes of communication and interfacing the virtual world with the real world.

MPEG-V.
DOI: http://dx.doi.org/10.1016/B978-0-12-420140-8.00005-6

When a user starts using a virtual world, they create their own virtual character, called an avatar, by configuring its appearance, and can even spend money to decorate their avatar with clothes and accessories. Decorating an avatar is a generally interesting and pleasurable experience for users, but owing to a lack of interoperability among virtual worlds, it can be time-consuming work to have to create a new avatar for use in another new virtual world service. Moreover, created and/or purchased goods are also not transferrable to another virtual world, despite the user's time spent in creating or purchasing them.

As stated, various natural and intuitive interface methods between the real world and virtual worlds need to be provided for a more immersive experience. Such natural and intuitive interfaces may include gestures and natural language support for the control of, and interaction among, avatars. Even the key mappings for interaction differ among virtual worlds.

Rather than using the graphics data to support interoperability between virtual worlds, ISO/IEC 23005-4 proposed a common transferrable data format for metadata. Therefore, proprietary contents themselves may not need to be transferrable, but some metadata that help in creating new virtual characters more easily should be. For example, imagine that a user has created a female avatar with long blond hair for use in one virtual world and wants to export this character to another virtual world. The information transferred to the other virtual world would include the gender and hair attributes such as the length and color. Finally, the second virtual world can automatically create its own avatar based on the transferred metadata, although the realized character may differ graphically. For natural interactions such as the avatar control, physical body-motion-based controls can be used. To support such interactions, the motion retargeting should be conducted in real-time. Such information requires the user's skeletal motion as well as the skeletal structure of the avatar.

Virtual worlds are composed of virtual characters and virtual objects. Virtual characters can be categorized into players, which are characterized versions of the users in the virtual environment (VE), or nonplayer characters, which are not controlled by any players. The virtual objects are any individual objects other than virtual characters inside the environment. In order to define the common characteristics shared by both virtual characters and virtual objects, ISO/IEC23005 introduced a virtual-world object as a comprehensive term containing both characters and objects.

5.2 VIRTUAL-WORLD OBJECT METADATA

5.2.1 Introduction

Virtual-world object metadata are containers for common descriptions of avatars and virtual object characteristics within a VE. They define the root element, the base type of virtual-world object characteristics, and the common data types of the virtual-world objects themselves.

The root element is VWOCInfo, which is specified by its own type, VWOCInfoType, which contains the two elements AvatarList and VirtualObjectList. AvatarList specifies a list of avatars, and VirtualObjectList specifies a list of virtual objects. In other words, an XML instance can start with a VWOCInfo tag. This instantiation allows a list of multiple avatars and virtual objects to be imported from one virtual world to another. The base type, VWOBaseType, contains the common attributes for specifying the characteristics of both avatars and virtual objects. The common data types are the basic building blocks used to specify the data types, such as the haptic properties, animation descriptions, and other types of simple data.

VWOBaseType is the base type of attributes and characteristics of virtual-world objects, and is inherited by AvatarBaseType and VirtualObjectBaseType. The base type contains four different categories of information. The first category is a set of attributes associated with the media resources, such as the sound and scent resources. The second category is a set of descriptors related to the movement of a virtual object. The third category is a set of descriptors used to support interactions from the input devices, such as input events and a behavior model. The final category is the identification of a virtual-world object for support of the ownership, rights, and copyright. Figure 5.1 shows the definition of the VWOBaseType.

5.2.2 Sound and Scent Types

In terms of the media attributes, the data type of the sound resource, VWOSoundType, contains one element, ResourcesURL, which is a location link to a sound file. This type also includes soundID, intensity, duration, loop, and name as its attributes. The soundID attribute is an identifier for an object sound, such as "SoundID3." The intensity attribute describes the volume of the sound, the range of which is from 0 to 1, were 0 indicates

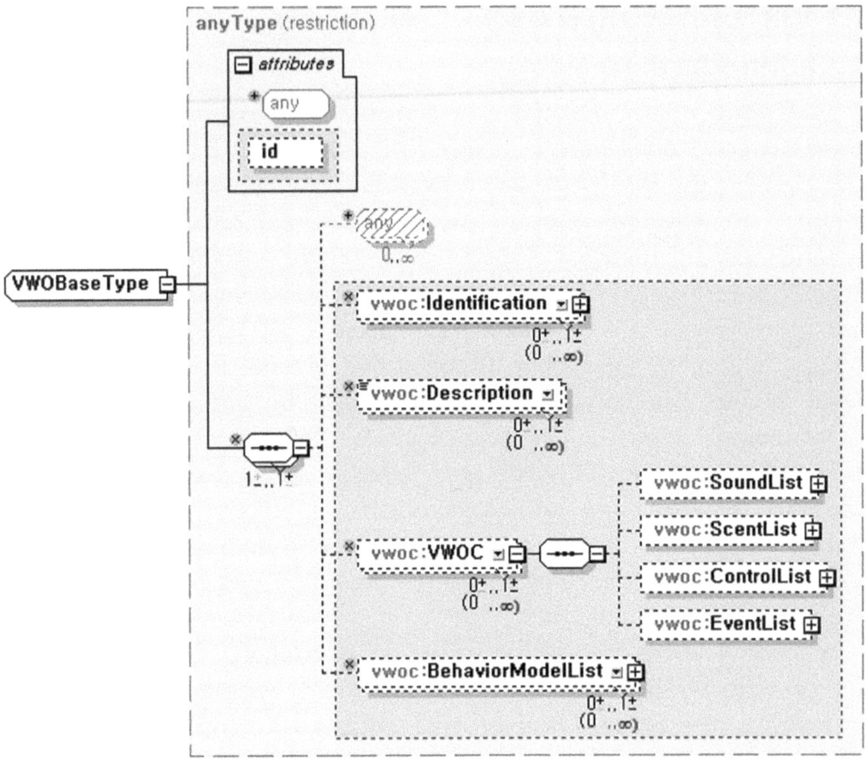

Figure 5.1 Diagram of `VWOBaseType`.

no volume and 1 indicates the same scale as the original volume of the sound resource. The `duration` attribute describes the length in time of the sound resource in ms. The `loop` attribute describes an option of repeated playing. A value of 0 indicates indefinite repetitions, whereas any positive integer indicates the number of repetitions. The `name` attribute describes the name of the sound and can be used to describe the actual sound name. The data type of the scent resource, `VWOScentType`, also contains the same element and the same list of attributes as `VWOSoundType`, with the exception that the referenced resource is of a different type.

5.2.3 Control Type

The data-type control, `VWOControlType`, contains the `MotionFeatureControl` element, and its associated attribute, `controlID`. `MotionFeatureControl` includes the position, orientation, and scale factors used to control the movement of a virtual object. Each of these parameters is represented by a 3D floating-point vector. `controlID` is a unique identifier of the associated `MotionFeatureControl`. Therefore, once `MotionFeatureControl` is defined, its pre-defined control can be used by referencing its identifier.

5.2.4 Event Type

One of the behavioral attributes, `VWOEventType`, is associated with the user's interactions, i.e., input events conducted by the user. `VWOEventType` supports input events from legacy input devices such as a keyboard and mouse, as well as any novel input devices. In detail, supported mouse events include a click, double click, down button, up of the left and right buttons, and mouse motions. Keyboard events are composed of both the key-code value of each key and its associated event. Note that the key code differs from the ASCII code, i.e., the codes for "a" and "A" are different in the ASCII code, but the two share the same key code of "65." Key code events "pressed," "clicked," and "released" are defined. Note that the corresponding events are also defined as "`keydown`," "`keypress`," and "`keyup`" in the W3C standards, as shown in Table 5.1.

For example, if an event is created through a combination of pressing the "ctrl" (key code, 17) and "c" keys (key code, 65) on the keyboard to copy an object (i.e., a possible event ID could be "copy"), the generated `VWOEventType` is as shown in Table 5.2.

In addition to mouse and keyboard events, any input event can be defined by the element, `UserDefinedInput`. Therefore, `VWOEventType` can support any input events by defining the events using the appropriate text strings. One example is hand-gesture-based input events. When a set of

Table 5.1 Keyboard event descriptions defined in MPEG-V and W3C

MPEG-V	W3C	Description
`"pressed"`	`keydown`	An event in which a key is continuously pressed
`"clicked"`	`keyclick`	An event in which a key is pressed and released
`"released"`	`keyup`	An event in which a key is released

Table 5.2 An example instance of `VWOEventType`: A keyboard event of "ctrl + c"

```
<vwoc:Event eventID="copy">
      <vwoc:Keyboard keyCode="17" event="pressed"/>
      <vwoc:Keyboard keyCode="65" event="clicked"/>
</vwoc:Event>
```

Table 5.3 An example instance of `VWOEventType`: A hand gesture support

```
<vwoc:Event eventID="handGestureUp">
      <vwoc:UserDefinedInput>
            up
      </vwoc:UserDefinedInput>
</vwoc:Event>
```

hand gestures is defined by five elements "up," "down," "left," "right," and "click," an input hand gesture can be defined using the same text as its command, as shown in Table 5.3.

Note that any combination of input events can be used to make `VWOEventType`.

5.2.5 Behavior Model Type

To control the behavior of a virtual-world object using any input device, `VWOBehaviorModelType` provides a mapping between a list of input events and a list of their associated output events for a virtual-world object. Thus, any input event can trigger any associated output event according to the mapping. For each input event in `VWOEventType`, `VWOBehaviorModelType` requires `eventID` as an identifier for the input event. The behavior model supports output events such as a sound event, scent event, control event, and animation event. Once the user sets their preferred combination of input events as a certain output event in one virtual world, this combination can be imported to another virtual world with the same configuration. In addition, a user can also combine different output events to make their own user-specific output events. For example, consider a keyboard control used to make an avatar greeting. Let the "g" key on the keyboard be an input event to activate a greeting. Let "greetAni" of the greeting animation identifier, and "hello," an identifier of a greeting-sound resource, reference and play the output animation clip and output sound effect, respectively. The behavior model type for such a greeting behavior is shown in Table 5.4.

5.2.6 Identification Type

This type provides two different functions. The first is to identify the association in the virtual world, such as the name, family, and user ID, and the second is to identify the association in the real world, such as the ownership, credits, and rights. `IdentificationType` provides the `name`, `family`, and `userID` attributes to support an association in a virtual world.

Table 5.4 An example instance of `VWOBehaviorModelType`: **How type can be defined by input and output events**

```
<vwoc:BehaviorModel>
      <vwoc:BehaviorInput eventIDRef="keyboardEvent-g_pressed"/>
      <vwoc:BehaviorOutput animationIDRefs="greetAni" soundIDRefs="hello"/>
</vwoc:BehaviorModel>

<vwoc:Event eventID="keyboardEvent-g_pressed">
      <vwoc:Keyboard keyCode="71" event="pressed"/>
</vwoc:Event>

<vwoc:Sound loop="0" soundID="hello" duration="30" intensity="0.5"
name="BigAlarm">
      <vwoc:ResourcesURL>http://sounddb.com/hello.wav</vwoc:ResourcesURL>
</vwoc:Sound>

<vwoc:Animation>
      <vwoc:Greeting animationID="greetAni">
            <vwoc:Name>urn:mpeg:mpeg-v:01-VWOC-GreetingAnimationCS-
NS:hello</vwoc:Name>
            <vwoc:Uri>http://avatarAnimationdb.com/hello.bvh</vwoc:Uri>
      </vwoc:Greeting>
<vwoc:Animation>
```

The `name` attribute describes the name of a virtual-world object within a virtual world. The `family` attribute describes the relationship with other virtual-world objects. If we take a virtual-world avatar as an example, the avatar has a clan associated with it. Its `family` attribute could be the name of the clan. Regarding such an association in the real world, the `IdentificationType` defines the `UserID`, `Ownership`, `Rights`, and `Credits` elements. The `UserID` element defines the user identification associated with the virtual-world object based on the `anyURI` type. The `Ownership` element defines the owner of the virtual-world object, and is based on `AgentType` defined in MPEG-7, ISO/IEC 15938-5:2003. The `Rights` element defines the rights of the virtual-world object based on `LicenseType` defined in rights expression language (REL), ISO/IEC 21000-5:2004. It can provide multiple licensing policies toward a virtual-world object, and therefore may provide multiple instantiations. The `Credits` element defines the contributors of the virtual-world object in chronological order based on `AgentType` in MPEG-7. There may be multiple contributors including the original creator, and therefore it also provides multiple instantiations.

5.3 AVATAR METADATA

5.3.1 Introduction

An avatar is a type of virtual character, defined as a (visual) representation of a user inside a VE. Therefore, users can directly characterize themselves and interact with/within a VE. Therefore, the characteristics of an avatar contain information used to set the visual and/or behavioral representation of the user inside the environment, in addition to the characteristics of the virtual-world objects. Therefore, avatar metadata provide the data types to support the following:

1. visible presence of a real user in a VE,
2. characterization of the user within the VE,
3. interaction with the VE.

In addition to the multimedia resources listed in `VWOBaseType`, an avatar is composed of appearance and animation metadata for a visual presence; communication skills and personality metadata used to characterize the users; and feature control, haptic properties, and control and event information metadata for user interactions. Note that the avatar metadata are an extension of `AvatarBaseType`, which is inherited from `VWOBaseType`. Similar to the virtual-world object metadata, the metadata related to multimedia resources can be used to describe the resources associated with a particular avatar.

5.3.2 Appearance Type

The `Appearance` element is defined by `AvatarAppearanceType`, which contains a high-level description of the avatar appearance. `AvatarAppearanceType` is defined to describe the appearance of the body parts and any other associated objects such as clothes, shoes, or accessories. In addition, `AvatarAppearanceType` also provides other attributes that can be used as variables to affect the appearance of the avatar, such as the locations of the appearance resources, facial calibration points, and physical conditions. Table 5.5 shows the categories of elements in `AvatarAppearanceType`.

A list of appearance descriptions is shown in Table 5.6. Note that the descriptions of each element contain a list of subelements to fully describe each element. The subelements are parametric if they are not descriptive.

Table 5.5 Categories for `AvatarAppearanceType`

Category	Type	Elements
Body parts	Physical appearance	Body, head, eyes, ears, nose, mouth, lips, body skin, facial skin, face, fingernails, toenails, body appearance, hair, eyebrows, facial hair, and body hair
Associated virtual objects	Any virtual objects that can be used with the avatar	Clothes, shoes, accessories, and skin marks
Conditional parameters	Information that can affect the appearance	Facial calibration points, physical condition, and appearance resources

5.3.3 Animation Type

The `Animation` element is defined by `AvatarAnimationType`, which contains a high-level description of the avatar animation. `AvatarAnimationType` provides a categorical list of possible animations, which is given in Table 5.7. The animations in each animation category reference the classification scheme of the corresponding category. For example, if there is a heavy-breathing pose animation available, its animation name will be listed as `bodyNoise` animation, which is one of the `Idle` animations defined through the classification scheme for this category.

Each avatar animation listed in Table 5.7 is defined by `AnimationDescriptionType`, as shown in Figure 5.2, and the corresponding categorical classification scheme for its naming.

`AnimationDescriptionType` includes two different options to describe the animation. The first option is to use the standardized description as specified in ISO/IEC23005. The other option is to use the proprietary but well-formed XML metadata itself as an `Extra` element. The first option contains a `Name` element, which is the type of animation as a reference to the classification scheme for the animation category, and an `Uri` element for a link to an animation file. There are three optional attributes included in this type, `animationID`, `duration`, and `loop`. The `animationID` attribute refers to the unique identifier of the animation. The `duration` attribute

Table 5.6 Descriptions of appearance elements

Element name	Type	Descriptions
Body	BodyType	Body height, body thickness, body fat (low, medium, or high), torso muscles (low, medium, or high), neck thickness, neck length, shoulders, pectorals, arm length, hand size, torso length, love handles, belly size, leg muscles, leg length, hip width, hip length, butt size, package (small, medium, or big), saddlebags (small, medium, or big), knee angle, and foot size
Head	HeadType	Head size, head stretch (%), head shape (square, round, oval, or long), egg head (Boolean, yes or no), head length, face shear, forehead size, forehead angle, brow size, face skin (dry, normal, or greasy), cheeks (small, medium, or big), cheeks depth, cheeks shape (high, chubby, or bone), the volume of the upper cheeks (small, medium, or big), the volume of lower cheeks (small, medium, or big), and cheekbones (down, medium, or up)
Eyes	EyesType	Eye size, eye opening, eye spacing, outer eye corner (down, middle, or up), inner eye corner (down, middle, or up), eye depth, upper eyelid fold (the degree of covering the eyes by the upper eyelid), eye bags, puffy eyelids (small, medium, or big), eyelash length, eye pop (the difference in size between the left and right eyes), eye color (defined in ISO/IEC23005-6), and eye lightness (percentage of reflectivity of the eyes)
Ears	EarsType	Ear size, ear position (low, medium, or high), ear angle, earlobes, and ear tips (degree of ear tip pointiness, i.e., pointed, average, not pointed)
Nose	NoseType	Nose size, nose width, nostril width, the size of the nostril division, nose thickness, the height of the upper bridge, the height of the lower bridge, bridge width, nose tip angle (up or down), and nose tip shape (pointy or bulbous)

`MouthLip`	`MouthLipType`	Lip width, lip fullness, lip thickness, lip ratio, mouth size, mouth position, mouth corner (low, medium, or high), lip cleft depth (height), lip cleft (width), mouth shift (left, middle, or right), chin angle, jaw shape (pointed, average, or not-pointed), chin depth, jaw angle, jaw jut (inside or outside), jowls, chin cleft (round or cleft), upper chin cleft (round or cleft), and chin neck
`BodySkin`	`SkinType`	Body skin pigment (very light, light, average, olive, brown, or black), body skin ruddiness (slight, average, heavy), and body skin rainbow color (defined in ISO/IEC23005-6)
`FacialSkin`	`SkinType`	Facial skin pigment (very light, light, average, olive, brown, or black), facial skin ruddiness (slight, average, heavy), and facial skin rainbow color (defined in ISO/IEC23005-6)
`Facial`	`FacialType`	Facial definition (level of facial brightness, i.e., 1 (light) to 5 (dark), freckles (5 levels: 1 (light) to 5 (heavy)), wrinkles (yes or no), rosy complexion (yes or no), lip pinkness (5 levels), lipstick (yes or no), lipstick color (defined in ISO/IEC23005-6), lip gloss (5 levels), blush (yes or no), blush color (defined in ISO/IEC23005-6), blush opacity (%), inner shadow (yes or no), inner shadow color (defined in ISO/IEC23005-6), inner shadow opacity (%), outer shadow (yes or no), outer shadow opacity (%), eyeliner (yes or no), and eyeliner color (defined in ISO/IEC23005-6)
`FingerNails`	`NailType`	Fingernail polish (yes or no), fingernail polish color (defined in ISO/IEC23005-6)
`ToeNails`	`NailType`	Toenail polish (yes or no), toenail polish color (defined in ISO/IEC23005-6)
`BodyLook`	`BodyLookType`	Body definition (small, medium, or large), body freckles (5 levels)

(*Continued*)

Table 5.6 (Continued)

Element name	Type	Descriptions
Hair	HairType	Hair size (short, medium, or long), hairstyle (9 different styles), hair color (defined in ISO/IEC23005-6), white hair (%), rainbow color (defined in ISO/IEC23005-6), blonde hair (%), red hair (%), hair volume (light, medium, or heavy), the degree of hair in front (short, medium, or long), the degree of hair on the sides (short, medium, or long), the degree of hair in the back (short, medium, or long), big hair front (short, medium, or long), big hair top (short, medium, or long), big hair back (short, medium, or long), hair front fringe (short, medium, or long), hair side fringe (short, medium, or long), hair back fringe (short, medium, or long), full hair sides (short, medium, or long), hair sweep (left, middle, or right), hair shear front (short, medium, or long), hair shear back (short, medium, or long), toupee front (short, medium, or long), toupee rear (short, medium, or long), rumpled hair (low, moderate, or high), pigtail (short, medium, or long), ponytail (short, medium, or long), spiked hair (short, medium, or long), hair tilt, the degree of parting at the middle front (low or high), the degree of parting on the right side (low or high), the degree of parting on the left side (low or high) the degree of parting in the middle (low or high)
EyeBrows	EyeBrowsType	Eyebrow size (short, medium, or long), eyebrow density (low, medium, or high), eyebrow height (low, middle, high), eyebrow arc (flat, average, or arced), eyebrow point (low, medium, or high)
FacialHair	FacialHairType	Facial hair thickness (low, average, or high), facial sideburns (defined in ISO/IEC23005-6), facial moustache (yes or no), facial chin curtains (yes or no), facial soul patch (yes or no)
BodyHair	BodyHairType	Hair color (defined in ISO/IEC23005-6), hair thickness (low, average, or high)
FacialCalibrationPoints	FacialCalibrationPointsType	Sellion, right infraorbitale, left infraorbitale, supramenton, right tragion, left tragion, right gonion, left gonion
PhysicalCondition	PhysicalConditionType	Body strength (%), body flexibility (low, average, or high)

Table 5.7 List of elements in `AvatarAnimationType`

Elements	Description
`Idle`	A container of various idle animations
`Greeting`	A container of various greeting animations
`Dance`	A container of various dancing animations
`Walk`	A container of various walking animations
`Moves`	A container of various movement animations
`Fighting`	A container of various fighting animations
`Hearing`	A container of various hearing animations
`Smoke`	A container of various smoking animations
`Congratulations`	A container of various congratulation animations
`CommonActions`	A container of various common action animations
`SpecificActions`	A container of various specific action animations
`FacialExpression`	A container of various facial expression animations
`BodyExpression`	A container of various body expression animations

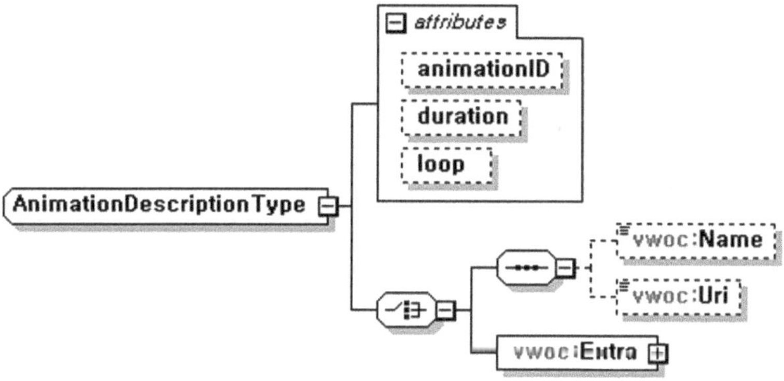

Figure 5.2 Structure of `AnimationDescriptionType`.

provides the length of duration of the animation. Finally, the `loop` attribute is used to provide a playing option for the number of repetitions.

Any other avatar animation that does not belong to any of these categories can also be defined by `AnimationResourceDescriptionType`, as shown in Figure 5.3. `AnimationResourceDescriptionType` has two elements, `Description` and `Uri`. The `Description` element defines the description of the animation resource in a text string. The `Uri` element defines a link to the animation file as previously defined. The three optional attributes of this type are the same as for `AnimationDescriptionType`.

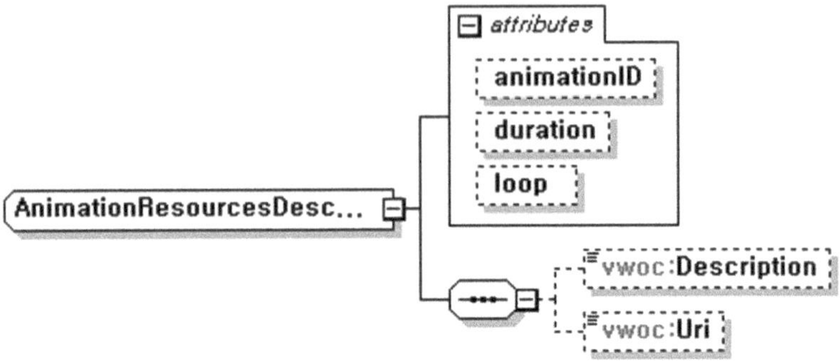

Figure 5.3 Structure of `AnimationResourceDescriptionType`.

5.3.4 Communication Skills Type

The `AvatarCommunicationSkills` element is defined by `AvatarCommunicationSkillsType`, which contains the user's communication preferences by means of two input and two output channels. The use of two input and output communication channels is to allow both verbal and nonverbal communication capabilities. The verbal communication capabilities for the input and output channels are defined by the `InputVerbalCommunication` and `OutputVerbalCommunication` elements, respectively. The verbal communication capabilities for both the input and output communication channels are defined by `VerbalCommunicationType`. The nonverbal communication capabilities for both the input and output communication channels are defined by `NonVerbalCommunicationType`. `AvatarCommunicationSkillsType` also has two optional attributes, `name` and `defaultLanguage`. The `name` attribute is used for addressing the particular user-specified communication type element, and the `defaultLanguage` attribute specifies the avatar's preferred language for all communication channels. Note that `defaultLanguage` can be overridden by a `language` attribute specified for each channel.

`VerbalCommunicationType` specifies the avatar's verbal communication skills and contains a `SecondaryLanguage` element, which defines a preferred secondary language for verbal communication. There are three optional attributes included in this type, `language`, `voice`, and `text`. The language attribute provides the preferred language for verbal communication. The `voice` attribute provides the level of preference to speak the preferred language. The level of preference is defined by `communicationPreferenceLevelType`, which contains three possible levels of preference, preferred, enabled, and disabled. Similar to the `voice` attribute defined by

Table 5.8 Five factors of the OCEAN model

Factors	Description
Openness	A tendency to be curious, creative, and more likely to experience novelty and variety
Conscientiousness	A tendency to be organized and dependable
Extraversion	A tendency to seek stimulation in the company of others
Agreeableness	A tendency to be compassionate and cooperative
Neuroticism	A tendency to experience unpleasant emotions easily

`communicationPreferenceLevelType`, the `text` attribute provides the level of preference to write in the preferred language.

The input and output nonverbal communication channels are defined by the `InputNonVerbalCommunication` and `OutputNonVerbalCommunication` elements, respectively. Both elements are defined by `NonVerbalCommunicationType`. `NonVerbalCommunicationType` specifies the avatar's nonverbal communication skills using the `SignLanguage` and `CuedSpeechCommunication` elements. Both elements are defined by `SignLanguageType`, which specifies the name of the language as an attribute, such as English sign-language and Spanish sign-language. The `name` attribute is defined by ISO 639, which contains short codes for language names. The `NonVerbalCommunicationType` also has an optional attribute, `complementaryGesture` which provides a list of complementary gestures during output verbal communications.

5.3.5 Personality Type

Avatar's personality is based on OCEAN model [1] which describes a specific personality through a set of characteristics. The possible characteristics are openness, conscientiousness, extraversion, agreeableness, and neuroticism. Table 5.8 illustrates the meaning of these characteristics [1]. This personality element can be used by virtual-world service providers to interpret the emotions and moods invoked by virtual-world events, i.e., automated avatar–avatar communication. For example, for a sample question given to multiple avatars, their answers may differ owing to the different values in their personality characteristics.

`AvatarPersonalityType` is composed of a set of personality characteristics as subelements. As shown in Figure 5.4, it provides five elements, `Openness`, `Agreeableness`, `Neuroticism`, `Extraversion`, and `Conscientiousness`. Each element is defined by `minusOneToOneType`, which

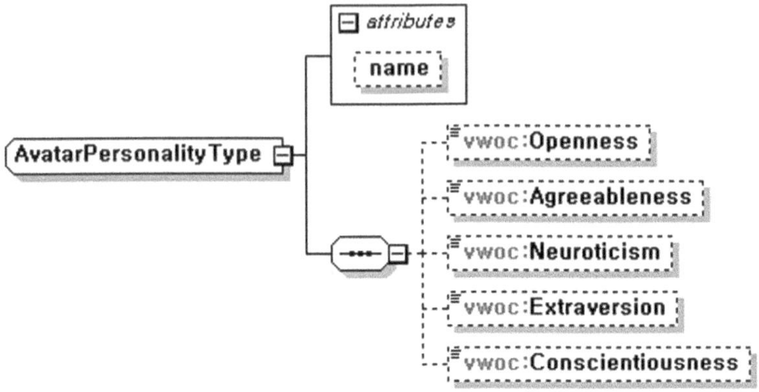

Figure 5.4 Structure of `AvatarPersonalityType`.

has a floating value between −1 and 1 for the range of characteristics. For example, `Openness` with a value of 1 indicates that the avatar shows its feelings and opinions freely, whereas `Openness` with a value of −1 indicates that the avatar does not show its feelings or opinions. In addition, `AvatarPersonalityType` also contains an optional attribute, `name`, which specifies the name of the particular personality defined by the five elements.

5.3.6 Motion Control Type

To control an avatar's motion based on the user's motion, the `ControlFeatures` element provides a set of descriptors that are possible place holders for control points on the body skeleton and for facial control points. This is defined by `AvatarControlFeaturesType`, which is composed of two elements, `ControlBodyFeatures` and `ControlFaceFeatures`. The `ControlBodyFeatures` element can be used to control the movements of the body skeleton and is defined by `ControlBodyFeaturesType`. The `ControlFaceFeatures` element can be used to control the facial expressions based on the facial control points.

`ControlBodyFeaturesType` is composed of four elements corresponding to four major body parts, i.e., the head, upper body, middle body, and lower body. The `HeadBones` element is the first element in `ControlBodyFeaturesType`, and is composed of neck bones, skull, eyelids, eyeballs, eyebrows, and jaw. This element is defined through multiple instantiations of `ControlBodyFeaturesDescriptionType`, which provides two optional attributes, `name` and `alias`. The `name` attribute describes the type of body features by referencing four classification schemes,

Table 5.9 Example instance of `ControlBodyFeaturesType`

```
<vwoc:ControlFeatures>
    <vwoc:ControlBodyFeatures>
          <vwoc:HeadBones name="urn:mpeg:mpeg-v:01-VWOC-HeadBonesCS-
NS:skull" alias="Head"/>
    </vwoc:ControlBodyFeatures>
</vwoc:ControlFeatures>
```

Table 5.10 Elements for facial feature control type

Element	Description	Resolution
`HeadOutline`	The outline of the head	Either 4 or 8 points
`LeftEyeOutline`	The outline of the left eye	Either 4 or 8 points
`RightEyeOutline`	The outline of the right eye	Either 4 or 8 points
`MouthLipOutline`	The outline of the mouth lips	Either 4 or 14 points
`NoseOutline`	The outline of the nose	Either 4 or 8 points
`LeftEyeBrowOutline`	The outline of the left eyebrow	4 points
`RightEyeBrowOutline`	The outline of the right eyebrow	4 points
`LeftEarOutline`	The outline of the left ear	4 points
`RightEarOutline`	The outline of the right ear	4 points
`FacePoint`	The control points for facial expression	5 points
`MiscellaneousPoints`	Any additional control points for advanced facial feature control	The same number of points as specified

`HeadBoneCS`, `UpperBodyBonesCS`, `DownBodyBonesCS`, and `MiddleBodyBonesCS`. The `alias` attribute can be used to assign a name to a specific type of body feature.

Table 5.9 shows the use of `ControlBodyFeaturesType` in defining “skull” in the `HeadBones` element with “Head” as the `alias` attribute.

`ControlFaceFeaturesType` is composed of 11 elements that correspond mostly to facial landmarks such as the eyes, nose, and lips. Table 5.10 shows a list of elements for this type. All elements with the exception of `MiscellaneousPoints` are of `OutlineType`, which can have four elements, `Outline4Points`, `Outline5Points`, `Outline8Points`, and `Outline14Points`, depending upon the number of contour points formed by each element. Note that `HeadOutline`, `LeftEyeOutline`, `RightEyeOutline`, `MouthLipOutline`, and `NoseOutline` have two different sets of outline points. That with more outline points supports higher-resolution outlines.

Each of the outline types is also defined by PointType, an abstract type providing a root for two different point types, LogicalPointType and Physical3DPointType. LogicalPointType is an extended type of PointType used to provide the name of the feature point, and has two attributes: name and sensorID. The name attribute is the name of the feature point, and the sensorID attribute is the sensor ID corresponding to this feature point. Physical3DPointType is an extended type of PointType for providing a 3D point vector value. Physical3DPointType has three attributes, X, Y, and Z to provide a value for each axis in the 3D coordinates.

When a user uses an intelligent camera to clone their avatar's facial motions from their own, the intelligent camera can provide a list of points that it tracks from the beginning. The names of the points on the list may be used as the sensorID in LogicalPointType to create a mapping between the avatar's facial control points and the sensed facial feature points from the camera.

5.3.7 Haptic Property Type

The haptic properties are listed in the VWOHapticPropertyLists element, which contains a list of high-level descriptors of the haptic properties. This element is defined by VWOHapticPropertyListsType, which contains multiple HapticProperty elements defined by VWOHapticPropertyType. The listed haptic properties are then associated with each body part in the Appearance element by referencing the identifier of each haptic property. As shown in Figure 5.5, each element in the AvatarAppearance type has an optional attribute, hapticIDRef, which contains an identifier that refers to the haptic property of each element. This configuration provides a way to assign a unique haptic property to each of the body parts in the avatar so that any body part can have its own different haptic property.

VWOHapticPropertyType is composed of three elements used to describe the haptic properties of a virtual object. These three kinds of information can be used to render haptic effects of both avatars and virtual objects. The first element, MaterialProperty, is defined by the MaterialPropertyType, which has six optional attributes: stiffness, staticFriction, dynamicFriction, damping, texture, and mass. The stiffness attribute describes the stiffness of the object. The staticFriction attribute describes the static friction of the object. The dynamicFriction attribute describes the dynamic friction of the object. The damping attribute describes the damping ratio of the object. The texture attribute contains a link to a texture file (usually an image). The mass attribute describes the

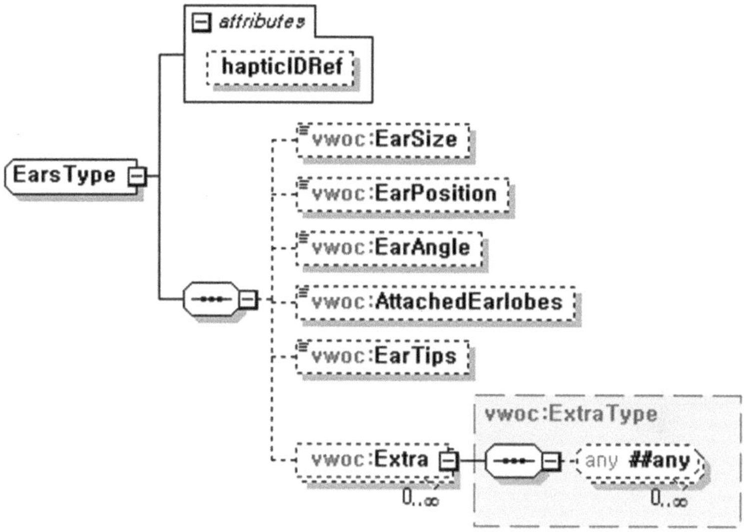

Figure 5.5 An example of a haptic property association in `EarsType`.

mass of the object. The second element, `DynamicForceEffect`, is defined by the `DynamicForceEffectType`, which has two attributes, `forceField` and `movementTrajectory`. The `forceField` attribute contains a link to a forcefield vector file (i.e., the sum of the forcefield vectors). The `movementTrajectory` attribute contains a link to a movement trajectory file (i.e., a sequence of motion data). The third element, `Tactile`, is defined by `TactileType`, which contains four attributes: `temperature`, `vibration`, `current`, and `tactilePatterns`. The `temperature` attribute describes the temperature of the object. The `vibration` attribute describes the vibration frequency of the object. The `current` attribute describes the electric current of the object. The `tactilePatterns` attribute describes a link to the tactile pattern file (e.g., grayscale video file).

5.4 VIRTUAL OBJECT METADATA

5.4.1 Introduction

Virtual object metadata characterize virtual objects inside an environment and inherit `VirtualWorldObjectBaseType`, which is also shared by the avatar metadata. `VirtualWorldObjectBaseType` does not provide any container for characterizing users because virtual objects are not used for representing users in a VE. In addition to the elements provided by its base

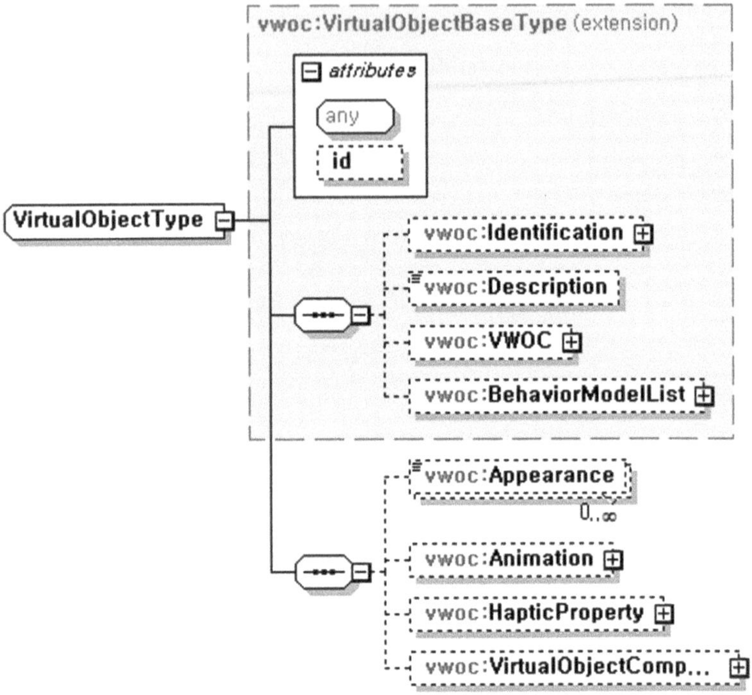

Figure 5.6 Structure of `VirtualObjectType`.

type, `VirtualWorldObjectBaseType`, the virtual object metadata also provide appearance, animation, haptic property, and virtual object components as its elements, as shown in Figure 5.6.

5.4.2 Appearance Type

The `Appearance` element provides one or more links to appearance files describing the visual and tactile elements of the virtual object through the `anyURI` type. Table 5.11 shows an example of how to provide a link using an element.

5.4.3 Animation Type

The `Animation` element provides a set of metadata including links to the resource file and its control describing the pre-recorded animations associated with a virtual object. `Animation` is defined by `VOAnimationType`, which includes three classified animation elements, `Motion`, `Deformation`, and `AdditionalAnimation`, as shown in Figure 5.7.

Table 5.11 An example instance of `VirtualObjectType` for an appearance-related resource description

```
<vwoc:VirtualObject xsi:type="vwoc:VirtualObjectType"
  id="virtualObject_001">
      <vwoc:Identification name="clothe"/>
      <vwoc:Appearance>http://db.com/clothe_001.clo</vwoc:Appearance>
</vwoc:VirtualObject>
```

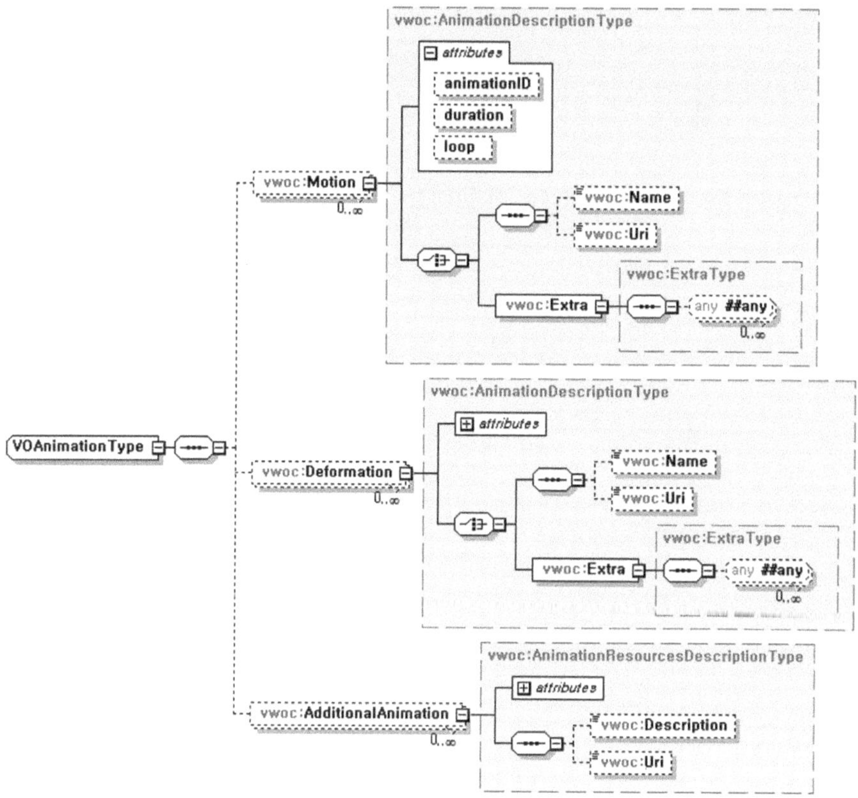

Figure 5.7 Structure of `VOAnimationType`.

The `Motion` element provides any rigid motion defined in the classification scheme, `VOMotionCS`. A list of rigid motions is shown in Table 5.12. The `Deformation` element provides a set of deformation animations defined in the classification scheme, `VODeformationCS`, a list of which is shown in Table 5.13. The `Motion` and `Deformation` elements are defined

Table 5.12 A list of rigid motions in `VOMotionCS`

Name	Description	Name	Description
moveDown	Move down	appear	Appear
moveLeft	Move left	away	Away
moveRight	Move right	disappear	Disappear
moveUp	Move up	falldown	Fall down
turn180	Turn 180	bounce	Bounce
turnback180	Turn back 180	toss	Toss
turnLeft	Turn left	spin	Spin
turnRight	Turn right	fly	Fly
turn360	Turn 360	vibrate	Vibrate
turnback360	Turn back 360	flow	Flow
freeDirection	Free direction		

Table 5.13 A list of deformation animations in `VODeformationCS`

Name	Description	Name	Description
Flip	Flip	roll	Roll
Stretch	Stretch	press	Press
Swirl	Swirl	fallToPieces	Fall to pieces
Twist	Twist	explode	Explode
Bend	Bend	fire	Fire

Table 5.14 An example instance of `VOAnimationType`

```
<vwoc:Animation>
        <vwoc:Motion animationID="TurnAnimation" duration="30" loop="1">
                <vwoc:Name> urn:mpeg:mpeg-v:01-VWOC-VOMotionCS-
NS:turn360</vwoc:Name>
                <vwoc:Uri>http://voAnimationdb.com/turn_180.bvh</vwoc:Uri>
        </vwoc:Motion>
</vwoc:Animation>
```

by `AnimationDescriptionType`, which is the same type used in defining the elements in `AvatarAnimationType`.

The third element, `additionalAnimation`, simply provides one or more links to any other types of animation not covered by the other two elements using `AnimationResourceDescriptionType`, which uses the same types of elements as `AvatarAnimationType`.

Table 5.14 shows an example of how to describe object motion animation information. Among the types of virtual object animation, a

180-degree turning animation (i.e., the motion animation category) is available for a virtual object. The animation resource is located at http://voAnimationdb.com/turn_180.bvh. The animation ID is `TurnAnimation`, the duration is 30 s, and a single loop is used.

5.4.4 Virtual-Object Components

The `VirtualObjectComponents` element is defined by `VirtualObjectListType`, which contains a list of virtual objects. Multiple virtual objects can be formed into a single virtual object. `VirtualObjectListType` supports such types of composed virtual objects, and provides a list of identified subcomponents concatenated in `VirtualObjectComponents`.

5.5 CONCLUSION

This chapter described the metadata of a virtual-world object. The common characteristics of avatars and virtual objects are defined by `VWOBaseType`, which contains resource descriptions (sound and scent resources), event descriptions, and the identification of the object. This base type is then extended into two base types for avatars and virtual objects. Because an avatar is a reflection of its user in a virtual world, the avatar type contains not only descriptions of the avatar itself but also descriptions regarding the user's preferences, such as their preferred mode of communication.

The metadata defined in this chapter can be used to import avatars and virtual objects from one virtual world into another. The characteristics in the metadata can help users start creating much faster since a virtual world may have already set up a new avatar with the same characteristics. In addition, the users may not need to learn any additional keyboard maps for controlling the effects of their avatars owing to the use of an imported behavior model that contains a list of input events, including mouse and keyboard events, and the associated output events.

REFERENCES

[1] R. McCrae, O. John, An introduction to the five-factor model and its applications, J. Pers. 2 (1992) 175–215.
[2] R. Schroeder, Virtual worlds research: past, present, & future, J. Virtual Worlds Res. (July 2008). ISSN: 1941-8477.

CHAPTER 6

Common Tools for MPEG-V and MPEG-V Reference SW with Conformance

Contents

6.1 INTRODUCTION

MPEG-V, Part 6: Common Types and Tools (ISO/IEC 23005-6) [1] specifies the syntax and semantics of the data types and tools that are common to more than one part of the MPEG-V standard. Therefore, Part 6 provides definitions of the terms, common headers for the binary representations of the MPEG-V instances, the basic data types, color-related data types, time stamp types, and classification schemes.

MPEG-V, Part 7: Conformance and Reference Software (ISO/IEC 23005-7) [2] specifies the conformance and reference software, which serves three main purposes, which are as follows:

1. validation of the written specification of several parts of MPEG-V;
2. clarification of the written specifications of several parts of MPEG-V;
3. conformance testing for checking the interoperability of various applications against reference software that aims to be compliant with MPEG-V.

MPEG-V.
DOI: http://dx.doi.org/10.1016/B978-0-12-420140-8.00006-8

The information provided is applicable for determining the reference software modules available for the different parts of MPEG-V, understanding the functionality of the available reference software modules, and utilizing the available reference software modules. The available reference software modules are specified in the form of an application programming interface (API) according to MPEG-M (ISO/IEC 23006, 1st edition, referred to as MPEG extensible middleware [MXM], and 2nd edition, referred to as multimedia service platform technologies).

Furthermore, Part 7 of MPEG-V provides the means for conformance testing, that is, the bit-streams, namely, XML descriptions, that conform or do not conform to the normative clauses of the other parts of MPEG-V or the informative descriptions thereof, including scripts for automated conformance testing.

6.2 COMMON TYPES AND TOOLS

As common types, mnemonics for binary representations, common headers for binary representations, basic data types, color-related data types, and timestamp units are defined in Part 6 of the MPEG-V standard.

6.2.1 Mnemonics for Binary Representations

Each type and element has its binary representations defined in the specifications in Parts 2–6. In the specifications of the binary representations, the encoding scheme of the data is simply noted as being a mnemonic scheme. For example, Table 6.1 shows the specifications of the binary

Table 6.1 Example specifications of a binary representation of a sensory effect

`TemperatureType {`	**Number of bits**	**Mnemonic**
`EffectBaseType`		`EffectBaseType`
`intensityValueFlag`	1	`bslbf`
`intensityRangeFlag`	1	`bslbf`
`if(intensityValueFlag) {`		
`intensityValue`	32	`fsfb`
`}`		
`if(intensityRangeFlag) {`		
`intensityRange[0]`	32	`fsfb`
`intensityRange[1]`	32	`fsfb`
`}`		
`}`		

representation for TemperatureType defined in MPEG-V, Part 3: Sensory Information [3]. In this example, the binary specifications should be interpreted as discussed further in this section. TemperatureType is composed of EffectBaseType and five other fields: intensityValueFlag, intensityRangeFlag, intensityValue, intensityRange[0], and intensityRange[1]. EffectBaseType should be encoded as specified in the EffectBaseType specifications. Both intensityValueFlag and intensityRangeFlag take 1 bit and are encoded in bslbf. If the value of intensityValueFlag is true (or 1), then 32 bits are allocated for intensityValue, and are encoded in fsfb. If the value of intensityRangeFlag is true, then 32 bits are also allocated for both intensityRange[0] and intensityRange[1]. The intensityRange[0] and intensityRange[1] fields are encoded in fsfb. Descriptions of these mnemonics, such as bslbf and fsfb, are given in Part 6 of MPEG-V, and the mnemonics are also defined in Part 3 of MPEG-7 [4].

Descriptions of the mnemonics are also given in Table 6.2.

Table 6.2 Summary of the mnemonics for binary representations [1]

Mnemonics	Description
bslbf	Bit String, Left Bit First "Left" indicates the order in which the bits are written in ISO/IEC 23005
vluimsbf5	Variable Length Unsigned Integer Most Significant Bit First The binary representation encoded in this type consists of two parts. The first part defines the number n of 4-bit fields used for the value representation, encoded by a sequence of $n-1$ "1" bits, followed by a "0" bit signaling its end. In this specific mnemonic, it should be noted that n is given as 5. The second part contains the value of the integer encoded using the number of bit fields specified in the first part
uimsbf	Unsigned Integer, Most Significant Bit First
simsbf	Signed Integer, in two's complement format, Most Significant Bit (sign) First
fsfb	Float (32 bit), Sign Bit First. The semantics of the bits within a float are specified in the IEEE Standard for Binary Floating Point Arithmetic (ANSI/IEEE Std 754-1985)
UTF-8	Binary string encoding defined in ISO 10646/IETF RFC 2279, preceded by its size in bytes coded as vluimsbf5

Table 6.3 Common header specifications [1]

HeaderInfo{	Number of bits	Mnemonic
Signature	40	bslbf
Version	16	bslbf
Reserved	14	
ProfileIdentifier	8	uimsbf
ElementIdentifier	8	bslbf
}		

6.2.2 Common Header for Binary Representations

The definitions of every type and element have their binary representations defined in Parts 2–6. When the instances of the control information, sensory information, virtual-world object characteristics, device command, or sensed information are transmitted in a binary representation, it may be confusing for the decoder to recognize the instance and decode the representation properly. To help decoders recognize an MPEG-V binary stream and identify the profile and element, common header specifications for all of the MPEG-V binary instances are defined as shown in Table 6.3.

The common `HeaderInfo` is composed of five fields: `Signature`, `Version`, `Reserved`, `ProfileIdentifier`, and `ElementIdentifier`. The 40-bit `Signature` field is assigned to signal the decoder that this is the beginning of the binary representation of the MPEG-V description. The value is fixed to 0x4D 0x50 0x45 0x47 0x56, representing the ASCII code for "MPEGV." The first 8 bits of the `Version` field are assigned to signal the version of the schema to which the root element belongs, and the last 8 bits of the `Version` field are assigned to signal the version of the schema for the common tools defined in Part 6. The next 14 bits are reserved for future use and byte alignment of the header. The 8-bit `ProfileIdentifier` field is used to identify the profile of the MPEG-V description to which the given binary stream is conformant. Currently, there is only one profile, i.e., a full profile, which is fixed at 0x01. The last field is `ElementIdentifier`, which is used to identify the 8-bit root element of the description. The assignment of the identifiers for various root elements is given in Table 6.4.

6.2.3 Basic Data and Other Common Types

In Part 6, the three data types that are commonly used in various parts or multiple types of the MPEG-V descriptions are defined as the basic

Table 6.4 Assignment of the identifiers for each root element

ElementIdentifier	Element name (Part)
0000 0000 - 0001 0011	Reserved
0001 0100	ControlInfo (Part 2)
0001 0101 - 0001 1111	Reserved
0010 0000	Declarations (Part 3)
0010 0001	GroupOfEffects (Part 3)
0010 0010	Effect (Part 3)
0010 0011	ReferenceEffect (Part 3)
0010 0100	Parameter (Part 3)
0010 0101	SEM (Part 3)
0010 0110 - 0010 0111	Reserved
0010 1000	VWOCInfo (Part 4)
0010 1001 - 0011 0001	Reserved
0011 0010	InteractionInfo (Part 5)
0011 0011	SensedInfo (Part 5)
0011 0100	DeviceCommand (Part 5)
0011 0101 - 1111 1111	Reserved

data types. `unitType` is of MPEG-7 `termReferenceType` for referencing one of the terms specified in `UnitTypeCS` given in A.2.1 of MPEG-V, Part 6. `InclineAngleType` is an integer type allowing values of between −360 and 360. Finally, `Float3DVectorType` has three float-type elements, i.e., `X`, `Y`, and `Z`, each of which denotes the value in that particular direction.

There are also six type definitions related to color representations. `colorRGBType` is defined as a sequence of six characters belonging to a specific range, such that a 24-bit RGB color can be represented by a 3 byte hexadecimal representation of the R, G, and B color component. The other color-related types are `ToneReproductionCurvesType` for the representation of a tone reproduction curve, `ConversionLUTType` for a definition of the color conversion look-up table, `IlluminantType` for the white point setting of the input display device, `InputDeviceColorGamutType` for a description of the input device color gamut, and `ChromaticityType` for a description of the chromaticity.

`TimeStampType` is defined as an abstract type, and `AbsoluteTimeType`, `ClockTickTimeType`, and `ClockTickDeltaTimeType` are the three types extending `TimeStampType`. `AbsoluteTimeType` has two attributes, `absTimeScheme` and `absTime`, and is used to specify the time using one of the absolute time schemes defined in the other standards. The absolute time scheme used can be specified in the `absTimeScheme` attribute in a text string format using the time scheme syntax specified in ISO/IEC 21000-17 [5]. The time itself can be specified in the `absTime` attribute using the format specified in the absolute time scheme given in the `absTimeScheme` attribute. By default, the `hh:mm:ss:ff` format is used, where `hh` represents hours in a 24 h scheme, `mm` represents minutes in two digits, `ss` represents seconds in two digits, and `ff` represents fractions of 1/100 s in two digits. When possible, the fraction of seconds can be omitted. `ClockTickTimeType` specifies the timing information using the number of clock ticks since the origin of the target device using the `timeScale` and `pts` attributes. The optional attribute, `timeScale`, represents the number of clock ticks per second, and the `pts` attribute represents the number of clock ticks since the origin of the target device. `ClockTickTimeDeltaType` specifies the timing information by providing the number of clock ticks since the last time in which the timing information was provided. The optional `timeScale` attribute represents the number of clock ticks per second, and the `ptsDelta` attribute represents the number of clock ticks since the time point at which the last timing information was provided.

6.3 CLASSIFICATION SCHEMES

Various classification schemes are defined in the annex of Part 6. `UnitTypeCS` currently provides 102 units for reference of various descriptions, such as specifying the unit for the values acquired by a sensor. `ColorCS` currently specifies 312 colors, which can be directly referenced from `colorType` instead of specifying the RGB values. `LocationCS` specifies a position in space using five positions in the width direction, three positions in the height direction, and three positions in the depth direction. These terms in `LocationCS` are usually referenced in the `location` attribute of `SEMBaseAttributes` and in the `locator` attribute of `SensoryDeviceCapabilityAttributes`. `ScentCS` specifies 640 different kinds of scents. `ShakeDirectionCS` specifies heaving, swaying, and surging as its terms, and `SpinDirectionCS` specifies six spin directions based on the forward and backward movements in the *X*, *Y*, and *Z* directions. Currently, only water is defined in `SprayingTypeCS`. `TactileEffectCS` has three effects: vibration, temperature, and pressure. `WaveDirectionCS` specifies only two directions, left–right and front–rear. `WaveStartDirectionCS` also specifies only two directions, i.e., up and down. `TactileDisplayCS` specifies vibro-tactile, electro-tactile, pneumatic-tactile, piezoelectric-tactile, and thermal-type displays. `HeadBonesCS` specifies 14 bones located in the head, UpperBodyBonesCS specifies 51 bones located in the upper body, DownBodyBonesCS specifies 15 bones located in the lower body, and MiddleBodyBonesCS specifies 18 bones located in the middle of the body. OdorSensorTechnologyCS currently defines five technologies, and CameraFilterTypeCS specifies five types of filters.

6.4 BINARY REPRESENTATIONS

In each part of the standard, binary representations of the descriptions are specified. The binary representations are defined for each type and are based on the following five rules.

Rule 1: Use of the defined types—For each data type, a binary representation is defined. If a data type is based on an existing data type, then the binary data are defined by referring to the defined data type.

Rule 2: Treatment of the string type variables—The string type variables are binarized using UTF-8 encoding.

Rule 3: Treatment of the optional attributes and elements—For each optional attribute and element, a flag is defined to signal the instantiation of a specific optional attribute or element. If a flag is set, then the binary representation of the corresponding attribute or element is provided.

Rule 4: Treatment of the recurring elements—A field is added to specify the number of recurring elements, and repeat these elements the corresponding number of times.

Rule 5: Treatment of enumeration and classification schemes—Create a mapping table using binary indices, and replace the terms with the corresponding indices.

As an example, the binary representation of ScentCapabilityType shown in Table 6.5 is given in Table 6.6.

As shown in Table 6.5, there is one optional element, Scent, and three optional attributes, maxIntensity, unit, and numOfLevels. Therefore, there are four flags, i.e., ScentFlag, maxIntensityFlag, unitFlag, and numOfLevelsFlag, defined in the binary syntax, as shown in Table 6.6. If any of these flags are set, then the corresponding element or attribute should appear in the binary representation. In addition, because the Scent element can appear an indefinite number of times, the LoopScent field is introduced to signal the number of recurrences of the Scent element. Using a for-loop construct, the Scent element is repeated LoopScent times. Note that, as SensoryDeviceCapabilityBaseType is defined elsewhere,

Table 6.5 Schema of ScentCapabilityType

```
<!-- ################################################ -->
<!--  Scent capability type                                 -->
<!-- ################################################ -->
<complexType name="ScentCapabilityType">
  <complexContent>
      <extension base="cidl:SensoryDeviceCapabilityBaseType">
            <sequence>
                  <element name="Scent"
  type="mpeg7:termReferenceType" minOccurs="0"
                        maxOccurs="unbounded"/>
            </sequence>
            <attribute name="maxIntensity"
  type="nonNegativeInteger"
                        use="optional"/>
            <attribute name="unit" type="mpegvct:unitType"
  use="optional"/>
            <attribute name="numOfLevels"
  type="nonNegativeInteger"
                        use="optional"/>
      </extension>
  </complexContent>
</complexType>
```

Table 6.6 Binary syntax of ScentCapabilityType

ScentCapabilityType {	**Number of bits**	**Mnemonic**
ScentFlag	1	bslbf
maxIntensityFlag	1	bslbf
unitFlag	1	bslbf
numOfLevelsFlag	1	bslbf
SensoryDeviceCapabilityBase		SensoryDeviceCapabilityBaseType
if(ScentFlag){		
LoopScent		vluimsbf5
for(k = 0;k < LoopScent;k++){		
Scent[k]	8	blsbf
}		
}		
if(maxIntensityFlag){		
maxIntensity	16	uimsbf
}		
if(unitFlag){		
unit	8	bslbf
}		
if(numOfLevelsFlag){		
numOfLevels	16	uimsbf
}		
}		

Table 6.7 Overview of MPEG-V reference software

Name	Definition
`Org`	Java package name for reference software provided by organizations such as ISO/IEC, W3C, or a similar group
`org.iso`	Java package name for reference software provided by ISO/IEC
`org.iso.mpeg`	Java package name for reference software provided by ISO/IEC JTC 1/SC 29/WG 11
`org.iso.mpeg.mpegv`	Java package name for reference software provided in the course of the development of MPEG-V. Subsequent packages for the individual MPEG-V parts use non-capitalized abbreviations as defined in the standard, e.g., org.iso.mpeg.mpegv.cidl for MPEG-V, Part 2; org.iso.mpeg.mpegv.sedl and org.iso.mpeg.mpegv.sev for MPEG-V, Part 3; org.iso.mpeg.mpegv.vwoc for MPEG-V, Part 4; or org.iso.mpeg.mpegv.iidl for MPEG-V, Part 5
`org.iso.mpeg.mxm`	Java package name for reference software provided in the course of the development of MPEG-M. The actual API is defined within this package

and `ScentCapabilityType` extends `SensoryDeviceCapabilityBaseType`, the `ScentCapabilityBase` field of `SensoryDeviceCapabilityBaseType` is introduced in the binary representation to make room for the inherited attributes and elements from `SensoryDeviceCapabilityBaseType`.

6.5 REFERENCE SOFTWARE

The reference software of MPEG-V defines an API compliant with MPEG-M (ISO/IEC 23006), enabling the means for the creation of and access to normative description formats defined in several parts of MPEG-V. Therefore, for each part of MPEG-V, an engine and different interfaces providing the aforementioned functionality are defined. An actual implementation of the engine and these interfaces is also provided. An overview of the MPEG-V reference software is shown in Table 6.7.

6.5.1 Reference Software Based on JAXB

The reference software is developed based on the Java Architecture for XML Binding (JAXB), which can make it easier to access XML documents from applications written in the Java programming language.

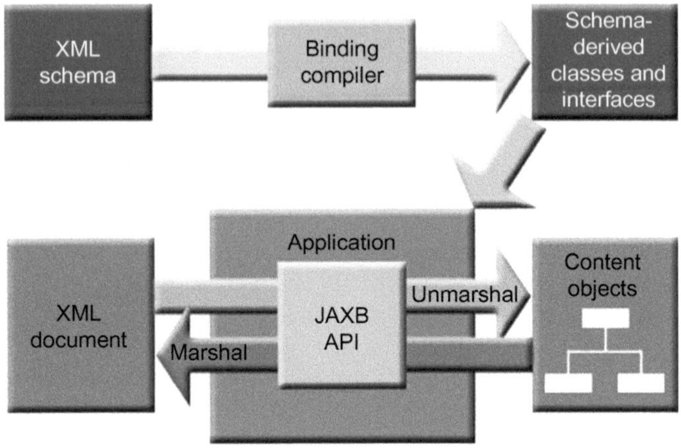

Figure 6.1 Java architecture for XML binding.

The first step in this process is to bind the schema for an XML document into a set of Java classes that represents the schema. Binding the schema means generating a set of Java classes that represents the schema. All JAXB implementations provide a tool called a binding compiler to bind the schema (the method for binding the compiler invoked can be implementation-spccific).

JAXB conducts the unmarshaling and marshaling (Figure 6.1). Unmarshaling an XML document means creating a tree of content objects that represents the content and organization of the document. The content tree is not a DOM-based tree. In fact, content trees produced through JAXB can be more efficient in terms of memory use than DOM-based trees. Marshaling is the opposite of unmarshaling. It creates an XML document from a content tree. Figures 6.2–6.5 depict the structure of the reference software and its main modules.

- **Creator**: Using the unmarshaling and marshaling modules, the creator generates MPEG-V XML instances (Figure 6.3).
- **Parser**: Using the unmarshaling module, the parser extracts the XML information (e.g., sensory information, sensed information, capability information, preference information, actuation command information, and virtual object information) and shows the description on the display device (Figure 6.4).
- **Modifier**: Using the unmarshaling and marshaling modules, the modifier creates an MPEG-V schema-valid XML instance based on the changed description objects (Figure 6.5).

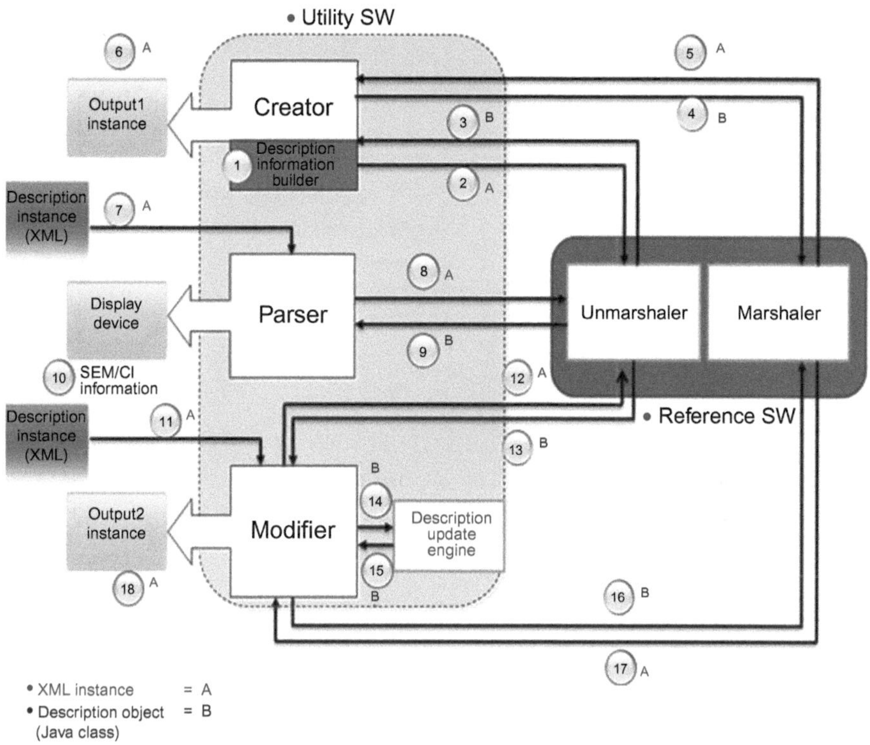

Figure 6.2 Diagram of the system structure.

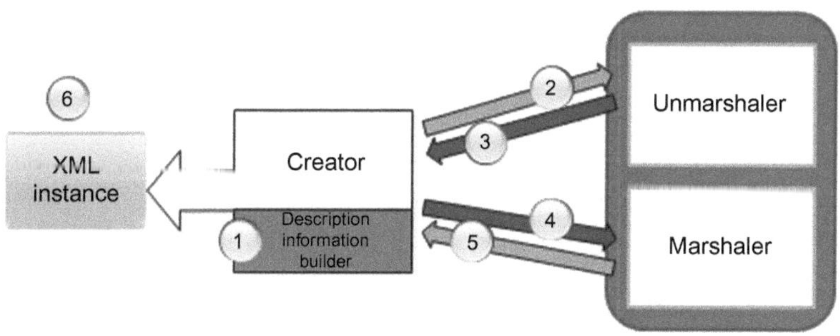

Figure 6.3 XML instance creation module.

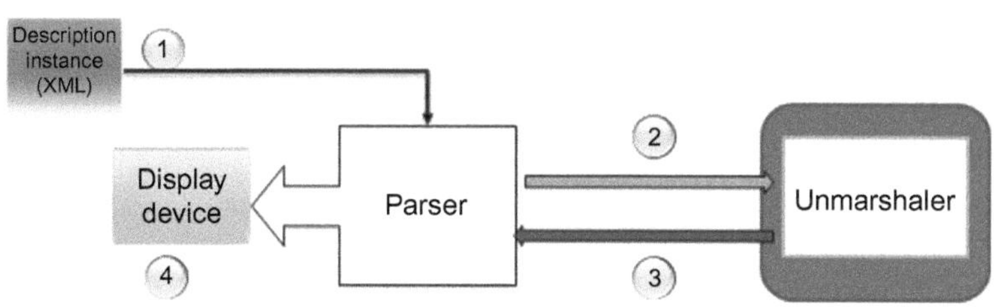

Figure 6.4 XML parser module.

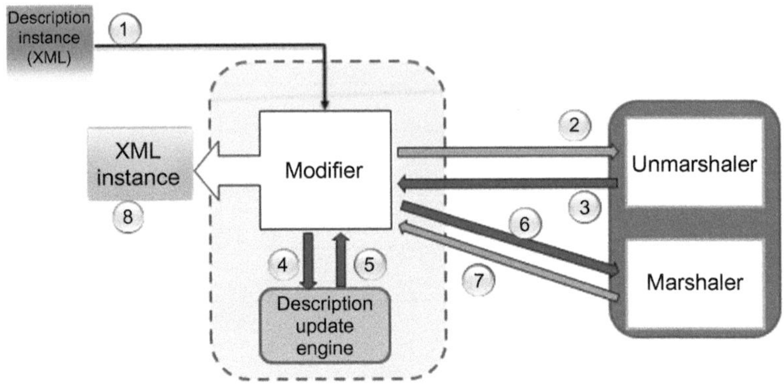

Figure 6.5 XML modifier module for a description instance.

6.5.2 Reference Software for Binary Representation

This clause specifies the API to the ISO/IEC 23005 reference software for a binary representation. The API is defined in Java, and follows the following package structure:

Name	Definition
`org.iso.mpeg.mpegv.binary.core`	Java package name for the API of the ISO/IEC 23005 reference software for a binary representation

The BinaryIO interface defines the methods used for operating over data structures defined within ISO/IEC 23005. Classes implementing the BinaryIO interface act as factories, creating instances of classes performing the following functionalities:

- Classes used to generate a binary structure from an MXM object tree, by means of the construct binary structure function.
- Classes used to generate a binary file from a binary structure, by means of the write binary function.
- Classes used to generate a binary structure from another binary structure, by means of the read binary function.
- Classes used to restore an MXM object tree from a binary structure, by means of the create MXM object function.

The DefaultBinaryIO class defines the "Encode" and "Decode" functions. The root elements of the other parts (e.g., Parts 2, 3, and 4) can be extended from this DefaultBinaryIO class. DefaultBinaryIO involves the following functions:

- Encode, i.e., a function defining the methods used to create a binary file from an MXM object tree;
- Decode, i.e., a function defining the methods used to restore an MXM object tree from a binary file.

6.6 CONFORMANCE TEST

Conformance to MPEG-V is defined as the schema and rule validity. The former requires checking whether a bit-stream is valid against its schema (in the sense of XML validity), and the latter defines a validation schema based on a Schematron (ISO/IEC 19747-3). The validation schema based on a Schematron implements additional validation rules as specified in several parts of MPEG-V, and allows for additional conformance testing that is not possible through XML validity checking. Therefore, this standard defines the actual validation schema, as well as a more readable version of the rules and assertion messages. Table 6.8 shows an example of

Table 6.8 Validation schema based on a Schematron for GroupOfEffects

```
<pattern name="GroupOfEffects elements">
   <!-- R2.*: Check the conformance of GroupOfEffects -->
   <rule context="sedl:GroupOfEffects">
     <!-- R2.0 -->
     <assert test="if ( not(parent::sedl:Declarations) and not
  (@si:pts or @si:ptsDelta or @si:absTime) ) then false() else
  true()">
       A GroupOfEffects outside of a Declarations shall have a
  timestamp (i.e., pts, ptsDelta, or absTime).
     </assert>
     <!-- R2.1 -->
     <assert test="if ( not(parent::sedl:Declarations) and
  (@si:pts and @si:absTime) ) then false() else true()">
       A GroupOfEffects outside of a Declarations shall not have
  both a pts and an absTime at the same time.
     </assert>
     <!-- R2.2 -->
     <assert test="if ( parent::sedl:Declarations and (@si:pts or
  @si:absTime) ) then false() else true()">
       A GroupOfEffects within a Declarations shall have only a
  ptsDelta for a timestamp.
     </assert>
   </rule>
</pattern>
```

the validation rules and their schema based on a Schematron, and provides a more readable version of the rules and assertion messages (e.g., description of the rules). Finally, the actual conformance bit-streams, i.e., XML descriptions, are provided along with a description of the conformance testing process.

Description for `GroupOfEffects`:

No.	Rule	Description
R2.0	if (not(parent::sedl:Declarations) and not(@si:pts or @si:ptsDelta or @si:absTime)) then false(); else, true()	A GroupOfEffects outside of a Declarations shall have a timestamp (i.e., pts, ptsDelta, or absTime).
R2.1	if (not(parent::sedl:Declarations) and (@si:pts and @si:absTime)) then false(); else, true()	A GroupOfEffects outside of a Declarations shall not have both a pts and an absTime at the same time.
R2.2	if (parent::sedl:Declarations and ((@si:pts or @si:absTime)) then false(); else, true()	A GroupOfEffects within a Declarations shall have only a ptsDelta for a timestamp.

6.7 CONCLUSION

Part 6 of MPEG-V is defined to provide tools common to other parts, or not belonging to a specific part, of the standard. For example, the common header syntax for binary representations and the basic data types are defined in Part 6, as are various types of classification schemes. Therefore, Part 6 should accompany any reading of the MPEG-V standard.

Part 7 provides reference software and conformance rules. By providing reference software, the MPEG-V standard provides every developer interested in MPEG-V a chance to easily start the development of relevant software. Part 7 also provides conformance rules using the Schematron technology. When utilizing the Schematron tools, the specific rules that cannot be forced using only an XML schema can also be enforced throughout the use of the MPEG-V standard.

REFERENCES

[1] ISO/IEC 23005-6:2013 Information technology—Media context and control—Part 6: Common types and tools.
[2] ISO/IEC 23005-7:2014 Information technology—Media context and control—Part 7: Conformance and reference software.

[3] ISO/IEC 23005-3:2013 Information technology—Media context and control—Part 3: Sensory Information.
[4] ISO/IEC 15938-3:2002 Information technology—Multimedia content description interface—Part 3: Visual.
[5] ISO/IEC 21000-17:2006 Information technology—Multimedia framework (MPEG-21)—Part 17: Fragment identification of MPEG resources.

CHAPTER 7

Applications of MPEG-V Standard

Contents

7.1 INTRODUCTION

The system architecture of MPEG-V can be used to serve different types of media exchanges. There are two types of media exchanges occurring between the real world (RW) and virtual worlds (VWs), i.e., real-to-virtual (R2V) world information adaptation, and virtual-to-real world information adaptation. Another type of media exchange is an information exchange between VWs. In this chapter, the potential applications for these three types of media exchanges are introduced. More detailed applications and their instantiations were introduced in MPEG-V, Part 1: Architecture [1].

7.2 INFORMATION ADAPTATION FROM VW TO RW

7.2.1 System Architecture

The overall system architecture for a virtual-to-real world information adaptation is depicted in Figure 7.1, which presents V→R adaptation comprising the sensory effects metadata, VW object characteristics, sensory

MPEG-V.
DOI: http://dx.doi.org/10.1016/B978-0-12-420140-8.00007-X

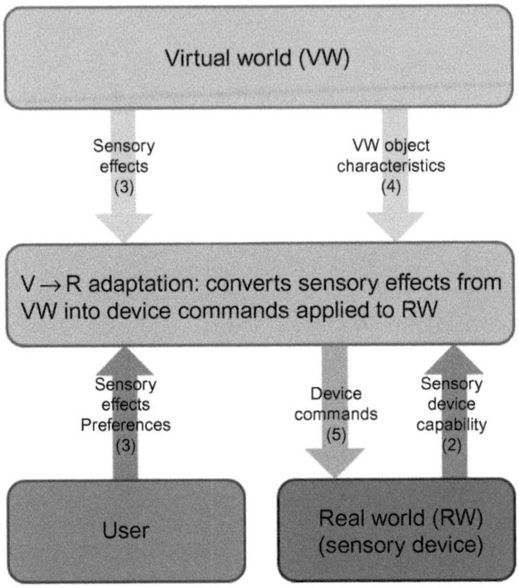

Figure 7.1 (Possible) system architecture for information adaptation from a virtual world into a real world.

device capability (actuator capability), device commands, sensory effects preferences, and a V→R adaptation engine, which generates output data based on the input data.

It is important to note that the sensory effects metadata, sensory device capability, device commands, sensory effects preferences, and VW object characteristics are within the scope of the standardization, and thus are normatively specified. On the other hand, the V→R adaptation engine, VW, and sensory devices (actuators) are informative, and have been left open for industry competition.

A VW within this framework is referred to as an entity acting as the source of the sensory effects metadata and VW object characteristics, such as a broadcaster, content creator/distributor, or even a service provider. The V→R adaptation engine is an entity that takes the sensory effects metadata, the sensory device (actuator) capability, and the sensory effects preferences as inputs and generates the device commands based on them for consumer device control, providing a worthwhile and informative experience to the user.

RW devices (sensory devices) are entities that act as a sink for the device commands, and as a source of sensory device (actuator) capability. Additionally, entities that provide preferences of sensory effects toward the

RoSE engine [1] are also collectively referred to as RW devices. Note that sensory devices (actuators) are a sub-set of RW devices including fans, lights, scent devices, and human-input devices such as a TV set with a remote control (e.g., for user preferences).

The actual sensory effects metadata provide the means for representing so-called sensory effects, i.e., effects augmenting a particular feeling by stimulating the human sensory organs during a particular scene of a multimedia application. Examples of sensory effects include scent, wind, and lighting. The means for transporting such kind of metadata is referred to as the sensory effect delivery format, which can be combined with an audio/visual (AV) delivery format, e.g., an MPEG-2 transport stream, a file format, or a Real-time Transport Protocol (RTP) payload format.

Sensory device capability defines the description formats used to represent the characteristics of sensory devices (actuators) in terms of which sensory effects they are capable to perform and in what manner. A sensory device (actuator) is a consumer device by which the corresponding sensory effect can be generated (e.g., lights, fan, heater, etc.). Device commands are used to control the sensory devices (actuators). For the sensory effects metadata, as well as for the sensory device (actuator) capability and device commands, the corresponding means for transporting such assets are referred to as the sensory device capability and command delivery format, respectively.

Finally, the preferences for different sensory effects that allow for describing the preferences of actual (end) users with respect to the rendering of sensory effects, as well as to the delivery format, are provided.

7.2.2 Instantiation A: 4D Broadcasting/Theater [2]

Advances in media technologies have brought about the so-called 4D movie experience to our neighborhood theaters. 4D movies represent movies (preferably in 3D) with additional sensory effects, such as motion chairs and wind effects. The key technologies of the 4D broadcasting framework required to provide sensory effects through a home theater consisting of creating sensory effects synchronized with AV content, delivering the sensory effects along with the content to the home theater devices, recognizing the home devices for rendering the sensory effects, and rendering the content through a home theater system using sensory devices connected in a synchronized manner.

In the framework for a 4D broadcast, as shown in Figure 7.2, in the first step, the author or creator creates sensorial effect data for a given AV content using MPEG-V, Part 3: Sensory Information [3].

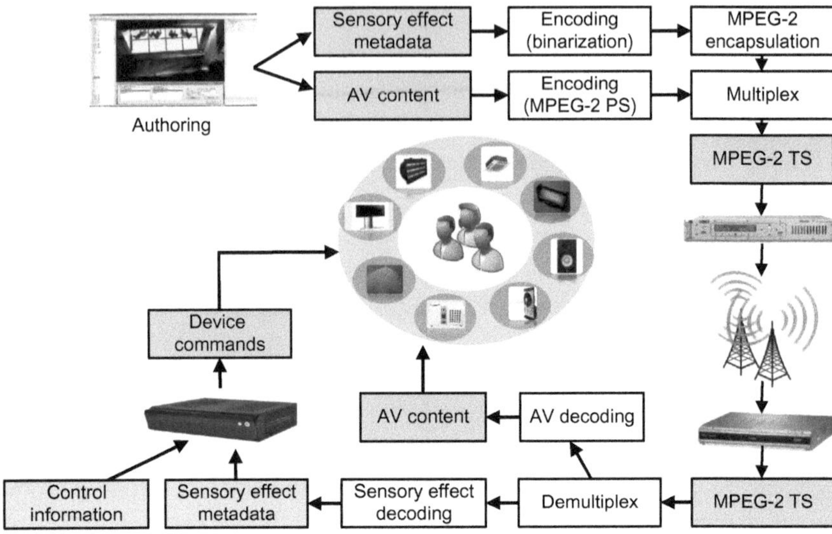

Figure 7.2 4D broadcast framework.

The authored sensorial effect data are then binarized as defined in MPEG-V, Part 3. The binarized sensorial effect data are then encapsulated into an MPEG-2 file and multiplexed with the AV content to form an MPEG-2 Transport Stream. The multiplexed MPEG-2 Transport Stream is then modulated and sent through the broadcast network. The receiver receives the stream and demultiplexes the stream to extract the binarized sensorial effect data. The extracted sensorial effect data are then decoded. The adaptor scans the user environment to configure the available actuators, and generates actuator commands for the actuators available, possibly by considering the user's actuation preferences. These actuator capabilities and user preferences are defined in MPEG-V, Part 2: Control Information [4]. The adapter acquires the sensed information from the environment sensors, as defined in MPEG-V, Part 5: Data Formats for Interaction Devices [5]. The generated (and adapted) actuator commands, as defined in MPEG-V, Part 5 are delivered to the appropriate devices to render the sensory effects for the users (Figure 7.3).

7.2.3 Instantiation B: Haptic Interaction [6]

For many years, holograms have been largely seen in sci-fi movies and TV shows such as *Star Wars* and *Star Trek*. The display setup shown in these

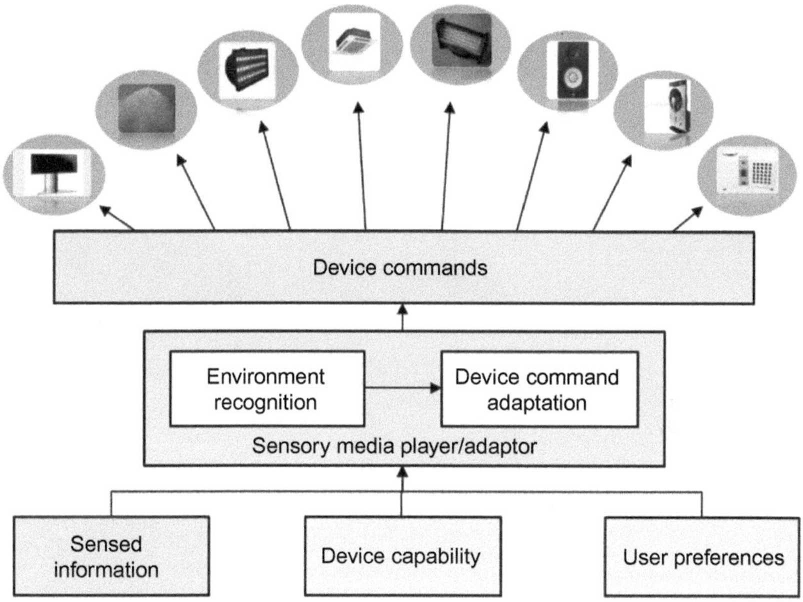

Figure 7.3 Adaptation to the environment.

sci-fi movies allows a person to view a hologram at multiple angles, but there is a limitation in terms of tactile interaction.

Many recent studies have focused on improving the quality of interaction between users and holograms. HoloDesk [7] demonstrates a rich emergent 3D interaction allowing users to interact directly with 3D graphics. Furthermore, the addition of touch capability is required to move to this next level of realism. Haptic feedback permits direct contact with virtual objects and provides the perception of attributes such as weight, texture, and volume. For realistic tactile feedback in a virtual object manipulation, Holo-haptics [6] was introduced. Holo-haptics supports intuitive 3D positioning and direct manipulation with haptic feedback, as shown in Figure 7.4. To generate haptic feedback, a thimble-formed pneumatic balloon display is used to generate the tactile sensation of contact, direction, and movement.

For interactive haptic sensible media, the sensors include position, velocity, acceleration, orientation, angular velocity, force, torque, and pressure sensors. The actuators used for this instantiation include haptic sensory effects such as rigid body motion, tactile, and kinesthetic effects. More detailed use case scenarios with haptic information are presented in

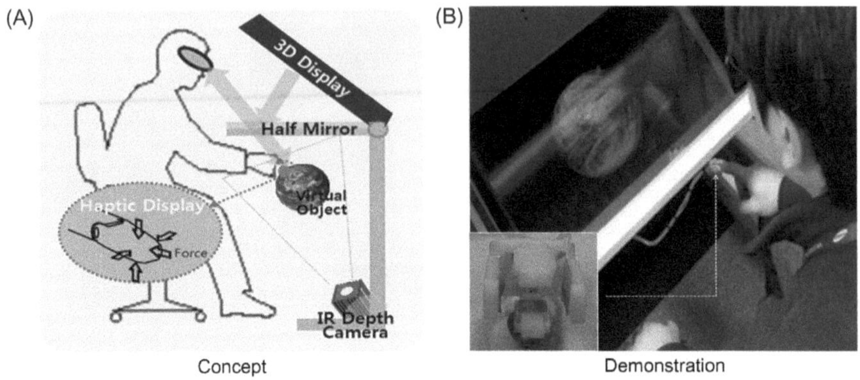

Figure 7.4 Haptic interaction with a see-through 3D display (Holo-haptics).

MPEG-V, Part 1: Architecture [1] to describe how haptic contents can be applied in an MPEG-V system through kinesthetic and tactile devices.

7.3 INFORMATION ADAPTATION FROM THE RW INTO A VW

7.3.1 System Architecture

The system architecture used for an information adaptation from the RW into a VW is shown in Figure 7.5, which represents R2V adaptation comprising VW object characteristics, sensed information, sensor capability, sensor adaptation preferences, and an R→V adaptation engine, which generates output data based on the input data.

It is important to note that the VW object characteristics, sensed information, sensor capabilities, and, sensor adaptation preferences are within the scope of standardization, and shall thus be normatively specified. On the other hand, the R→V adaptation engines, VWs, and sensors are informative and are left open for industry competition.

An entity that processes the sensed information from the RW for consumption within the context of a VW takes the sensed information with/without the sensor capabilities from sensors, the sensor adaptation preferences from the users, and/or the VW object characteristics from the VW; and controls the VW object characteristics or adapts the sensed information by adapting it based on the sensor capabilities and/or the sensor adaptation preferences.

There are two possible implementations used to adapt information from the RW into a VW. In the first system implementation, R→V adaptation takes the sensor capabilities as inputs, the sensed information from the sensors, and the sensor adaptation preferences from the users; and

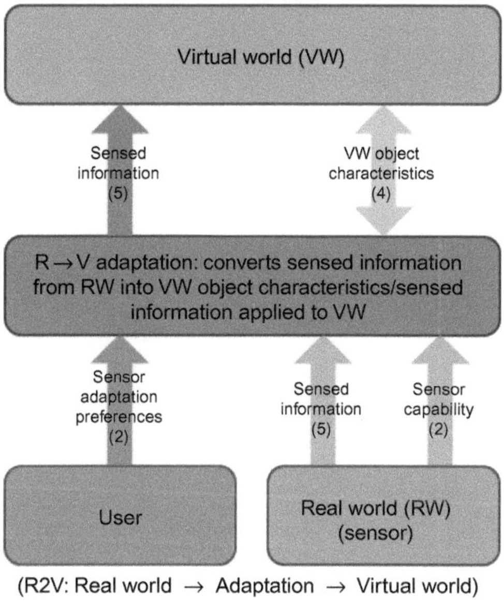

Figure 7.5 (Possible) system architecture for information adaptation from the real world into a virtual world.

adapts the sensed information based on the sensor capabilities and/or sensor adaptation preferences.

In the second system implementation, R→V adaptation takes the sensed information with/without the sensor capabilities from the sensors, the sensor adaptation preferences from the users, and/or the VW object characteristics from the VW; and controls the virtual-world object characteristics by adapting the sensed information based on the sensor capabilities and/or the sensor adaptation preferences.

7.3.2 Instantiation C: Full Motion Control and Navigation of Avatar or Object With Multi-Input Sources [8]

Full motion control and navigation of an avatar or object using multi-input sources allows for full motion control and navigation within a VW. Based on large volumes of recent research, user interest in human–computer interaction has grown considerably. Through the development of VR technology, such interaction has been applied to various fields. In particular, the entertainment area has commercialized such interactions through 3D virtual online communities such as *Second Life* and 3D game stations. A graspable user interface offers an elegant solution to the problems of manipulating 3D objects and moving avatars within a virtual environment. By simply grasping a handheld device, the user can

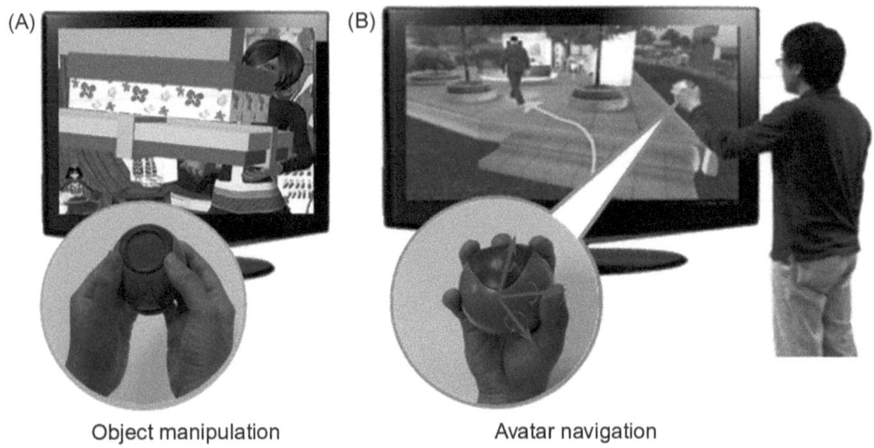

Figure 7.6 Applications of Grip-Ball.

pick up a virtual object, rotate it, move it around, and even deform it, all without the need for arbitrary key strokes. As illustrated in Figure 7.6, Grip-Ball [8], which is a spherical multimodal interface, enables the intuitive manipulation of 3D virtual objects and the direct navigation of avatars within VWs. It is a spherical input device based upon capacitive multitouch sensing and three-axis motion tracking.

The Grip-Ball system comprises two major subsystems, as shown in Figure 7.7, one for touch sensing and the other for motion sensing. The main components of the capacitive touch-sensing subsystem are the sensing means, the measurement circuit, and the signal-processing algorithm. The sensing means comprise a set of electrodes and a panel upon which electrodes are arranged. The measurement circuit converts the measured capacitance into voltage or current values. The signal-processing algorithm maps these values to the position, area, and other factors to be used by the user interface application. Determining a single-touch area may require reading measurements from multiple electrodes depending on the sensing architecture. The main components of the motion-sensing subsystem are the ultrasonic receiver and transmitter, and the inertial sensors (accelerometers and gyroscopes). Together, these components provide accurate and reliable 3D position and orientation data on the Grip-Ball. The resulting six degrees-of-freedom (6 DOF) motion data are transmitted to the main VR system (not shown in the figure) through a wireless Bluetooth network.

As shown in Figure 7.8A, Grip-Ball can sense the grip on its surface and recognize the grip patterns. The classification of these patterns is based

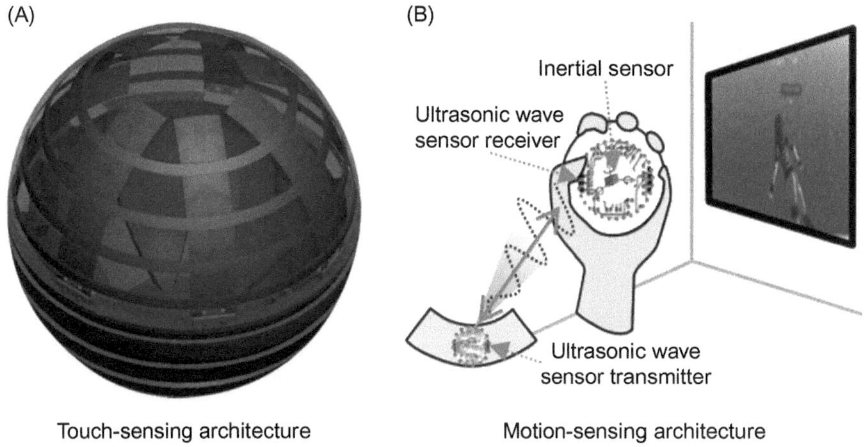

Figure 7.7 System architecture for Grip-Ball.

on Cutkosky's grasp taxonomy, which separates grasps according to their purpose (power-grip or precise-grip) and object size, and thereby distinguishes most of the grasps required for manufacturing tasks. The control of avatars and cameras in a 3D virtual space requires more complex methods than conventional input devices such as a mouse, keyboard, or joystick can provide. As illustrated in Figure 7.8B, the Grip-Ball system detects the position and orientation of the user's hand and triggers the avatar and/or camera motion accordingly.

7.3.3 Instantiation D: Facial Expressions and Body Gestures [9,10]

A life-scale VW presentation and the intuitive interaction between users and VWs will provide a more natural and immersive experience for users. The strong connection between the RW and a VW will also provide an immersive experience to users. Such a connection can be provided using a large-scale display where the objects in the VW are represented at life-scale of the RW, and by natural interactions using facial expressions and body motions of the users when controlling their avatar, which is their representation or alter ego within a VW. Recently, Microsoft announced its Project Natal, which is known to sense the full-body motion of users using a 3D-sensing camera. Through the sensing of their full-body motion, the users can control a character within a game using their own body movements. The project is expected to develop even more precise facial expression and motion-sensing technologies. VW services adapting

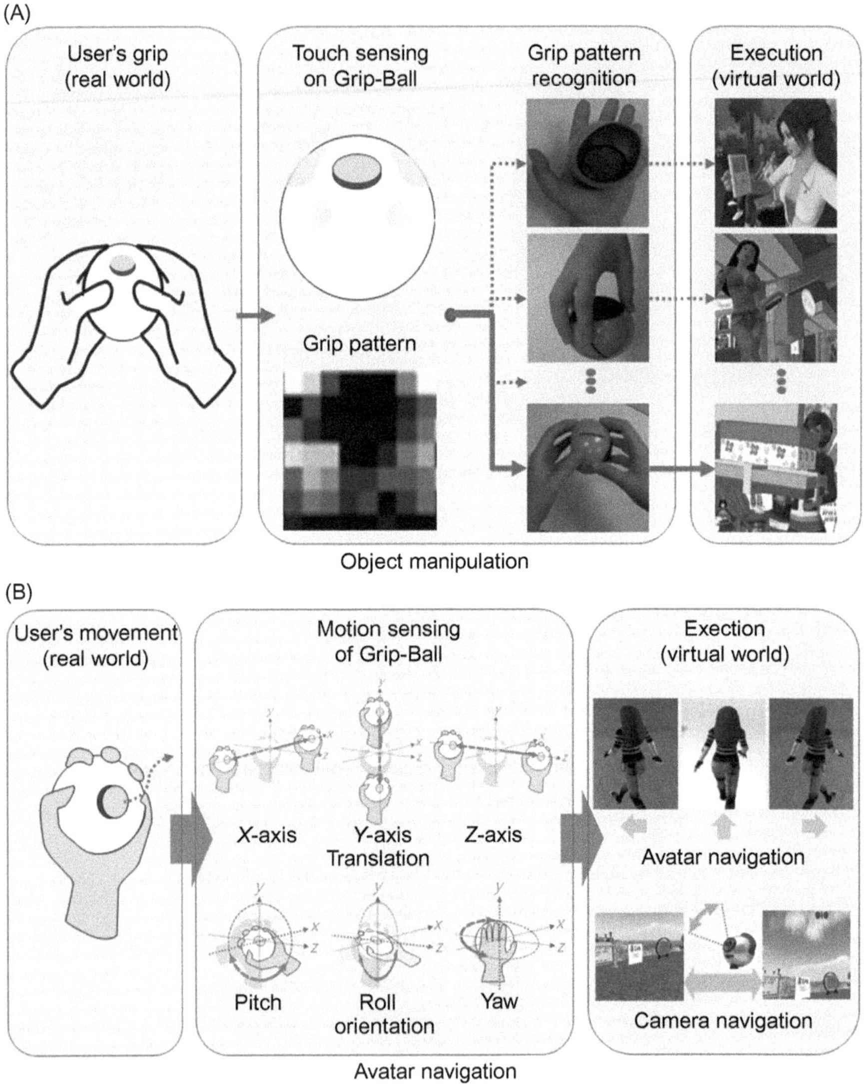

Figure 7.8 Grip-Ball procedure.

such precise and natural interaction technologies will be able to provide various types of experience, such as virtual tours, which will enable users to travel back in time to a virtual version of ancient Rome, or embark on a simulated astrophysical space exploration, providing them the experience of walking or flying within an enormous space.

MPEG-V R2V supports interaction and control information from interaction devices for the purpose of controlling one or more entities within a VW. In particular, control of the body motions and facial expressions of an avatar within a VW is being considered. Avatar motions can be generated by either pre-recorded animation clips or through a direct manipulation using a motion-capturing device. Figure 7.9 shows an example of a facial expression- and body-tracking application using an intelligent camera. The intelligent camera detects/tracks the feature points of both the face and body, and then analyzes the time series of the detected feature points to recognize the body gestures and/or facial expressions. The detected feature points of the user in the RW provide the user's body motion and facial expression information. To control the motion of the avatar using such information, the avatar should also have similar feature points for proper rendering. As a simplest case, the sensed feature points of the user and the feature points of the avatar will be identical. Therefore, the description of the avatar should provide the feature points for both its body and the face. To support the direct manipulation of an avatar, VW object characteristics contain animation and control-feature elements for the avatar characteristics. The animation element contains a description of the animation resources, and the control-feature element contains a set of descriptions for body and facial control of the avatar. To efficiently render RW effects in a VW, MPEG-V R2V also provides the architecture to capture and understand the current status of the RW environment. For example, a VW acquires the sensed temperature or light level of a room in the RW based on the sensed information, and renders the same effect in the VW.

7.3.4 Instantiation E: Seamless Interaction Between RW and VWs [11]

VWs can be controlled using information sensed from RW sensors. The sensed information (e.g., temperature, humidity, light intensity, gas intensity) obtained from a user's vicinity plays an important role in the generation of environmental changes, the main character's reactions, and storyline changes within a VW. In [11], a method for transforming sensed information from the RW into standardized XML instances and to control VW objects was proposed. Figure 7.10 shows the overall architecture of the VW control system using the sensed information from RW sensors. The sensed information from the RW is transformed into XML instances standardized by the schemes in MPEG-V, Part 5 [5], and then delivered to

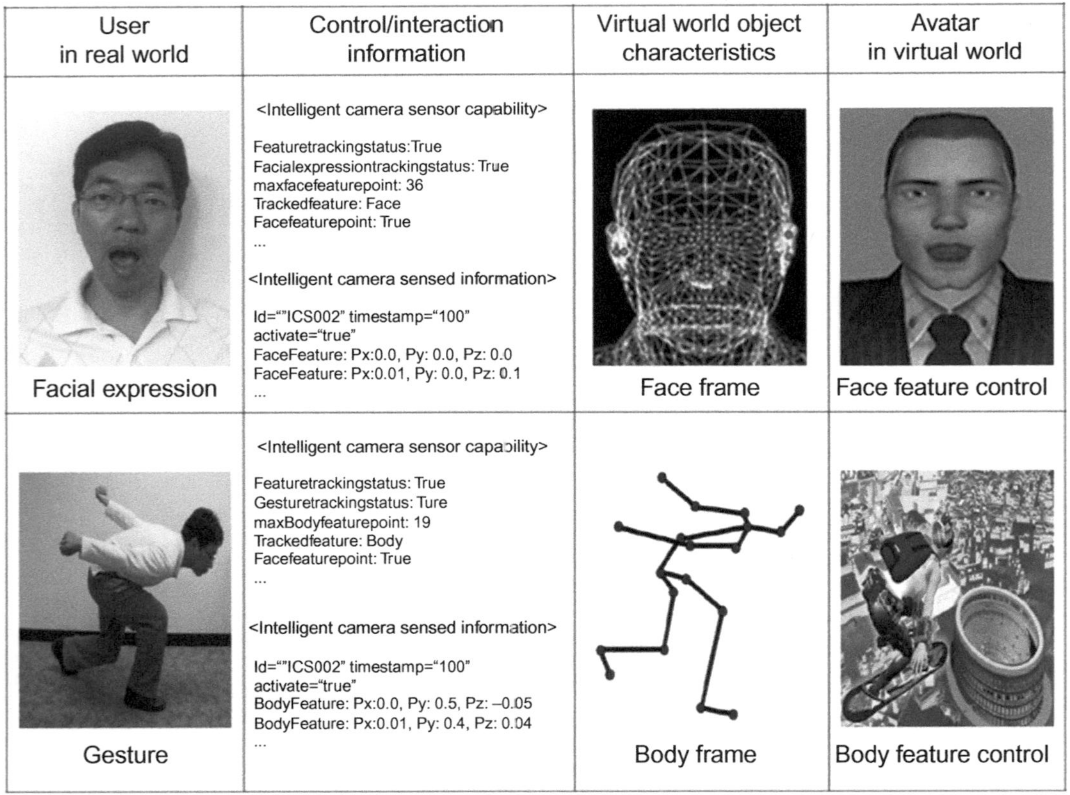

Figure 7.9 Use scenario with an intelligent camera.

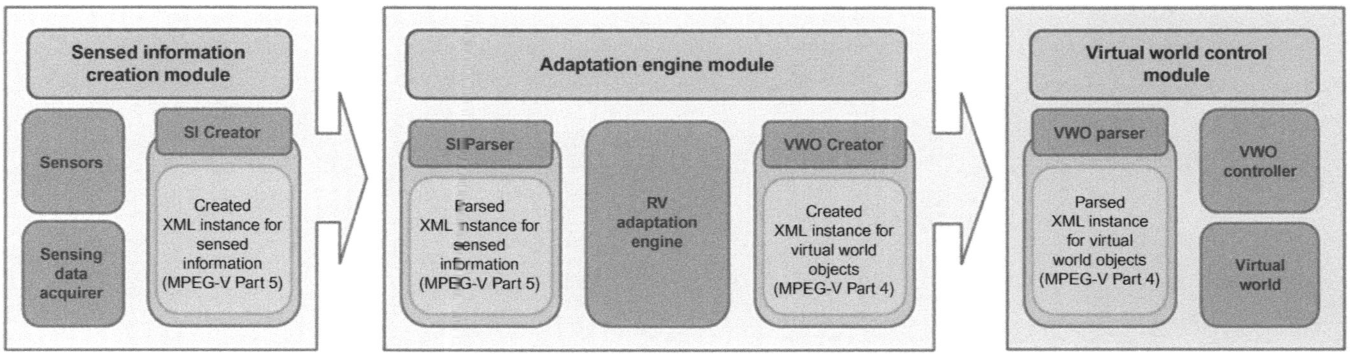

Figure 7.10 Architecture of a virtual-world control system.

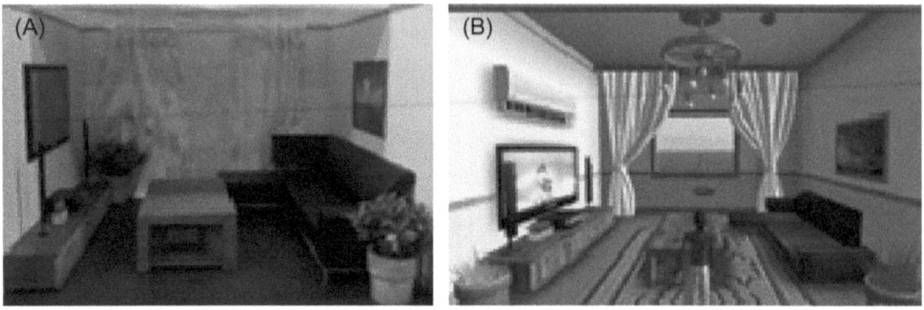

Figure 7.11 A real-world environment mock-up w/sensors (A), and its virtual world implementation (B).

a R2V adaptation engine (Sensed Information Creation Model described in Figure 7.10). The engine generates another XML instance standardized by MPEG-V, Part 4: Virtual World Object Characteristics [12], which describes the control information of avatars and objects within a VW (Adaptation Engine Module described in Figure 7.10). Finally, the Virtual World Control Module parses the standardized descriptions of the control information from the Adaptation Engine Module and converts them into proprietary control commands of the target VW.

Figure 7.11 shows a RW mock-up equipped with a set of sensors (e.g., light, temperature, humidity, noise, and vibration sensors), and a virtual space such as that found in *Second Life*. The virtual avatar and objects react based upon the values from the sensors of the RW mock-up. For example, when the value from a light sensor is greater than or equal to 150 lux, the lamp in the VW is switched off. Otherwise, it is switched on. When the decibel level from an ambient noise sensor is larger than 35 dB, the background music within the VW is turned on. Otherwise, it is turned off. When the value from the vibration sensor (e.g., a one-axis accelerometer) is greater than 200, a siren within the VW begins flickering.

7.4 INFORMATION EXCHANGE BETWEEN VWs

7.4.1 System Architecture

The system architecture for information exchanges between VWs is shown in Figure 7.12. This architecture represents an information exchange comprising VW Object Characteristics, which generate exchangeable information within a VW.

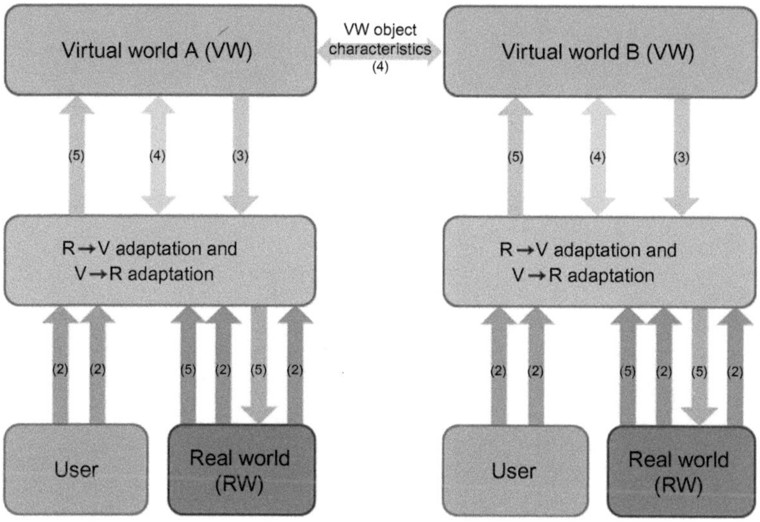

Figure 7.12 (Possible) system architecture for (bidirectional) exchange of information between virtual worlds.

It is important to note that the VW Object Characteristics are within the scope of standardization, and thus are normatively specified. On the other hand, VWs are informative and are left open for competition by the industry.

V→V adaptation adapts proprietary VW object characteristics from a VW into VW Object Characteristics, and sends the VW Object Characteristics from one VW to another for interoperability support. Based on the data provided in the Virtual World Object Characteristics, the Virtual World will internally adapt its own representation for a virtual object or avatar.

7.4.2 Instantiation F: Interoperable VW [13]

To support interoperability between VWs, a common schema is needed to establish the possible mapping or transfer between different attributes of avatars and virtual objects. As described in [13], the appearance and animation of virtual characters can be transferred from one VW to another using the appearance and animation schemas described in MPEG-V, Part 4 [12]. The subcategorical elements of both elements are shown in Figure 7.13. The standardized appearance schema is designed to contain 150 different parameters of different VWs in 14 attribute groups to describe the appearance features shown in Figure 7.13A. Regarding the avatar animation,

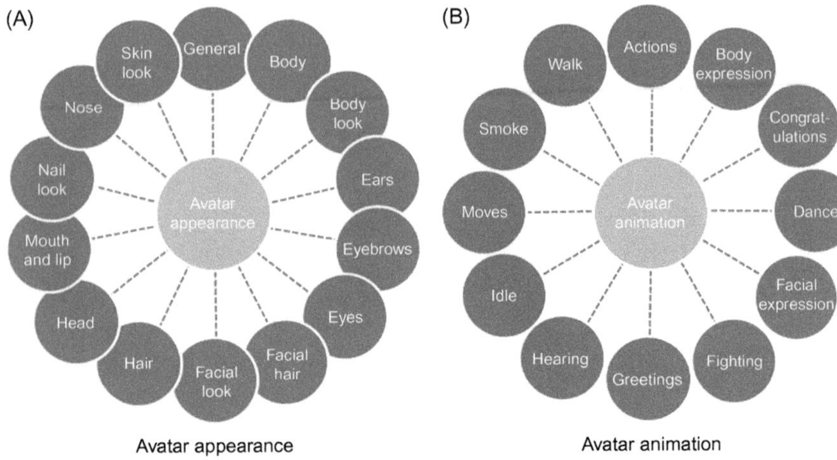

Figure 7.13 (A) Avatar appearance and (B) animation elements.

several VWs provide a rich set of animation parameters describing mainly the emotional state related to the facial expressions and body gestures, as shown in Figure 7.13B.

As shown in Figure 7.14A, an avatar in the original VW contains its own proprietary appearance parameters. The original avatar can be portable by mapping the parameters associated with it into the parameters of the standardized elements. For example, if an avatar in one VW has the following parameters, height, 165 cm; body fat, 15%; head shape, egg-shape; clothes, a brown jacket with a clothes id of 1; and geometry resource location, *my-mesh.mp4*, then the generated XML element using the standardized schema is as follows:

```
<Appearance>
        <Body>
                <BodyHeight value=165/>
                <BodyFat value=15/>
        </Body>
        <Head>
                <EggHead value="true"/>
        </Head>
        <Clothes ID=1 Name="jacket_brown"/>
        <AppearanceResources>
                <AvatarURL value="my_mesh.mp4"/>
        </AppearanceResources>

</Appearance>
```

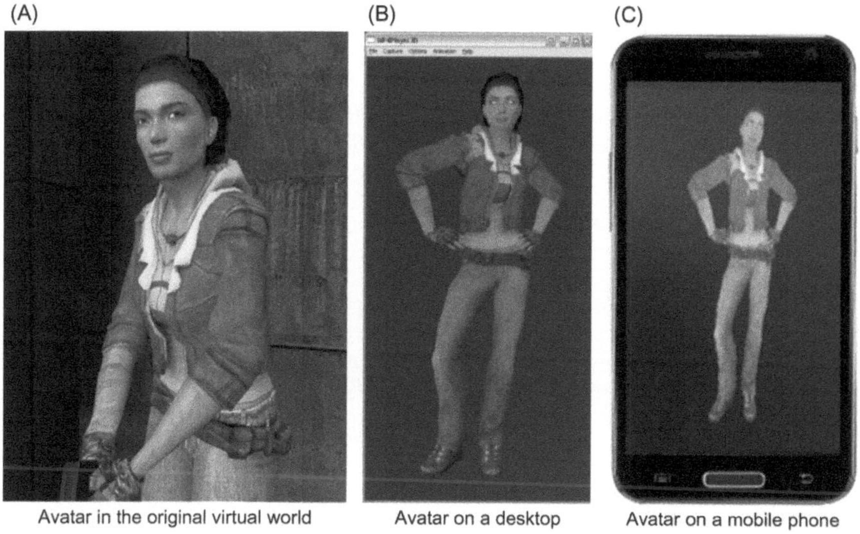

Figure 7.14 Transferring an avatar from (A) one virtual world into an MPEG-4 player on both (B) a desktop and (C) a mobile phone.

Finally, these parameters can be imported to a second VW that also understands these standardized elements. The second VW then automatically adjusts its own avatar template based on the imported parameters, as shown in Figure 7.14B and C.

REFERENCES

[1] ISO/IEC 23005-1:2014 Information technology—Media context and control—Part 1: Architecture, January 2014.
[2] K. Yoon, End-to-end framework for 4-D broadcasting based on MPEG-V standard, Signal Process. Image Commun. 1 (2012) 127–135.
[3] ISO/IEC 23005-3:2013 Information technology—Media context and control—Part 3: Sensory information, November 2013.
[4] ISO/IEC 23005-2:2013 Information technology—Media context and control—Part 2: Control Information, November 2013.
[5] ISO/IEC 23005-5:2013 Information technology—Media context and control—Part 5: Data formats for interaction devices, November 2013.
[6] S. Han, J. Park, Holo-Haptics: Haptic interaction with a See-Through 3D display, IEEE International Conference on Consumer Electronics (ICCE) 2014, pp. 522–523, January 2014.
[7] O. Hilliges, D. Kim, S. Izadi, M. Weiss, A.D. Wilsonn, HoloDesk: Direct 3D interactions with a Situated See-Through display, ACM SIGCHI Conference on Human Factors in Computing Systems 2012, pp. 2421–2430, May 2012.

[8] S. Han, J. Park, Grip-Ball: A spherical multi-touch interface for interacting with virtual worlds, IEEE International Conference on Consumer Electronics (ICCE) 2014, pp. 600–601, January 2013.
[9] S. Han, J.-J. Han, Y. Hwang, J.B. Kim, W.C. Bang, J.D.K. Kim, C. Kim, Controlling virtual world by the real world devices with an MPEG-V framework, IEEE International Workshop on Multimedia Signal Processing 2010, pp. 251–256, October 2010.
[10] S. Han, J.-J. Han, J.D.K. Kim, C. Kim, Connecting users to virtual worlds within MPEG-V standardization, Signal Process. Image Commun. 28 (2) (2013) 97–113.
[11] S.-K. Kim, Y.S. Joo, M. Shin, S. Han, J.-J. Han, Virtual world control system using sensed information and adaptation engine, Signal Process. Image Commun. 28 (2) (2013) 87–96.
[12] ISO/IEC 23005-4:2013 Information technology—Media context and control—Part 4:Virtual world object characteristics, November 2013.
[13] M. Preda, B. Jovanova, Avatar interoperability and control in virtual Worlds, Signal Process. Image Commun. 28 (2) (2013) 168–180.

TERMS, DEFINITIONS, AND ABBREVIATED TERMS

TERMS AND DEFINITIONS

actuation preferences description schemes and descriptors to represent users' preferences with respect to rendering of sensorial effects

actuator consumer device by which the corresponding sensorial effect can be made

actuator capability description to represent the characteristics of actuators in terms of the capability of the given actuator

actuator command description to control actuators

adaptation engine VR adaptation and/or RV adaptation

interaction device device that accepts inputs from users and/or gives output to users in the form of various modalities

RV adaptation entity that takes the sensed information from sensors, the sensor capabilities and/or the sensor adaptation preferences as inputs and adapts the sensed information and/or the virtual world object characteristics based on those inputs

sensed information information acquired by a sensor

sensor consumer device by which user input or environmental information can be gathered

sensor adaptation preference description of user's preference on individual sensed information

sensor capability description to represent the characteristics of sensors in terms of the capability of the given sensor such as accuracy or sensing range

sensorial effect effect to augment perception by stimulating human senses in a particular scene of a multimedia application

sensorial effect data description schemes and descriptors to represent sensorial effects

sensory device consumer device (actuator) by which the corresponding sensory effect can be made

sensory device capability actuator capability

sensory device command description to control actuators used to generate sensorial effects

sensory effect sensorial effect

sensory effect metadata sensorial effect data

sensory effect preference description schemes and descriptors to represent user's preferences with respect to rendering of sensorial effects

sensory information standardized representation format to describe sensorial effect data defined in ISO/IEC 23005-3

virtual world object characteristics standardized representation format to describe virtual world objects defined in ISO/IEC 23005-4

VR adaptation entity that takes the sensorial effect data, the virtual world object characteristics, the actuator capabilities, the sensor capabilities, the sensed information, and/or the actuation preferences as inputs and generates actuator commands based on those inputs

ABBREVIATED TERMS

AC Actuator Capability
ACmd Actuator Command
AP Actuation Preference
CIDL Control Information Description Language
DCDV Device Capability Description Vocabulary
DCV Device Command Vocabulary
IIDL Interaction Interface Description Language
SAP Sensor Adaptation Preference
SAPV Sensor Adaptation Preference Vocabulary
SC Sensor Capability
SCDV Sensor Capability Description Vocabulary
SE Sensorial Effect
SEDL Sensory Effect Description Language
SEM Sensory Effect Metadata (i.e., Sensorial Effect [SE] data)
SEPV Sensory Effect Preference Vocabulary
SEV Sensory Effect Vocabulary
SI Sensed Information
SIV Sensed Information Vocabulary
VWOC Virtual World Object Characteristics

INDEX

Note: Page numbers followed by "*f*" and "*t*" refer to figures and tables, respectively.

T

FSC
www.fsc.org
MIX
Papier | Fördert
gute Waldnutzung
FSC® C083411

Kolibri 360 GmbH
Ferdinand-Jühlke-Straße 7
99095 Erfurt, Deutschland
produktsicherheit@kolibri360.de